It is widely accepted that "the eyes are the mirror of the soul," a proverb so ingrained in common knowledge that we often take it for granted, seldom contemplating its profound implications. Fortunately, scholars like Isabella Poggi exist to illuminate the beauty and complexity of our behavior, particularly when it is camouflaged in plain sight, making it challenging to discern. Similar to the allegory of Plato's cave, Poggi guides us to comprehend how limited our understanding is regarding the use of our eyes, providing a thorough and scientific exploration of their role in our social lives. Upon completing this book, one inevitably perceives others' eyes through an entirely different lens.

**Alessandro Vinciarelli**, Full Professor,
University of Glasgow – School of Computing Science

Poggi provides a profoundly original treatment which has the potential to revolutionize the fields it addresses. The book is bound to make the reader think and reconsider many assumptions they have been taking for granted, while at the same time it is written in clear language that will be accessible even to beginners.

Applying a variety of methodologies, Poggi produces a coherent proposal for the bold, maybe even daring, thesis that gaze can be described as a language, not in a metaphorical sense, but literally, that it is organized like language, hence with the equivalent of phonemes, morphemes, words, meanings, pragmatics, and so on, through much of gamut of linguistic constituents. This book has the potential to bring together several different fields (the study of gesture, gaze, and emotions, Ekman's FACS, ethology, some areas of robotics and of eye tracking) in an integrated field. The book is groundbreaking and a synthesis at the same time. Poggi's effort is a refreshing example of scholarship and theory building.

**Salvatore Attardo**, Professor, Texas A&M University

Isabella Poggi's *The Language of Gaze* offers powerful new insights into the role of gaze in human interaction. Attardo and Pickering's recent *Eye-tracking in Linguistics* focuses on eye movements when a person describes a visual scene and, more relevantly, gaze patterns between two people during a humorous conversation. There has been much study in the past of manual gesture as a complement to the use of spoken language (as distinct from the use of hands, face and other parts of the body in signed languages) as well as study of facial expressions of emotion, with cross-species accounts going back to Darwin. Recent work has seen facial expression (including the direction of gaze) studied not only in relation to emotion but also as a complement to language use in signaling syntactic information and managing turn taking. Poggi contributes to such studies but carries them further by not only highlighting the role of gaze in multimodal communication but also suggesting how "talking with the eyes" – and facial expression more generally – can have an important impact on how humans interact in everyday life, politics, education, and more. In this way, Poggi builds upon and greatly extends her exploration – in her book with Francesca D'Errico, *Social Influence, Power, and Multimodal Communication* – of how democratic leaders and dictators use words, voice, gesture, face, gaze, and posture to boast about their own merits or insult and ridicule rivals.

**Michael Arbib**, University of California, San Diego

# THE LANGUAGE OF GAZE

How do you feel if someone gives you a seductive glance or looks down on you? What do we mean when we look sideways at someone? How can we solicit another person's attention? This book analyses the communicative system of gaze in depth, investigating its structure and functions the same way that words and gestures are studied, and shows how to do so by establishing a phonology, a morphology and a semantics of eye communication, before finally outlining a lexicon of gaze.

Poggi provides a detailed semantic analysis of lexical items, highlights the role of gaze in multimodal communication, and illustrates its uses in everyday life, politics, education and musical performance. The meanings we communicate by gaze are intertwined with the multimodality of our communication, thus integrating, complementing, sometimes contradicting, whether deliberately or inadvertently, what we say with words or gestures.

Starting from a robust theoretical framework, this book also provides an overview of the methods that can be exploited to study gaze, ranging from ethno-semantics to observation and simulation, and provides examples of their use.

A timely and original contribution that is essential reading for advanced students, scholars and researchers of multimodal communication, pragmatics, social psychology and related areas.

**Isabella Poggi** has been a Full professor of Psychology at Roma Tre University, and a member of European Networks on Embodied Communication, on Emotions, and Social Signal Processing.

# THE LANGUAGE OF GAZE

## Eyes that Talk

*Isabella Poggi*

Routledge
Taylor & Francis Group

LONDON AND NEW YORK

Designed cover image: vitranc

First published 2025
by Routledge
4 Park Square, Milton Park, Abingdon, Oxon OX14 4RN

and by Routledge
605 Third Avenue, New York, NY 10158

*Routledge is an imprint of the Taylor & Francis Group, an informa business*

© 2023 Parlare con gli occhi by Carocci editore, Roma

© 2025 Isabella Poggi

*British Library Cataloguing-in-Publication Data*
A catalogue record for this book is available from the British Library

ISBN: 978-1-032-67833-7 (hbk)
ISBN: 978-1-032-67832-0 (pbk)
ISBN: 978-1-032-67834-4 (ebk)

DOI: 10.4324/9781032678344

Typeset in Sabon
by Apex CoVantage, LLC

*To my (blue-eyed!) beloved Master*
*Cristiano Castelfranchi*

# CONTENTS

# 1
# A FIRST GLANCE

What do your eyes say? We all talk with our eyes: our gaze is a language, and one with a rich and systematic structure, more than you might think – it includes a phonology and possibly a morphology – and it can convey a wide range of meanings. The eyes are the mirror of the soul, but not only of the soul: they reflect our mind and sometimes even the world around us.

We all know that we talk with our eyes. And yet in the vast literature on bodily communication, the gaze is not the most studied of all possible communicative systems, and, what is more, even its status as a signal is not considered central by scholars, even when they speak of the "duality of the gaze", attributing to it two functions: one as a cue and the other as a signal.

Among the works devoted to the gaze, which have become increasingly numerous since the 1970s, four strands of research can be distinguished that mark the points of the following outline: besides the specific parts of the eye region (section 1.1), studies on three aspects of the gaze: its informational or cue function (1.2), its effects (1.3) and finally its communicative or signal function (1.4).

## 1.1   The region of the eyes

The parts of our body by which our gaze is produced form what we can call the "eye region". The iris is the membrane of the eyeball, in the form of a circular, pigmented disc – the one that makes the eye blue, green, brown; it is bordered by the sclera, the white of the eye, and crossed by the pupil, a circular hole that expands and contracts to let in more or less light, precisely thanks to the action of the iris muscles.

DOI: 10.4324/9781032678344-1

The upper and lower eyelids are thin, flexible, muscular-cutaneous folds that open and close over the eyeball and on whose edges grow the eyelashes, curved hairs that act as sensors of external agents from which they protect the eye. Above the eye, the eyelids are separated from the forehead by the eyebrow arch, a hair-covered skin relief whose function is to prevent external or bodily fluids from entering the eye and blurring vision. Let's have a look at the studies devoted to these parts of the eye and the surrounding region (for accurate and detailed overviews of the anatomy and physiology of the eye and of eye movements, see Hyönä, Radach & Deubel, 2003; Attardo & Pickering, 2023).

*The iris.*  The shape and colour of the iris has been studied mainly in the context of biometric authentication, for example, to verify that the person withdrawing money from an ATM is the account holder. However, some research has also attempted to establish the relationship between eye colour and personality (Larsson, Pedersen & Stattin, 2007). By looking at two parts of the iris, crypts and contraction furrows, it was found that different types of crypts correspond to different approach behaviours, such as warmth, tenderness, trust and positive emotions, while furrows are associated with impulsivity. Such an association may be due to the fact that the gene *Pax6* induces changes in the tissues of both the iris and the left anterior cingulate cortex, which is responsible for approach behaviour.

The colour of the eyes is determined by the amount of neuromelanin, a substance in the brain that facilitates the exchange of nerve impulses, speeds up their transmission and, in high proportions, gives darker colours. Light eyes seem to correlate with shyness and inhibition, dark eyes with disinhibition. People with dark eyes tend to react more strongly to events, prefer complex figures and are better at sports with a low reaction threshold; in psychotherapy, they prefer experiential and engaging treatment. People with light eyes are more impassive, prefer simple figures but are more sensitive to colours and are more prone to physical activities of precision and concentration; in psychological treatment, they prefer dialogue and intellectual exchange (Pacori, 2010).

*The pupil.*  The pupil is the black circle at the centre of the eye: controlled by the iris muscles, it performs the same function as the aperture of a camera, dilating to let in more light when there is little light and contracting when there is a lot of light. But in addition to this basic function of vision, it also has a function as a cue or signal, being a symptom of emotions and other internal states. The dilation of the pupils can indeed be determined by dopamine, the hormone of happiness, but also by other states of physiological activation: this is why, as studies using pupillometry techniques have shown, the pupils dilate when we experience happiness or love but also when we experience anxiety (Sirois & Brisson, 2014; Mathôt, 2018), fear or anger, difficulty in making decisions (Kret & Sjak-Shie, 2019) and finally sexual arousal.

In women, pupils dilate when looking at photographs of naked men but also of small children or babies with their mothers; in men, when looking at naked women and landscapes (Hess & Polt, 1960). Hess (1965, 1975) showed heterosexual students photographs of attractive girls, but in some the girl's pupil diameter was normal, and in others the same photograph was manipulated to make the pupil appear much more dilated. The students judged the girls with dilated pupils to be prettier, sweeter and sexier, not realising that it was the eyes that made them more attractive.

On the other hand, if the dilated pupil induces sexual arousal, this in turn causes the dilation of the pupil of the person looking at it: it is thus a signal that, although it is completely below the threshold of consciousness, "calls" for a similar reaction in the other person, thus determining a synchronisation effect and consequently a similar reciprocal attitude.

Such synchronisation, which takes the form of equal pupil size, also occurs in the narration of personal memories, where the pupils of the narrator and the listener breathe together, so to speak, when attention is shared, dilating as emotional intensity increases and contracting at times of less involvement in the narrative: a synchronisation that is a cause, effect or symptom of greater empathy (Kang & Wheatley, 2017).

However, pupil size also provides information about a person's current cognitive processes and can therefore provide clues to deception (Dionisio et al., 2001): the pupil dilates more under higher cognitive load, including when answering a question by lying.

*The sclera.* Few but important studies have looked at the white part of the eye: Tomasello et al. (2007) hypothesise that the white sclera, which makes the eye particularly conspicuous, a trait found only in humans among other primates, has evolved to allow conspecifics to follow the direction of an individual's gaze, thus enhancing shared attention and communication. In an experiment with children and great apes, the experimenter looked at the ceiling and the monkey followed his gaze primarily by the direction of his head, while the child followed the direction of his eyes. Tomasello thus formulates the "cooperative eye" hypothesis: human eyes also evolved with the function of facilitating cooperative social interactions.

This is precisely what ultimately creates a "primary intersubjectivity" between mother and child (Trevarthen, 1979): they can establish shared attention precisely thanks to the direction of their gaze. When the child wants to make a request to his mother, he "catches" her gaze by looking at her, almost "pulling" her gaze towards the object of his attention (Baumgartner, Devescovi & D'Amico, 2000).

But the colour of the sclera also has other functions, more self-protective than cooperative: Whalen et al. (2004), in a study in which the whites of the eyes of stimulus faces were more or less masked, found that the amygdala, a brain structure that responds to biologically relevant stimuli, reacts more readily when the whites of the eyes are more extensive, as in the expression of fear, than when they are more restricted, as in happiness: a person who is afraid is a more threatening stimulus for us, which should be a greater prompt for us to act.

*The eyelids and eyelashes.*  In the literature on nonverbal communication, some of the few studies on eyelids and eyelashes refer to the blink: a movement of rapid closure of the eyelids that we make very often because it is necessary to moisten our eyes. However, the frequency of this blink generally increases or decreases during deception, making it a reliable indicator that one is lying. In "guilty knowledge" experiments ("guilty knowledge" is information that the suspect should not know if he were innocent but to which he instinctively reacts, if guilty, thus unmasking himself), the blink rate differs between relevant and irrelevant stimuli (Fukuda, 2001). When lying, the blink rate decreases, probably due to the cognitive load of lying, while it increases immediately after telling the lie (Leal & Vrij, 2008). These clues appear during and after deception, but the blink rate also reveals deception about the future, that is, about one's intentions. In people who lie when answering a question about their intentions, there is suppression of the blink during the question, and in the following 10 seconds the blinks are shorter and less frequent than average (Marchak, 2013).

*The eyebrows.*  As we shall see, the eyebrows are the part of the eye region most often attributed with a communicative function. But they also have a simple informative function. When they are close together, forming vertical wrinkles on the forehead, the A-shape, with the inner parts of the eyebrows raised, expresses sadness, whereas the V-shape expresses anger and is therefore perceived as threatening; the latter is recognised much more quickly than the A-shape but only in the context of faces, not in other types of figures (Tipples, Atkinson & Young, 2002), precisely due to the human need for early detection of dangerous situations.

## 1.2  What do eyes tell us?

Sometimes we understand something relevant from someone else's eye behaviour, even though they have no intention of letting us understand anything. But it is important, though not always easy, to distinguish such cases from those in which the one who produces the ocular behaviour does so because, even without realising it, she wants to let us know something. We can call the former the informative function of the eyes and the latter the communicative gaze proper. Let us focus first on the former: what can we understand from the eyes of others, even despite their will and consciousness?

A seminal work on this subject is Argyle and Cook's book (1976). As they point out, the very fact that A is looking at B means that A is paying attention to B, who might do something for A; therefore, A expects a response from B, be it aggression, sex, play, the establishment of power relations.

A newborn child reacts not only to a face but even to the image of two eyes and begins to have a social relationship with them. The use of the gaze is universal, but cultures differ in the duration of the gaze: Arabs and Greeks look longer at their interlocutors, but generally there is an unwritten rule that we should not look at a stranger for more than 2 seconds at a time. When we do look at someone in the face, we give only brief glances, exploring the face quickly and in repeated cycles, then stopping at the eyes (Exline, 1963). In conversation, speakers intermittently look at each other, at grammatical boundaries between sentences, and at the end of utterances to get feedback from the other person. The listener, on the other hand, lingers with his gaze for twice as long as the speaker in order to supplement the auditory information with visual information. This is also why the cases in which the eyes are averted are particularly communicative.

Women look at others more than men (Cook, 1977), extraverts more than intraverts; psychiatric patients (but generally only when in hospital) look at others less often than other people do; while autistic children tend either not to look or to look very briefly.

Looking is apparently related to attraction: we look more at those we like – and the more we look at them, the more we like them – while we reserve a look of hatred for individuals we are hostile to.

Argyle and Cook (1976) propose the 'equilibrium theory', which governs the level of intimacy between people: turning one's gaze to the other serves to control the level of intimacy or affiliation with the other and compensates for the level of intimacy produced by other behaviours, such as physical proximity, in order to achieve balance. Animals use strategies to reduce contact; rats and birds turn their heads, close their eyes, pretend to be asleep, and interrupt visual interaction during times of aggression or courtship to reduce aggression or the urge to flee. Among primates, it is usually the non-dominant that looks at the dominant. The dominant has a confident posture, and if he looks, he may do so with a slight frown; whereas the submissive averts his gaze to avoid being attacked. But let us take a closer look at what information we can glean from the other person's eyes.

*A cue of attention.* It is important for me to see where you are looking, not only when you are looking at me but also when you are looking elsewhere. As pointed out by McKay et al.'s (2021) "cueing effect", your gaze is a cue to me that something relevant is happening around me. Given the vast amount of information that reaches me at any given moment in my daily life, my attention has to sort out the relevant stimuli from the irrelevant ones, and seeing what someone else is looking at tells me where to look and what to pay attention to: indeed, healthy adults tend to look at what others are looking at. But the cues provided by the gaze of others are even more specific: by following the eyes of a waiter or a nurse working in a hospice, I can work out who is the next customer or patient at the table to be served (Yamazaki et al., 2016). Furthermore, if I am in a dangerous situation, I am more likely to follow the gaze of a dominant male than that of a non-dominant female (Ohlsen, van Zoest & van Vugt, 2013).

*Conversation.* Observing where the gaze is directed is also important for understanding the course of the conversation (Rossano, 2013), especially in three-way conversations, where the leader gives a longer look to the person he or she is about to give the turn to (Kalma, 1992); but "gaze density", even between people who are not speaking, says a lot about their level of involvement (Jokinen, 2011). Moreover, glances are more frequent in conversations between native and non-native speakers: listeners look at the speaker more often when speaking in a foreign language because the speaker's gaze indicates who will have the next turn but also because looking at the speaker complements the understanding of his or her speech with clues of bodily communication (Ijuin et al., 2015, 2018).

*Cognitive processes.* People's gaze not only reveals their interactional intentions but also their cognitive processes. The first and most basic is attention (Peters et al., 2005): not only when X directs his gaze to object O, I understand that he is paying attention to O, but his way of looking at O tells me whether X is distracted or concentrated: this is why the teacher scrutinises the students' eyes to understand how engaged they are in the lesson (De Carolis et al., 2019).

But even the teacher, when "professionally" observing students to get information about them, looks at them individually during the lesson, concentrated and with a few side glances, whereas when reviewing them in a video, she looks at a larger number of students, as if for a more "comprehensive" control (Minarikova et al., 2021).

On the other hand, students also gain information from the teacher's gaze: they attribute more dominance or interpersonal agentivity to the teacher when she looks them in the eye while asking questions – thus revealing cognitive processes of attention – whereas they see her as more friendly when she looks at them in the eye while lecturing (McIntyre, Mulder & Mainhard, 2020).

Gaze also reveals thought processes: for example, looking away is sometimes an indication of cognitive difficulty, such as when you have to answer a difficult question. In this case, not looking may also relieve the emotional burden of fear of looking bad, but primarily it relieves the cognitive load required by the task (Doherty-Sneddon & Phelps, 2005).

However, even in the case of revealing thoughts, gaze seems to be influenced by cultural rules. In an experiment in which they had to answer questions, subjects from Canada and Trinidad looked up when thinking about their answers, while the Japanese looked down (McCarthy et al., 2006).

According to NLP theorists (neuro-linguistic programming; Bandler & Grinder, 1979), looking up before speaking reveals the cognitive apparatus from which the speaker is drawing the information he or she is about to give: if I look to the bottom left, I am engaged in an inner dialogue; if I look to the top left, I am looking for real images retrieved from memory; if I look to the top right, I am looking for constructed images; and the latter may indicate the invention of details, hence deception.

Fixational eye movements also provide information about the cognitive processes involved in reading. Analysis of the eye movements of experienced readers showed that the main verb of the sentence received more sustained attention than other grammatical elements (Rayner, 1977). This suggests that the semantic processing of the sentence influences eye movements in a top-down manner, and that it is not just the pure visual input that determines interpretation. Given the intervention of eye movements in cognitive processes, eye tracking and pupillometry (the use of technological tools that capture eye movements and pupil size; Brône & Oben, 2018; Mathôt, 2018; Ansani, 2020; Attardo & Pickering, 2023) have made it possible to reveal, for example, the triggering of a cognitive process, such as case encoding in Basque or German (Egurtzegi et al., 2022), increases in cognitive load when processing syntactic ambiguity (Engelhardt, Ferreira & Patsenko, 2010) or the typical eye movements in describing visual scenes and the gaze patterns between people during a humorous conversation (Attardo & Pickering, 2023).

Eye movements are also a cue for ongoing decision-making processes, including the consideration and evaluation of possible alternatives (Glaholt & Reingold, 2011). After initial judgements, there is a (possibly unconscious) "cascade effect": the more you look, the more you lean towards one alternative, and the more you tend to prefer it over the other (Shimojo et al., 2003).

*Emotions.* Even when gaze does not intentionally communicate emotions, it informs us about them: if basic emotions are more easily recognised by looking at the whole face rather than just the eyes or just the mouth, complex emotions can be recognised as well by the eyes alone as by the whole face, and more so than by the mouth alone (Baron-Cohen, Wheelwright & Jolliffe, 1997).

Moreover, as it is an important evolutionary advantage for us to be able to detect threats in the environment, the eyes are crucial for the recognition of threatening faces (Fox & Damhanovic, 2006): the mere fact of seeing eyes can convey a sense of threat. But the eyes are also crucial for the emotions of sadness and happiness. In the former case, tears flow from the lacrimal glands, a cue – but also a biological communicative signal – of sadness or grief (Miceli & Castelfranchi, 2003; Miceli, 2008). Furthermore, it is the moisture in the eye that makes it shiny and bright, an indication, albeit involuntary, of longing, joy or enthusiasm. Finally, the prototypical signal of happiness, the smile, involves not only the muscles of the mouth but also the muscles around the eyes: only in the genuine smile, the "Duchenne smile" (1862), or the smile of happiness, do they cause the skin at the corners of the eyelids to wrinkle; this gives rise to the so-called crow's feet, which are difficult to simulate and do not appear in fake smiles, making it possible to distinguish them from genuine smiles (Ekman & Friesen, 1982).

*Social relationships.* Eye contact is crucial in social relationships, whether intimate or not: this is clear from our everyday lives, but it is also demonstrated by the link between liking someone and looking at them (Argyle & Cook, 1976). Wellens (1987) found that mutual gazes between participants and people they liked or disliked determined changes in their heart rate. When a confederate who was either liked or disliked by a male participant asked him intimate questions and then looked away or looked directly at him, the subject's heart rate increased when looked at by a disliked confederate but slowed when looked at by the liked confederate, while there was no change in heart rate when the confederate did not look at him.

Furthermore, different power relations correspond to different gaze behaviours (Dovidio et al., 1988): men and women with high power look at the interlocutor as often when speaking as when listening, whereas those with low power look more when listening than when speaking. When there are no power differences, there are gender differences: men look as if they have power, while women look as if they do not. Moreover, the more dominant one is, the more one tends to look longer when confronted with an angry face (Terburg et al., 2011).

Indeed, the attribution of dominance is influenced by gaze: neutral or angry faces, but not happy or disgusted faces, appear more or less dominant depending on the direction of gaze, whereas a face with averted gaze is more likely to be judged as angry (Shang, Liu & Fu, 2008). There is a bidirectional link between gaze and competitive relationships (Giacomantonio et al., 2018): the rate of looking towards the opponent predicts defection in the Prisoner's Dilemma; looking into the other's eyes rather than the face in an ultimatum game increases competitive behaviour; and a competitive negotiation elicits more mutual looking, which in turn increases competitiveness. Symmetrically, looking away causes the other person to experience feelings of exclusion and relational devaluation (Wirth et al., 2010).

*Personality and mental disorders.* Some personality traits can be inferred from gaze behaviour. Extraverted people look at the other person in an interaction much more often than intraverted people, and people with high affiliative motivation do so more than others, especially in pleasant and cooperative situations (Argyle, 1990; Ijuin & Jokinen, 2020). People with an internal *locus of control* look less because, attributing the causes of their successes and failures to themselves, they are less interested in observing others and gaining their help (Lefcourt & Wine, 1969; Rajecki, Ickert & Tanford, 1981).

A shy person looks at you less often when speaking (Iizuka, 1994) or looks at your face but at the level of your chin, as if tangentially, without going so far as to look into your eyes. A child with a shy temperament, characterised by anxious and vigilant behaviour and a perception of social novelty as threatening, tends on the one hand to look away more often (attentional avoidance) and on the other hand, paradoxically, to look more often (attentional vigilance), as if to check and defend against the threat, thus alleviating the respiratory arrhythmia induced by his social anxiety (Poole & Schmidt, 2021).

In terms of gaze perception (Tsuji & Shimada, 2018), people with high levels of social anxiety tend to interpret as threatening any gaze that expresses even mildly negative emotions.

When it comes to psychiatric and neurological patients, gazing, both physically present and on the screen, seems to be clearly dangerous for the psychotic, while the frequency of gazing is low for the depressed (Brossard, 1992). In an experiment by Feyereisen and Lignian (1981), patients with Broca's aphasia looked little during verbal production, which requires more concentration, whereas in fluent aphasics, who produce automatic and stereotyped verbal expressions, the amount of gazing was constant from beginning to end – in contrast to normal subjects, who look at the interlocutor only during the utterance of the comment, the most important part of the sentence.

Gaze behaviour is particularly studied in autism, where its peculiarities are considered a diagnostic symptom. Autistic people avoid looking into other people's eyes (Dalton et al., 2005), but they also do not tend to follow other people's gaze (Emery, 2000; Nation & Penny, 2008), nor do they benefit from the memorisation opportunities provided by eye contact to normal people (Falck-Ytter, Carlström & Johansson, 2014).

This may also be the reason why autistic people are less expert at emotion recognition: in an experiment by Baron-Cohen, Wheelwright and Jolliffe (1997), non-autistic adults recognised some complex emotions either from the whole facial expression or from the eyes alone but not from the mouth alone, whereas in adults with Asperger's syndrome the usual recognition difficulties were exacerbated when the pictures showed only the eyes.

Various theories, supported or not by neurological studies, have been proposed to explain this tendency of autistic people not to look into the eyes of others: do they feel the need to look away because eye contact causes them anxiety or fear, as evidenced by the concomitant hyperactivation of the fusiform gyrus and amygdala (Dalton et al., 2005), or simply because they are not interested in the eyes as a social stimulus (Moriuchi, Klin & Jones, 2017)?

## 1.3 Effects of gaze

The direction of gaze, our own and that of others, has very significant effects on us, on others and on our relationship.

*What are you looking at?* The direction of our gaze influences the attractiveness of a face. In a study by Ewing, Rhodes and Pellicano (2010), male subjects preferred faces of women looking directly at them to those looking away, especially if they were attractive women. But this preference is such that an object – for example, an object to be advertised – is also considered more desirable when paired with an attractive face looking directly at it, compared to an attractive face looking away and an unattractive face, regardless of the direction of gaze (Strick, Holland & van Knippenberg, 2008).

Of course, gaze is strongly determined by attractiveness (Leder, Mitrovic & Goller, 2016): the more attractive a face is, especially of the opposite sex, the longer and more frequently gaze is directed at it. Moreover, attractiveness, especially when combined with a direct gaze, activates dopaminergic regions linked to the reward system involved in initiating social interaction (Kampe et al., 2001): the perceived attractiveness of an unfamiliar face increases brain activity in the ventral striatum when its gaze is directed at you, whereas it decreases it when it is directed elsewhere.

Being looked at is such a relevant experience that even a cartoon is more persuasive or engaging when it looks us in the eye (Musicus, Tal & Wansink, 2015). In an experiment in which a rabbit advertised cereal, adult volunteers chose the advertised brand more often when the rabbit looked them in the eye.

This is also the reason why teachers or popularisers of public speaking (Ravinal, 2022) recommend looking the audience in the eye: on the one hand, it helps the speaker to concentrate, makes him appear more authoritative, more convinced of what he is saying, and makes him not only appear but actually feel more confident; on the other hand, it induces the audience to look at him in turn, not to be distracted, to follow him with greater concentration and to adopt a more active attitude, participating in the speaker's speech, thus increasing the likelihood of being persuaded.

Direct gaze is also very important in the perception of anger expressions: comparing angry, frightened and neutral faces, Ewbank, Jennings and Calder (2009) found that those with direct gaze at the observer were significantly more often interpreted as expressing anger than the others, and, vice versa, angry faces were perceived as faces looking at the observer. This effect again reminds us of the evolutionary importance of threat perception and the centrality of eyes as threat signals.

*Feeling watched.* When we feel looked at, we often tend to change our behaviour for reasons of image and self-awareness: on the one hand, because we want to make a good impression but sometimes also simply because we suddenly draw more attention to ourselves (Cañigueral & Hamilton, 2019). Of course, there must be a reputational factor at work: just put a two-eyed figure on a collection box for drinks in the university cafeteria and three times as many students contribute (Bateson, Nettle & Roberts, 2006).

*Eye contact.*   Looking into each other's eyes is much more than just looking at each other. Eye contact occurs very rarely: only in situations of great intimacy – between two lovers or between mother and child – or of competition – the two bullies in the alley about to come to blows, challenging each other with their eyes. In all other cases, we can't bear to look into each other's eyes for more than about 2 seconds, then we have to look down or away.

Looking into the eyes has an almost magical power – hypnotic or magnetic, as we will see in Chapter 10. If you look at me, you appear more attractive: in a study where participants looked at artificial agents on a computer, when the agent looked at them, they looked at it longer and found it more attractive (Palanica & Itier, 2012). And when you look at me, you're asking for my attention, so you tense me up because you're making a request, and I feel compelled to respond; but when I'm trying to lie, it's harder to do so when you look me in the eye (Hietanen et al., 2018).

In some cases, eye contact is distracting: if you ask me a question and look me in the eye, I take longer to answer because this contact uses the same cognitive resources as language (Kajimura & Nomura, 2016). But, conversely, it can also increase cognitive performance: direct gaze improves memorisation, albeit differently in men and women (Lanthier et al., 2019) and in normotypic and autistic children (Falck-Ytter, Carlström & Johansson, 2014); and it facilitates the retrieval of people's names in both normal and Alzheimer's patients (Lopis & Conty, 2019). This effect may be due to increased arousal, positive emotions or increased motivation induced by being observed (Niedźwiecka, 2020).

## 1.4   When our eyes talk

The first systematic reflections on the communicative aspects of the gaze go back to Aristotle, Cicero and Quintilian, who describe its use by orators. Fornés Pallicer and Puig Rodríguez-Escalona (2011, 2019, 2024) group the speaker's eye gestures identified by the authors of ancient rhetoric into classes, distinguishing between gazes with eyelid, iris or eyebrow movements. In particular, they examine the cases of the oblique gaze and the gaze into the eyes, identifying their descriptions in Cicero, Quintilian and other Latin authors, and the meanings and contributions to discourse that these authors ascribe to them. The slanted gaze, with its somewhat furtive flavour, is used to convey hostile feelings such as hatred or envy in Horace, and contempt, accompanied or not by pride, in Ovid and Ammianus Marcellinus; while Propertius and Apuleius use its potential for seduction. With regard to the gaze, Virgil testifies to its importance as a sign of attention, Statius notes that it can be a sign of understanding or an invitation to speak, Suetonius recalls the expression of dominance widely used by the Emperor Augustus: a gaze that could not be sustained, like a dazzling sun. On the basis of ancient authors, Fornés Pallicer and Puig Rodríguez-Escalona (2024) also examine a rich repertoire of eyebrow signals: four movements – contracting, raising, relaxing and lowering – conveying arrogance and humility, anger or seriousness, assent or disapproval, or finally identifying specific characters.

Descartes (1649) argued that "all passions are revealed by some particular action of the eyes", and Darwin, in his seminal book *The Expression of the Emotions in Man and Animals* (1872), noted that emotions such as pride, humility, guilt, conceit, cunning and suspicion could be inferred from the eyes alone.

In the nineteenth century, early pioneering work by Kendon (1967) and Kendon and Cook (1969) attributed to the gaze, in addition to its functions of regulating turn-taking, that of monitoring the conversation, which is expressed in an asymmetry of gaze between speaker and listener – the listener looks at the speaker much more than vice versa – but the reciprocal gaze allows each participant to control the other's facial expressions and attention to ensure mutual understanding and to gain approval. But its control also allows both to regulate their level of arousal, for example, by averting their gaze at times of excessive emotion.

Two works deal specifically with the gaze as a form of communication: in Russia, Kreidlin's (2002) book on oculesics, the study of the eyes and their behaviour as a semiotic system, and, in France, Brossard's (1992) book, which ascribes to the gaze an "exchange" function of communication in conversation, a "socio-referential" one of sharing the point of reference with the interlocutor in order to share the object of communication, and a "socio-emotional" one of informing about the intensity of the emotions felt.

In the region of the eye, the part that has been studied the most as a communicative element is the eyebrow. Eibl-Eibesfeldt (1972) identifies the "eyebrow flash" as a signal of openness to interaction: a rapid raising of the eyebrows that we instinctively make when greeting someone we meet, but also when nodding or offering something. Ekman (1979) shows that the emotions most typically expressed by the eyebrows are anger, sadness, surprise, but he also recognises the conversational functions of their movements, including marking a question, finding words, agreeing or disagreeing with the interlocutor – including the intriguing "sceptical eyebrow", a one-sided raising of a single eyebrow that communicates scepticism. Moreover, as other authors have pointed out, raising one's eyebrows emphasises a word to signal its importance, in parallel with the emphasis given by the accent on a tonic syllable (Cavé et al., 1996; Krahmer et al., 2002). Goodwin (1981), Jokinen et al. (2013) and Rossano (2013) further specify how the gaze is used to request, grant and accept the speaking turn, as well as to provide a backchannel, the return of information by which the listener lets the speaker know whether he or she understands, follows or agrees.

More recent studies have attributed to the gaze referential functions such as pointing, iconic communication of physical and metaphorical properties (Poggi, 2006a, 2006b, 2007), and pragmatic functions such as expressing the performative of a sentence or providing metadiscursive information (Poggi, Pelachaud & de Rosis, 2000; Poggi & Pelachaud, 2002; Pelachaud & Bilvi, 2003; Poggi, Spagnolo & D'Errico, 2010; Vincze & Poggi, 2011; see chapters 4, 6 and 7), as well as persuasive functions (Poggi & Vincze, 2009a, 2009b; see Chapter 10).

The high communicative value of the eyes is demonstrated, among other things, by the fact that it can be communicative even when the gaze is inhibited or blocked, not only by looking away but also by using socio-emotional artefacts (Viola, 2022) such as dark glasses, which metacommunicate (communicate about one's communication): "I don't want my eyes to communicate". In this way they can convey a great deal of information: e.g., "I don't want you to know my feelings" because feelings are weakness whereas, actually, "I want to have power over you"; or else "I don't want you to see me crying at the funeral", but, quite paradoxically, by doing so I let you know that I am crying (Mizzau, 1997).

## 1.5    A grammar of gaze?

To date, the literature on the gaze has emphasised its informational functions and effects rather than its use as a communicative system. And even then, only a few aspects of it have been considered, such as eyebrow movements and gaze direction, which are used as key parameters in all three strands of research. But other equally interesting features of the gaze, such as the position of the eyelids or the position of the iris within the eye, have been almost completely overlooked by contemporary studies; even in terms of communicative functions, not all the relevant semantic aspects of the use of the gaze have been studied; above all, although some authors – including Baron-Cohen – have sometimes spoken of a "language of the eyes", no one has yet analysed this communication system with the tools used by linguists to study all the languages of the world: no one has studied its semantics, its pragmatics, its phonology, or even its morphology. This is what we will try to do in the following chapters.

# 2

# GAZE AND COMMUNICATION

As gaze research has shown, the eyes have a dual function, as a cue and as a signal. But we can find more than that. It often happens in evolution that an organ that is specialised for one function is also used for something else, becoming a polyfunctional organ. For example, we use our mouth to eat, to breathe, to kiss, and eventually speech became one of its basic functions.

## 2.1  How many things do we do with our eyes?

Similarly, with our eyes we perform different kinds of actions. Communication is just one of them, and not the most typical: we can see, look, feel, think . . . and communicate.

- *Seeing*. First, our eyes have an input function: to store information through visual perception. When I am waiting for the bus, I see three people at the bus stop, but I do not pay any attention to them. In this case, my eyes only have a receptive function: to receive information about the outside world.
- *Looking*. To look is to see with the intention of seeing. If a teenager is at the bus stop, I look at him to see what his hairstyle is, just to keep up to date with current hairstyles. If a man seems mentally disturbed, I keep an eye on him to be ready to flee if he does something strange. The conductor of an orchestra looks at all the musicians before the start to make sure they are ready and concentrated: a 'check look'. Looking is often used to check, to control, that is, to monitor whether the state of the world around us corresponds to our wishes.
- *Feeling*. Visual perception also allows us to feel positive and negative sensations and aesthetic pleasures (Argyle & Cook, 1976). This is true for

DOI: 10.4324/9781032678344-2

the voyeur who peeps through a keyhole but also when you stop to look at the sunset, a handsome man, a beautiful picture, a scabrous detail or a gruesome scene.

So far, the eyes fulfil a receptive, an input function, aimed at storing information potentially useful for our (practical, aesthetic or simply cognitive) goals. In all these cases, the transfer of information is from the world to our mind. But eyes are also involved in the production of thought and in communication.

- *Thinking*. The cognitive processes that take place in our minds are not only signalled by our eye movements, they are in some way facilitated by them. In order to concentrate, we close our eyes or look away; when we are lost in our thoughts, we let our eyes wander into the void. In short, the eyes accompany and assist our thought processes.
- *Communicating*. Through the movements and morphological features of our eyes, eyelids, eyebrows and eye sockets, we communicate information to other people, either consciously or unconsciously, about our desires, emotions and mental states. If a boy steps on my foot on the bus, I can electrocute him with my gaze, a deliberate, conscious communicative behaviour; if I've been up all night, even if I don't want to, my dark circles manifest it: an involuntary communication about my tired state.

## 2.2   Towards a model of communication

In order to clarify when and how our gaze is a communicative tool, I will now present the theoretical model of communication that I adhere to in this book: a socio-cognitive model based on the notions of goal and belief.

### 2.2.1   Action

We start from the idea of communication as a form of action, as suggested by Austin (1962), who saw all sentences in a language as speech acts. From this intuition it follows that the same mechanisms that govern action are at the basis of communication.

According to Miller, Galanter and Pribram (1960), the life of any system, whether natural or artificial (a baby or a boiler), whether individual or collective (my grandmother or an anthill), is governed by goals. A goal is a regulatory state, i.e. one that does not exist in the real world, and the system starts to act just in order to make that state real. Actions have a hierarchical structure in that a goal is often pursued by means of a more or less complex plan, where each action has a goal, but each goal can be a means to a further goal, which Castelfranchi and Parisi (1980) call a supergoal, and all actions with their goals and supergoals lead to the final goal of the plan.

Starting from this abstract and general notion of goal as a regulatory state, we can also see as goals (Castelfranchi, 1981) the instincts of animals (such as a seagull flying away to warn the flock of an approaching predator) or the aims of a human institution (such as maintaining health for the Ministry of Health or public safety for the Ministry of the Interior), unconscious impulses (mistreating a friend of whom one is jealous), needs (hunger, knowledge), the norms of an institution (paying taxes) (Conte, 1997), the duties that individuals impose on themselves (taking care of ageing parents).

In order to achieve its goals, the system relies on external resources, such as the conditions of the world, including material resources, which can prevent or favour the pursuit and achievement of goals; but it mainly uses internal resources, its beliefs and action skills, which allow it to overcome the lack of resources in the world through planning and problem solving.

These resources give power to the system, i.e. they increase its likelihood of achieving its goals. This is why, for example, experience and learning – the acquisition of new beliefs and skills – are forms of empowerment.

### 2.2.2 Beliefs

Beliefs are representations in a system's mind of external or internal objects or events, and they are represented in a sensorimotor or conceptual format. A chair is represented in my mind as a visual image of some chair I have seen but also as a motor programme of my action of sitting down and finally as a set of abstract concepts in the form of propositional structures: predicates (properties or relations) with their arguments. Here are the propositional structures contained in the meaning of "chair":

X object
X artefact
X is made to sit on
X has a seat
X has four legs
X has a back

Very important kinds of belief are evaluations: beliefs about whether and how much a particular object, event or person has or gives us power for a particular goal. I might judge a knife to be a bad knife if it does not cut salami well; consider today a nice day if I want to learn new things and I attend an interesting conference; I think my boyfriend is nice if he makes me feel happy; I say a politician is dishonest if he does not meet my goal of not having corrupt administrators.

Beliefs are useful to the system at all stages of the decision-making and planning processes. First of all, even to decide which of several goals to pursue, we have to evaluate their benefits (other goals to which they are conducive) and their costs (what other goals their pursuit might thwart). To be vaccinated or not? If I do, I am protected from the pandemic (a benefit), but I risk the side effects of the vaccine; if I do not, I risk infection, but this is better than giving up my free choice. So I choose my goal by considering how valuable its supergoals are to me.

Once I have decided which goal to pursue, I need beliefs about the conditions for pursuing and achieving it (how to sign up for the vaccination, where to go for it) in order to plan effectively.

Given the importance of beliefs, for humans more than for any other animal, the goal of acquiring and processing them becomes vital; we acquire and process beliefs through sensation and perception, inference, signification and communication, and we store and connect them in memory.

Sensation and perception are our first interface with the world. Through our senses, we come into contact with patterns of matter/energy: acoustic, optical, chemical and mechanical which, once processed together with information from the brain – the laws of perception – give rise to sensory-motor representations that are stored in our long-term memory and connect to each other in belief networks, so that from one belief we can derive another.

But if (relatively few) beliefs are acquired through perception, new beliefs, which we call inferences, are autonomously generated by our mind on the basis of different kinds of inference rules (different kinds of reasoning, e.g., deductive, inductive, abductive, . . .). Inferences concerning relations of place, time, class-example, part-whole, cause-effect, means-end, contrast allow us to combine a newly arrived belief in our working memory with others retrieved from long-term memory in order to generate further new beliefs, often as reliable as perceived and memorised ones. The ability to make inferences, i.e. to autonomously generate new beliefs, allows for an enormous increase in knowledge; in fact, perception excludes our access not only to all beliefs about events far away in time and space (the colour of Napoleon's horse or the shape of my newborn grandson's eyes in Australia) but also to abstract beliefs (such as altruism or dictatorship). Furthermore, we can use reasoning and inferences to create possible or imaginary worlds.

Besides inference, another source of belief is signification: meaning. A signified belief – a meaning – is a finally automated inference. The first time I saw smoke, it was only then that I understood that it was caused by fire, but after this cause-effect connection has occurred repeatedly, I stored it in my memory, and in the end I came to know that "smoke 'means' fire": I no longer need to go through the whole process of reasoning, but I immediately connect the presence of one event (which I perceive) with another event (which I do not directly perceive): "smoke" stands for "fire".

Finally, communication comes from signification. When I communicate something to you, I produce a perceptible stimulus – a word, a gesture, a look – from which (I believe) you can derive a meaning, i.e. another belief that is inextricably linked to that stimulus.

As for the beliefs in our minds, we also have meta-beliefs, i.e. beliefs about beliefs: for example, we assign different degrees of certainty to them, depending partly on the source from which they come, be it perception, inference, memory, signification or communication.

I generally trust most what I have seen with my own eyes; often (especially if I am a very critical person) I trust something I have deduced myself more than something I have heard from other people. But if I blindly trust the person who told me, I feel even more confident about it than if I thought it myself.

The degree of certainty we attach to our beliefs depends not only on their source but also on a comparison with our previous beliefs.

If a new belief contradicts my previous ones or cannot be deduced from them, I must either reject it or restructure the whole network. The first is what people (and the Church) initially did in the face of Copernicus's theory; the second is what they eventually came to accept. But the rejection of a belief can also be motivated by the fact that accepting it is too painful; like someone who is afraid of vaccination, cannot accept the shameful belief that he is afraid, and tries to find all the information that proves that he is right not to want to vaccinate.

### 2.2.3 You and others

The other "external" resource the system draws on is other systems. Social interaction arises from our finitude, from our lack of omnipotence (Conte & Castelfranchi, 1995). If we were endowed with all the material resources, beliefs and agency we need to achieve our goals, we would be self-sufficient. But this is not the case for human beings from the moment of birth: a new-born child could not survive on its own: it is dependent on another for food and care. Lack of power leads to dependence on other systems, and in particular on their 'goal adoption'. Goal adoption is the fact that one system takes care of the goals of another system, i.e. it pursues them as if they were its own goals. Cases of this are: a mother with her child (adoption by affect); a man who rescues an unknown child drowning in the sea (altruism); but also the grocer who sells me sandwiches (exchange), or the schoolmates who summarise different parts of a book (cooperative adoption), or when I stop for the red traffic light (normative adoption).

However, when two systems are present, another social device is triggered: social influence, i.e. the fact that one system tries to make the other pursue (or not pursue) certain goals, whether for selfish or altruistic reasons, i.e. in one's own interest or in the interest of the other. And various ways to influence exist: from hypnosis to education, from manipulation to the use of force, from threat to seduction, adulation and persuasion.

Communication is part of these two mechanisms of social interaction: it is an act of adoption, a gift, because when you communicate, you provide others with beliefs that they can use for their purposes. But it is also an act of influence because every sentence is requesting the other to do something, to provide information or to believe what you say (Castelfranchi & Parisi, 1980; Castelfranchi & Poggi, 1998; Poggi, 2007, 2022a).

## 2.3 Communication

Communication is a process by which we acquire new beliefs from others. According to this model, an act of communication takes place when a system S (sender) has the goal of having another system A (addressee) acquire a belief B and, in order to achieve this goal, produces a signal $s$ that is (or S believes is) associated in the minds of both sender and addressee with belief B, which is the meaning of the signal $s$. A signal is a perceptible stimulus – a sentence, an intonation, a pause, a gesture, a gaze, a posture; but also a statue, a strike, a letter of resignation, a like on social media. It can be produced by S in different productive modalities, i.e. by different bodily organs – mouth, face, eyes, hands, trunk – and it is perceived by A in different sensory modalities – sight, hearing, touch, smell, taste. Each signal is linked to its corresponding meaning by a system of communication: a set of rules for linking meaning to signals, which may be a verbal language, a sign language of the deaf but also a system of gestures or of facial expressions, postures, glances.

### 2.3.1 *Goal of communicating*

The criterion for considering an event as a communicative event is that the sender of a belief has the goal of transmitting this belief to some addressee: thus we can distinguish this from cases in which a system comes to have a belief by itself, no thanks to others, and perhaps simply generates it by inference or signification. If I see my grandfather looking around the room, I may infer that he is looking for his glasses, but he is not communicating this to me, he had no goal to communicate it (a case of inference). If I am a violinist and I see the conductor looking around, it means that he is checking if we are ready, then he will give the start (signification); but if I see that he is looking at me, I feel that he is asking for my attention, as if he were saying "be ready to start": this is communication, since the conductor has precisely the goal of letting me know that he is going to give the start.

In this view of communication, it is not necessary for the goal of the sender to be a conscious intention to convey information. The goal of communicating can also be an unconscious goal – you have it, but you don't know you have it because it might hurt to know it, so you hide it from yourself – or else a "tacit" or silent goal – one you automatically pursue because conscious attention to it would entail cognitive overload.

A personal case of an unconscious communication goal dates back to my early years at university. As a young assistant professor, I was quite lenient, and sometimes perhaps a little too sympathetic, with students who did poorly in oral examinations. As I would look students in the face when giving them a low grade or even a failing grade, they would invariably begin to haggle over the grade: they probably saw in my eyes some uncertainty or flash of sympathy that I did not know I felt, and they tried to take advantage of it. When I started to communicate the grades by looking down, without staring at the other person, the haggling stopped as if by magic.

Here, instead, is a case in which the goal of communicating is "tacit": often, to emphasise a passage of speech, we drop our hands down, or emphasise a syllable, or raise our eyebrows. The latter is a signal of our own surprise that we want to convey to the interlocutor in order to attract his attention, and it means "pay attention, because this is the most important part of what I'm saying"; but it would require too much cognitive load to consciously decide that we want to communicate this every time we raise our eyebrows: so the signal is produced at a low level of consciousness, in an automatic, silent, "unspoken" way.

Finally, the goal of communicating may even be a biological function, such as behaviours or morphological traits that are not determined by the individual's will but are functional to adaptive goals. This is common in many animals, such as the stickleback fish, whose abdomen reddens to signal mating readiness. In humans, the signal of pupil dilation, which conveys sexual arousal, is not only not subject to conscious will, it is even received unconsciously: in Hess's study (1965; see Chapter 1), male students judged the girls with dilated pupils to be sexier, without realising that it was only the eyes that made them so attractive. Thus in humans, as in fish, what signals mating readiness is a transient morphological trait that is not only emitted by the sender but also perceived by the addressee without consciousness.

### 2.3.2 Meaning

The minimal unit of communication is the communicative act, i.e. an act by which a sender asks the addressee to perform an action and which includes performative and propositional content (Castelfranchi & Parisi, 1980; Poggi, 2022a). The performative conveys the kind of action one is asking the other to do: by a request, such as the imperative "Put on your new raincoat", one is asking the other to do something; by a question, such as "Is this your new raincoat?" and its interrogative intonation, one is asking the other a belief; by an informative sentence, such as "This raincoat is new", one is asking the other to believe what one is saying; by an optative sentence, such as "I wish I could buy a new raincoat", one is expressing a wish.

The propositional content is the content of the request: the action to be performed, the information to be given, the information to be believed, the desire expressed.

Within the structure of a communicative act, what are the meanings that a system may need to convey to others? The myriad meanings that human and animal communication convey can be grouped into three broad types. Firstly, information about the world, that is, information about entities and events external to the sender: actions or properties ("runs", "smokes", "is green") of concrete or abstract entities ("my watch", "democracy"); about real events ("the predator is approaching", "pollen is at an angle of 30° to the sun") or imaginary events ("Scrooge is very stingy") and general statements ("eagles are birds"). This kind of information can be conveyed by words but also by gestures and even by eye gaze: grandma squints her eyes when she says "she saw a teeny tiny house", thus also representing something small in this language.

Another important piece of information for humans and many animals is the identity of the sender. The peacock's wheel, a lizard's colour display and the jumps of some birds inform a potential mate of one's lustre. A politician putting his hand over his heart emphasises his honesty. But breasts or Adam's apple, the sound of a voice or a beard can also tell us a person's gender and age, and the shape of their eyelids can tell us their ethnicity.

Finally, another type of information is conveyed in every act of communication: information about the mind of the sender. Every time you talk to someone, as well as providing the information you are dealing with, you also communicate your goals (why you are talking about it and what you want the other person to do), your beliefs (how convinced, uncertain or confident you are about what you are saying) and your feelings about what you are saying. If you *look a person straight in the eye* when you ask him something, your request is imperative; if you *raise your eyebrows* when you say something, *without opening your eyes too much*, it means that you have some doubts; but if *your eyes sparkle* when you say it, the thing excites you.

However, all these meanings are not always communicated directly: sometimes I cannot understand what you mean simply from what you explicitly say or communicate by gestures, facial expressions, posture; I must make inferences, i.e. draw further beliefs beyond those literally present in your message. In some cases, making inferences allows us to imagine what the sender does not want us to know, as when a pickpocket on the bus tells me that I have dropped something in order to distract me and go through my bag. But very often what the sender does not say is what he wants to make clear, but he just prefers not to communicate it by explicit signals, for reasons of euphemism or politeness. This is indirect communication, as opposed to literal communication. Literally I say to you, *Can you pass the salt?*, i.e. I ask a question, but what I really mean is, "Give me the salt", that is, I want you to understand that this is a request. I mean "I apologise" (an act of submission to the interlocutor), but I say *I'm sorry*, literally an expression of a negative emotion of mine. I mean "I don't agree", but I say *I didn't understand*. Actually, we can do the same thing with body signals: if *I frown* while you are talking, I may simply want to convey "I didn't understand, please explain better", but I may instead mean "I understand very well, but I don't agree at all".

### 2.3.3 Communication systems

Any communication system is a set of rules for relating signals to meanings. But the communication systems used by humans are diverse and varied, not only because they use different productive modalities (hands, voice, face, eyes, bust, . . .) but also because the rules that make them up differ in terms of various parameters.

A first parameter is the "cognitive construction" of the signal, distinguishing between codified and creative communication systems: in the former, signals are linked in a stable way to their respective meanings and are therefore stored in long-term memory, where they form a lexicon. For example, in a verbal lexicon, the sound sequence (word) *chair* is associated with the meaning "artefact with the function of sitting, with four legs, a seat and a back"; in a lexicon of gestures (Poggi, 2002a), the hand movement of *moving the extended index and middle fingers back and forth, touching the mouth*, corresponds to the meaning of "smoking action" (to smoke) or "long and thin object to be smoked" (cigarette); the *rapid blinking of a single eye while looking at the interlocutor (wink)* means "to set complicity with the other".

Creative signals, on the other hand, are those we create on the spot, not memorised beforehand: for example, the gestures of pantomime, i.e. the use of gestures and the body to represent events in the world. If, when talking about an eagle, *I move my hands as* if they were *wings*, or if, when talking about a person whirling through the air like a trapeze artist, I *look up in the air from left to right* as if following her whirls, then I have created a new gesture or gaze that represents what I mean iconically, that is, by rendering the image of what I mean. Such an extemporaneously created gesture or gaze signal, not having been previously memorised in the minds of the sender and the receiver, must necessarily be iconic, i.e. represent its referent by imitation.

Another related distinction in communication systems, concerning the relationship between a signal and its meaning, is that between motivated and arbitrary signals. A signal is motivated if, even if you do not know it in advance, you can catch (infer, guess) its meaning; and it is arbitrary if you cannot guess its meaning, you must know it, have it already stored in a mental lexicon. The iconic signals, such as *moving hands like wings* to mean "bird", or *looking up here and there* to mean "trapeze artist", are motivated because there is a relationship of similarity between signal and meaning: the former imitates perceptible features of the latter.

Other signals are also motivated, not by iconicity, but rather by "mechanical determinism": see the bilabial sound of the word *mummy* in many languages, determined by the baby's sucking movements; the gesture of *rising and shaking the fist* when celebrating a victory, biologically induced by the high arousal of such a positive emotion; or the *wide opening of the eyes* in surprise, determined by the need to expand the visual field to acquire more information in order to understand the reasons for the unexpected event (Pelachaud & Poggi, 2002b; Poggi & Pelachaud, 2002).

Again, signals can be distinguished according to the part of the communicative act they convey. Some signals, which I call articulated (Poggi, 1981, 2022b), "segment" the communicative act into parts, and each single part is conveyed by a single signal. In the sentence *I assure you John is nice*, the word *assure* conveys the performative, *John* an argument of propositional content and *nice* a predicate attributed to that argument. Only a single class of words, interjections, are holophrastic signals, since they convey the meaning of a whole communicative act, comprising both performative and propositional content. Saying *Wow!* is equivalent to saying "I inform you (performative) that this event makes me pleasantly surprised and happy (propositional content)!"

Even among the gestures, some are articulated and others holophrastic: the movement of the *extended index and middle fingers back and forth, touching the mouth*, is an articulated gesture (a "word" gesture) meaning "cigarette" or "smoke"; the *hand palm downwards, moving the fingers repeatedly downwards*, is a holophrastic gesture (a "sentence" gesture) meaning "come here", i.e. a whole communicative act, composed of performative ("I ask you") and propositional content ("that you come here").

Among gaze items we can also find articulated signals, like the one meaning "trapeze artist", which conveys a single argument of a communicative act. But gaze items are much more often holophrastic: a *fixed look in the eye* means "I ask you (performative) to pay attention (propositional content)"; a *lazy eye* means "I inform you (performative) that I love you (propositional content)".

A final important distinction between signals concerns their origin. Some are universal because they are biologically determined: smiling, laughing, crying, but also some gestures, such as *raising and shaking the fist* as a sign of victory, and the facial expressions of primary emotions: joy, anger, sadness, fear, disgust, surprise. There are also many facial expressions, such as *frowning* as a sign of concentration or *raising the eyebrows* in perplexity. Some signals, on the other hand, are cultural, shared by one or more specific cultures but not universal: like the majority of words in all the world's languages but also the so-called symbolic gestures, which are used only in a specific culture and are incomprehensible in others. For example, the hand with the *palm up and the fingers closed, moving up and down*, which means "But what are you saying? What do you want?", is only used with this meaning in Italy. But even among the glances, some are not universal: the *wink* – the *rapid closing and opening of one eye* – has a meaning of allusion and complicity only in some cultures.

### 2.3.4 Lexicons of the words, lexicons of the body

A codified communication system is a lexicon, i.e. a list of rules of correspondence between signals and meanings, among which we can distinguish semantic rules and norms of use. A semantic rule is a signal–meaning pair in which a set of sounds produced by the voice or a set of movements of a body part corresponds to a set of beliefs that are the literal meaning of that signal. For example, the word *chair* corresponds to the belief "artefact with the function of sitting, with four legs, a seat and a back"; *staring at an interlocutor* corresponds to the belief "the sender asks the addressee to pay attention"; the *hand with the palm facing downwards repeatedly moving the fingers downwards* corresponds to the belief "the sender asks the addressee to come closer to the sender".

*/chair/*← → "artefact with the function of sitting on, with four legs, a seat, and a back"
*/staring at the other/*← → "I ask you to pay attention"

Often, however, the same signal can correspond to several different meanings: the signal is ambiguous. We can distinguish two types of lexical ambiguity: (1) homophony, where two meanings happen to correspond to the same signal, but there is no semantic relationship between them; as in the word *watch*, which means both "clock" and "to look at"; and (2) polysemy, where two or more meanings of the same signal share a semantic element. For example, the word *ring* means both "a jewel to wear on a finger" and "a platform for boxers", but both share the same semantic core, one or more common beliefs contained in both meanings, the image of a "closed boundary around an object or place". When confronted with an ambiguous signal, in order to understand which of its meanings is intended, we must rely on other beliefs drawn from the physical or communicative context (if it is a ring, in the context of jewellery, the intended meaning will be the former; in the context of boxing, the latter). A case of gestural polysemy is the Italian symbolic gesture of the *hands, palms down, with the index fingers extended, repeatedly approaching each other*, which means "there is an understanding between the two of them", or "they are accomplices", "they are lovers", but also "there is a connection between these two facts". Here the common semantic core, i.e. the belief contained in all these meanings, is the idea of some "relationship between two objects, persons or events". In Chapter 7 we will see some cases of polysemy in the gaze.

In addition to semantic rules, a lexicon also contains norms of use. A norm of use adds to the semantic rule information about when, in which situations, and to which addressees it is appropriate, permitted, or required to convey that meaning and thus to produce that particular signal. It is then a sociolinguistic norm, corresponding to Ekman and Friesen's (1971, 1978) "display rules". We all laugh at an amusing event; but if you are amused at a funeral, you must refrain from *laughing*. Thus the semantic rules are universal, but the norms of use may vary from culture to culture: a seductive look is always the same and is produced with the same muscular actions in the USA as in Sweden, in Japan as in the Samoan Islands, but in a culture where the norms of sexual morality are particularly restrictive, the seductive look will be more sanctioned and will have to be inhibited, whereas in a very free and emancipated culture a man and a woman will be free to look at each other as they wish.

## 2.4   The lexicon of gaze

To sum up, in my hypothesis the gaze involves both a creative and a codified communication system: the former with rules based on similarity that tell us how to create an entirely new signal, provided it is iconic (as in the trapeze artist example); the latter organised into memorised signal-meaning pairs: a lexicon.

Each signal in this lexicon is a set of movements or morphological features of organs in the eye region – pupil, iris, sclera, eyelids, eyelashes, eyebrows – corresponding to a particular meaning, i.e. a set of beliefs. In the following chapters, we will try to understand the meanings conveyed by these gaze signals in general, and for some of them, we will attempt an in-depth analysis of the beliefs they carry and the functions they fulfil.

We will do this both for the gaze signals that we all use in our everyday lives and for those that are exploited in particular types of communicative interaction, such as the gaze of teachers and the gaze of orchestra conductors.

But beyond discovering the principles that govern this lexicon, its semantic rules and norms of use, beyond analysing its communicative signals in terms of their meanings, we have to bear in mind that each signal is a physically perceptible stimulus produced by the features and movements of the ocular region, so we will also try to identify the rules that govern the construction of different signals: what distinguishes – in production and recognition – a *seductive look* from a *glare* or a *dirty look*? A *slanted look* from a *look down*?

Of course, these are different ways of looking at others, both in terms of their meaning and their interactional function, but they also differ in the physical ways in which we produce them and in the perceptual appearance they present to the interlocutor.

Therefore, in addition to the lexicon, we will have to study the "alphabet" of this language, or more precisely, the "phonology" of the gaze: the minimal elements that, combined in various ways, make up all the "words" of our ocular speech.

# 3

# METHODS

How can we describe the lexicon and "alphabet" of the gaze? How can we capture the many ways we can look at others, and what meanings correspond to each of these different gaze signals? Since this is not an easy task, we have to resort to all kinds of methods from linguistics, psychology, cultural anthropology, artificial intelligence and simulation.

Let us look at these methods in detail.

## 3.1  Ethno-semantic method

To describe the lexicon of gaze, we must first understand how many and what codified meanings it contains and then understand the physical properties of these signals. As Berlin and Kay (1969) have shown, we can define commonsense concepts by analysing how they are distinguished and organised in a language. A language is a mirror of our conceptualisation of reality, it is the way in which our culture "slices and dices" some semantic areas, i.e. some structures of meaning.

For example, if you list the words that describe the semantic field of deception, you will find verbs like *lie, deceive, cheat, adulate*, nouns like *bluff, bragging, fraud subterfuge, hoax, slander*, which distinguish innumerable ways of deceiving; but also nouns like *dupe*, or adjectives like *gullible, credulous*, which refer to the deceived person. These words already lead us to distinguish their underlying concepts.

So, in order to find out which meanings are expressed in the lexicon of the gaze, I start by looking for the words or idioms in a natural language that name communicative and noncommunicative acts performed by the gaze.

DOI: 10.4324/9781032678344-3

To sum up, if we are looking for the "words of gaze", we first need to find the "words on gaze" in our language: the verbal items that mention *eyes*, *gaze*, *looking*, such as *dirty look*, *oblique gaze*, *blink*, *stare of defiance* and the like. They all describe communicative acts that we perform with our eyes and thus allow us to list and partially characterise, if not all, at least many of the lexical items in our lexicon of gaze.

## 3.2  Deductive method

A second way of singling out lexical items in a body lexicon (Poggi, 2007) is to adopt a top-down strategy: one relies on a general taxonomy of possible meanings – such as the one presented in Chapter 2 – and then, for each type and subtype of meaning, one asks whether there is a signal in the lexicon under study that communicates that very meaning. For example, I might ask whether the lexicon of gaze contains signals that convey backchannel information, such as "I'm following you" or "I don't agree", and find that we can indeed communicate that we are following the present speaker by *briefly closing our eyelids*, and that we don't agree by *frowning our eyebrows*; but if I look for the same meanings in the lexicon of head movements, I might find that here too they are conveyed by two common signals: *head nodding* and *head shaking*.

Once a list of possible items in a body lexicon – in this case a list of "gaze words" – has been selected, it can be analysed both on the signal side (how each gaze item is physically produced) and on the semantic side (what meaning corresponds to each gaze item).

Various methods can be used to carry out this analysis.

## 3.3  The speaker's judgements

The simplest but also the richest method, since it provides very precise and detailed information about the form of a signal and its corresponding meaning, is the Chomskian method of speaker's judgements (Chomsky, 1965; Parisi, 1979), which is based on the linguistic intuition (here, more generally, the communicative intuition) of the native speaker. In his book *Aspects of the Theory of Syntax*, Noam Chomsky (1965) argues that every speaker can make judgements of acceptability, ambiguity and paraphrasis about the sentences of one's own language.

We can make the same judgements about our own and others' gaze signals.

In order to analyse the meaning of a word, a gaze or any other bodily signal, it is necessary to make judgements of acceptability (asking in which context a given gaze is acceptable or not), of ambiguity (whether a gaze item has one or more meanings and which ones) and of paraphrasis (if and which other elements of a lexicon, whether of the same or a different modality, have the same meaning of the signal under consideration) (Parisi, 1979; Poggi, 1983, 2022a).

The first piece of information you have when considering a particular gaze is whether or not it is appropriate in a given situation. For example, you may have an intuition about the norms of use, say, that it would be inappropriate to *wink* at the chair of your doctoral committee. But you also have intuitions about the "phonological rules" of the gaze system, about how "gaze words" are physically produced: you know that if you *squeeze your eye for too long*, the other person will not think that you are *winking* at him (communicative gaze) but that a mote has entered your eye (a noncommunicative action, a non-gaze): the same difference as between a word like *jump* and a non-word like *mump*.

Moreover, a look can also be ambiguous: if you *look at me with a frown*, you can either mean "I don't understand", or just say "I'm concentrating", or finally "I don't agree".

Finally, just as two sentences can be paraphrases of each other, i.e. they can have a similar meaning, so two different looks can be synonyms. To convey that you are thinking, you can either *frown* or *look up*.

The judgement of paraphrasis is also useful for the analysis of gaze because by paraphrasing each gaze item with a sentence in a verbal language, one already has a first idea of its meaning. This tells us, for example, that the majority of gaze items are holophrastic signals, i.e. they convey the meaning of a whole sentence.

Such communicative intuitions allow us to tease out both the construction rules of gaze signals (their "phonology") and the correspondences between individual gaze items and their relative meanings. For example, we could represent the ambiguity of a single gaze as follows: three possible meanings correspond to a single gaze signal.

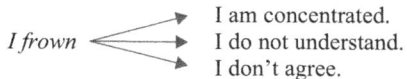

And we might represent the synonymy of two different gaze items: two different signals conveying the same meaning:

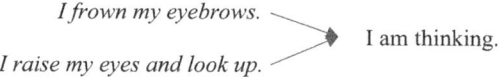

According to Chomsky (1965), the native speaker's intuitions are the conscious reflex of the underlying semantic and syntactic rules that govern the construction of sentences in a language, and it is only thanks to these intuitions, these judgements, that they can emerge. But these intuitions of acceptability, ambiguity and synonymy also allow us to analyse the meaning of individual items in the lexicon of the gaze.

Relying on the speaker's judgement is a very economical method of semantic analysis because the research can be carried out by a linguist on the basis of his judgements alone, on his communicative intuitions; but it is also a very effective method because it allows us to analyse very large areas of the lexicon and to carry out in-depth analyses. At the end of such an analysis, we have at least a picture of the communicative competence of that individual scholar, which is relevant on the scientific side anyway, because even the competence of a single person is a coherent system of communicative rules.

## 3.4  Corpora

Another approach to investigate the meaning of specific signals is through corpus research. You collect a corpus of texts or audio recordings (for words) or video recordings (for visual signals such as gestures, facial expressions, postures, glances). You select all the cases in which a given signal is used, trying to assess, on the basis of the context, the specific meaning that this signal assumes in each case, so that you identify the set of semantic features or components contained in the meaning of this signal. Finally, taking into account the differences that the meaning shows in the different contexts, you select the core of meanings, i.e. the minimum set of semantic elements shared by all uses of the signal (Kendon, 2004; Müller, 2004; Brookes, 2004; Vincze & Poggi, 2016, 2022).

For example, in a study on the meanings of the sigh, Poggi, Ansani and Cecconi (2018), in a corpus of Italian literary texts, selected 64 fragments of novels in which the root *sospir-* (sigh) occurs in verbs such as *sospirò* (sighed), *sospirando* (sighing), in nouns such as *sospiro* (sigh) or in complex expressions such as *tirò un sospiro* (he let out a sigh). In an attempt to assess the meaning of each occurrence of the word in its particular context, a wide range of mental states was identified that the sigh can express, including displeasure, regret, annoyance, boredom, resignation, worry, relief, desire, hope.

Another study carried out on the same corpus (Poggi & Ansani, 2018a), analysing the occurrences of the gaze item *occhi al cielo* (eyes heavenward), finally singled out meanings such as prayer, resignation, impatience, reflection and inference (see Chapter 9).

## 3.5  Observation

When the researcher uses a videorecorded corpus, he is carrying out an observational study of the possible meanings of a word or other bodily signal, so he has to select, describe and classify the occurrences of the observed signals, possibly even with the help of annotation schemes that allow analysis.

To give an example of an observation, let us consider the case of a "facial comment", that is a body signal usually produced during a talk show by a participant who is not the interlocutor but who nevertheless wants to comment on what the current speaker is saying and does so by means of a face or a gesture (Poggi, D'Errico & Vincze, 2013). A common facial comment is the combination of *sighing + eyes heavenward*, which, by expressing impatience with what the current speaker is saying, implies a negative evaluation of it as boring or useless repetition, thus diminishing the speaker's credibility and prestige.

For example, Matteo Salvini, leader of the right-wing Northern League party, argues that migrants who land on Italian shores should be sent back, while the left-wing deputee Laura Boldrini counters that the current situation of frequent landings is the result of previous mistakes by the right-wing government. While Boldrini speaks, Salvini *raises his eyes heavenward* and *sighs*, showing his impatience with his opponent's speech.

### 3.6 Empirical research

After an introspective analysis in which the researcher plays the role of an informant, or after formulating a hypothesis about the meaning of a signal in a real case, the researcher can test the hypotheses resulting from his intuitions or observations by using empirical methods (Morris et al., 1979; Serenari, 2003, 2004; Poggi, 2007): interviews and questionnaires, in which the speakers of a given social or cultural group are asked about the meaning attributed to a given bodily signal or the way it is used. Two methods can be used: encoding and decoding. In the case of decoding, you present a certain signal to the participants and ask them to decode it, to explain its meaning in words, to say in which situations it would be appropriate, or to point out other signals with the same meaning. For example, if, based on your communicative intuition, you have hypothesised that *opening one's eyes wide* in the context of conducting an orchestra means asking for attention, you can show a survey participants a picture of this gaze and ask them, by means of an open-ended question, to express its meaning in words and/or, by means of a multiple-choice question, which of three or four verbal expressions best paraphrases this gaze.

In the case of encoding, participants are given a specific meaning in words and asked how they would express it, e.g. through a gesture or a look. In their study of facial expressions, Ekman and Friesen (1971) presented Japanese, American, and Papuan subjects with situations that elicited fear, anger, or sadness and photographed their facial expressions. In a study of sighs, Teigen (2008) asked participants to describe a situation in which someone might sigh.

## 3.7 Simulation on artificial agents

Another way to test the adequacy of our hypotheses about the meaning of a given signal is to simulate it on an artificial agent (ECA, avatar or robot). As has been shown since the early days of AI and even more so in robotics and artificial life research, simulation is an excellent way to test empirical hypotheses (Parisi, 2010). Here is the underlying reasoning: if I can express my theoretical hypotheses in a very precise, rigorous and formalised way, so much so that I can reproduce some behaviours (communicative signals) on a computer, and if this computer finally outputs the same reactions (meanings) caused by these behaviours in humans, then my theoretical hypotheses are verified. Furthermore, simulation has the advantage of allowing me not only to know the input and output of the process but also to follow its intermediate steps in detail. Therefore, the simulation of communicative behaviour on an artificial system such as a virtual agent – a two or three-dimensional user interface that reproduces a human agent – allows us to demonstrate a hypothesis more strongly and better than interviews or surveys: for example, if a facial expression of the virtual agent evokes the same emotion or reaction in the participants as the human expression does, the hypothesised meaning is verified.

Simulation on virtual agents can involve different steps, possibly using the other methods just mentioned. A study by Ochs et al. (2012), based on hypotheses about the shape and movements of smiles of amusement, politeness and embarrassment, proposed an algorithm to distinguish between the different types of smile; then, an evaluation study tested whether human participants would accurately classify the different smiles generated by the algorithm into these three types.

The last two methods, empirical research and simulation, are particularly useful for semantic analysis when it comes to "intensive" research, i.e. in-depth analysis of single signals. However, for an "extensive" study, i.e. the construction of an entire lexicon of the gaze – as we propose in the following chapters – the most effective methods are the deductive, the ethno-semantic and, to some extent, the observational.

## 3.8 How to analyse the items of a lexicon

Whatever method is used, among those mentioned above, for the semantic analysis of verbal and bodily signals, the first step is always the speaker's judgements. But how can we analyse the meaning of a communicative signal in order to extract its semantic features or components? Here are the necessary steps:

1. Collect a number of real or invented situations in which this signal can be used. "*Exempla ficta*" (fictional, invented examples) are also very useful because we can express speaker's judgements even about them. In fact, our linguistic/communicative competence is made up of abstract and general rules, and this makes our judgements richer than both observation and empirical research. Empirical research and observation provide us with real cases – but not necessarily all possible cases. Instead, our competence, with its intuitions expressed in the speaker's judgements, is valid not only about what is real but also about what is possible – which is much broader.

   Example: In a video recording (case 1, real example) you see an interviewee *frowning* before answering a question. But later you also imagine yourself (case 2, invented example) *frowning* while asking a question.

2. For each situation listed, write down all the information that might be useful for interpreting the signal: the physical and social context, the reasons that might have led the sender to produce this meaning, i.e. her beliefs and goals in producing it, and also any other communicative signals (words, sentences, facial expressions, body movements) that might have been produced at the same time as the signal analysed.

   In case 1, the context is an interview, i.e. an interaction in which a speaker S asks a listener L for some information, and L, who is *frowning*, is concentrating to find it in her long-term memory.
   In case 2, the *frown* is produced by S, who does not have any information and therefore asks the listener L.

3. Reformulate in a verbal paraphrase what the signal means in each situation;

   In case 1, the *frown* means: "I'm concentrating".
   In case 2, it means: "I'm asking you a question".

4. On the basis of the paraphrases used to reformulate the signal in the different situations and of the information about the sender's goals and beliefs in producing it, you can make a hypothesis about the meaning of the signal occurring in all the given situations; in other words, you make a hypothesis about the semantic rules and constraints that govern its use:

   The sender of a *frown* is looking for a belief and either concentrates to retrieve it from memory (case 1) or asks others to provide it (case 2).

5. To test the hypothesis, you can invent a situation in which these rules or constraints are violated and try to use the signal. If the signal is unacceptable in this new, invented situation, then your hypothesis is plausible: you have probably found the right rules and constraints for using this signal, hence its meaning.

   Imagine that in case 1 the interviewee already knows how to answer the interviewer's question: in this situation the *frown* would be unacceptable. Or imagine that, in case 2, S does not want L to understand that S does not know something and wants to ask about it: in this situation too, S's *frown* would be unacceptable.

6. Finally, try to use, in these same situations, other signals whose meaning is similar but not the same as that of the analysed signal, asking yourself in which situations the two signals would be completely interchangeable and in which they would not. In this way, you will be able to carry out a differential semantic analysis of signals that are partially synonymic: the semantic comparison of two signals allows you to better understand their respective meanings.

   In case 1, the interviewee could be *looking far away*, thus communicating that she is thinking. In case 2, the person asking a question might *raise her eyebrows*, which also means: "I'm asking you about this". The difference is that the *frown* gives the question an air of urgency, perhaps of suspicion, of fear that the other person will not answer honestly or take the question seriously.

# 4

# A MINE OF WORDS

If the gaze is a system of communication, that is, a set of rules for relating signals to meanings, then in order to write a lexicon of it we need to identify, on the one hand, the meanings it conveys and, on the other, the signals, that is, the ways in which it communicates them.

In the following chapter, we will examine the signals of this system in detail; in this chapter, we will examine the semantics of the gaze, trying to answer the question: what meanings can be conveyed by our eyes?

## 4.1 Codified and creative signals

As mentioned in Chapter 2, the correspondences between signals and meanings in a communication system can be of two types, either codified or creative.

In the first case, when the sender wants to communicate a meaning M, he searches more or less consciously or automatically in his mental lexicon for a codified signal *s* (a word, a gesture, a look), i.e. one that is permanently linked in his long-term memory to the meaning M, and produces it, i.e. he imprints on an organ of his body – mouth, hands, eyes – those features or behaviours that make up the signal *s*. To express surprise, for example, he *opens his eyes wide* and *raises his eyebrows*.

In the case of the creative signal, on the other hand, the sender cannot find a ready-made signal associated with this meaning in his memory, and in order to create it on the spot, in the chosen modality, he produces a movement or displays a feature which, by resemblance, can recall the intended meaning and thus allow it to be inferred.

DOI: 10.4324/9781032678344-4

For example, to refer to a person who is not very bright, he might *open his eyes wide* and perhaps *roll them*, imitating a dumbfounded expression. In this case, the signal is not codified, but it can still be understood because it is iconic (from the Greek *èikon*, image): it imitates, i.e. resembles aspects of the meaning it wants to convey.

In fact, the codified signals make up a lexicon, that is, a set of correspondences between the displayed features or behaviours produced in the eye region and the meanings that a sender may have the goal of communicating. And this lexicon can be described in a "gazeionary": a dictionary of the gaze.

## 4.2 Ethno-semantics of gaze

What are the "words" of our gaze? To answer this question, we can first use the ethno-semantic approach (Chapter 3): we look for words and idioms that, in a given language, express meanings related to eyes, gaze, seeing, looking: such as *to look, to peek, to peer* but also *to ogle, to feast one's eyes on, to gaze, to stare, to glare*. Analysing the "words about gaze" will help us to identify the "gaze words". The lexicons of natural languages such as Russian, Italian, English contain many lexical entries of one or more words, i.e. single words or whole idioms, which either in their signal (e.g. in one word of an idiom) or in their meaning (in the denoted or implied concepts) refer to communicative or noncommunicative acts of looking or to its organs, such as eyes, eyelids, eyebrows: verbs such as *to scrutinise* or *to make sheep's eyes*, nouns such as *gaze, glance, evil eye*, adjectives such as *frowning, winking*, adverbs such as *to the eye, at first sight*.

In a list of 136 lexical entries in Italian, I have selected six types of these (see Table 4.1). Further examples are given in Table 4.1.

## 4.3 Eyes without gaze

In many words and idioms of a language that use terms related to eyes, seeing, or looking, their meaning often has nothing to do with looking or at least only in a metaphorical way. For instance, in Italian *in un battito di ciglia* (lit. in a blink of eyelashes = *in a blink of an eye*) means "very quickly"; *a occhio e croce* (literally, by an eye and a cross) means "roughly"; *dare fumo negli occhi* (lit. to put smoke in their eyes) means "to give unclear information in order to give a deceptively positive impression", *vedersela brutta* (literally, to see it badly = to have a bad time) means "to be afraid of dying"; *vedo nero* (lit. I see it black) means "I am pessimistic"; *vedo rosso* (lit. I see red), "I feel anger or hostility towards someone or something".

In many cases, the idiom uses a metaphor behind which there is an original meaning somehow related to seeing or looking, but the current meaning is very different from the literal one.

**TABLE 4.1** Words and Idioms Connected vs. Non-Connected to Gaze and Its Functions

| Non-connected (or only metaphorically connected) with gaze | Seeing | Looking | Feeling | Thinking | Communicating |
|---|---|---|---|---|---|
| a occhio e croce (by and large) | adocchiare (to eye) | scrutare (scrutinise) | guardone (peeper) | sguardo perso nel vuoto (staring out into space) | ammiccare (to wink) |
| vedersela brutta (to have a bad time) | | dare uno sguardo (to have a look) | rifarsi gli occhi (to feast one's eyes) | Occhio! (eye! = watch out!) | occhiata (glance) |
| guardare in faccia la realtà (lit. to look reality in the eye = to be realistic) | | sguardo (gaze) | | come la vedo io (as I see it = in my view) | sguardo (gaze) |
| | | fissare (to stare) | | | fissare (to stare) |

Some expressions are polysemic, i.e. they have a meaning related to the functions of the eyes and an unrelated one: *occhieggiare* (= *to wink, to ogle*) has an unrelated meaning "to appear in a discrete, not so obvious way" and a related one: "to look at someone repeatedly with short and insistent glances that reveal curiosity, interest or desire".

## 4.4  Eyes that see, look, feel, think . . . and talk

Taking the Italian language as an example (but this is presumably valid for all or most other languages), among the expressions related to the functions of the gaze, some, such as *adocchiare* (to spot = to look at with a glance), refer to the function of SEEING; others, such as *scrutare* (to scrutinise = to examine attentively with the eyes) or *dare uno sguardo* (to have a look = to look quickly, just passing by) refer to LOOKING; *guardone* (peeper = a person who enjoys looking at the erotic acts of others) and *rifarsi gli occhi* (to feast one's eyes = to feel an aesthetic pleasure in looking at something) refer to FEELING.

A large number of lexical entries, either words or idioms, are related to THINKING and other COGNITIVE PROCESSES: attention (*occhio!* = "watch out!"; *tenere gli occhi aperti*, lit. keep your eyes open = "be careful"); concentration and retrieval from memory (*sguardo perso nel vuoto* = look out into space), opinion (*agli occhi di . . .* = in the eyes of . . ., "according to"; *come la vedo io*, lit. the way I see it = in my view, "in my opinion"), judgement (*prendere sott'occhio*, lit. to take someone under one's eye = "to expect bad things from someone because of prejudice"; *vedere di buon occhio*, lit. to see something or someone with a good eye = "to make a good judgement of something or someone"; *la vedo dura*, lit. I see it hard = "I think it will be very difficult").

Finally, more than 60 words or idioms in my list, such as *occhiataccia* (dirty look), *guardare di sottecchi* (to look furtively), *guardare dall'alto in basso* (to look down at another), *fare l'occhiolino* (to wink), refer to the gaze as a way of COMMUNICATING (Table 4.1). Some of these, such as *fissare* (to stare), are polysemic lexical items, since they have two or more meanings that fall into two or more different categories: *fissare* in Italian is both a way of LOOKING (to look at something fixedly, with attention) and a way of COMMUNICATING: *fissare* a person means to stare at her with a continuous look to mean something or to ask for something.

## 4.5 "Words about gaze": on the signal, the meaning and both

Coming to the words "about gaze", which refer to its communicative uses, we need to make another distinction.

As a communicative act, a gaze is a signal, i.e. a visually perceptible physical stimulus, more specifically a set of morphological features or movements produced by muscular actions or physiological states in the eye region, which corresponds to a meaning, i.e., a set of beliefs about the world, the sender's identity or the sender's mind.

This dual nature of the gaze is also revealed by the words of a language: some, with their meaning, provide information about the gaze signal, how it is produced, its physical characteristics; other words provide information about its meaning; finally, others provide information about both the signal and the meaning (Table 4.2). For example, the meaning of the "word (idiom) about gaze" *guardare dritto negli occhi* (look straight into the eyes) does not tell us what this look means but only how it is produced physically; it barely mentions the direction of the eyes when looking at the other, but only in an indirect or metaphorical way does it tell us that the person looking in this way is addressing the interlocutor in a deliberate and serious way. On the contrary, an idiom such as *fare gli occhi dolci* (make sheep eyes) tells us what this gaze communicates (showing one's love) but not how it is produced.

**TABLE 4.2** "Words About Gaze" That Inform About the Signal, the Meaning, or Both

| Signal | Meaning | Signal and meaning |
|---|---|---|
| *guardare dritto negli occhi* (to look straight in the eye) *sguardo perso nel vuoto* (staring out into space) | *fare gli occhi dolci* (to make sheep eyes) *Sguardo di sfida* (defiant gaze) | *Guardare dall'alto in basso* (looking down to the other) *Accigliato* (frowny) *Fare l'occhiolino* (to wink) *Distogliere lo sguardo* (to avert gaze) |

Finally, *guardare dall'alto in basso* (looking down at someone) contains information both on the meaning of this type of gaze ("to show contempt for someone") and on the signal itself, that is, on the actions one performs in order to produce this gaze: the person who *looks down at someone* else usually *raises his chin* – a typical expression of pride and superiority (Tracy & Robins, 2004; Poggi & D'Errico, 2012; D'Errico & Poggi, 2013) – in such a way that, in order to look at the other person, the eyes must necessarily look down! Again, one who is *accigliato* (frowny) is a person who generally has his eyebrows closer together because he very often *frowns* (signal) but is also one who is often in a bad mood, one who is always very critical of others (meaning).

## 4.6   Gaze words

By adopting an ethno-semantic method, among the Italian words and idioms that, as to signal or as to meaning, refer to the organs and functions of gaze, I selected a subset of 66 items that mention communicative gaze actions (Table 4.3). At a very *first glance* (!), the semantic richness and precision both of gaze communication per se and of its conceptualisation in Italian (but probably in the words of many natural languages) *leap to the eye* (!!).

To find an order among these multifaceted meanings, we may resort to the deductive method (see Chapter 3) to group them into semantic types, the general classes of meaning proposed in Chapter 2. So we distinguish the types of gaze lexicalised in Italian on the basis of their bearing information on the world, the sender's identity, or the sender's mind. For each word or idiom concerning communicative gaze (Column 1), Table 4.3 explains the meaning by a verbal paraphrase (Col. 2) and its classification into types and subtypes of meanings (Columns 4 and 3, respectively).

For example, *indicare con lo sguardo* ("pointing with the gaze") (line 1) is a way to construct a referent, that is, an object to communicate something

**TABLE 4.3** Meanings of the Words About Gaze

| | 1. Word or expression | 2. Meaning | 3. Subclass of meanings | 4. Class of meanings |
|---|---|---|---|---|
| 1 | *Indicare con lo sguardo* (to point with one's eyes) | I refer to that thing/person there | Reference | Information about the world |
| 2 | *Sguardo serio* (serious gaze) | I am serious, I'm not kidding. | Certainty | Beliefs |
| 3 | *Aggrottare le sopracciglia 1* (frowning eyebrows) | I am concentrating/ I'm trying to understand. | Metacognitive information | |
| 4 | *Occhiata* (glance) | I address you (but I do not want others to see me). | Request for attention | Goals |
| 5 | *Rivolgere lo sguardo* (to turn gaze to someone) | I am addressing you. | | |
| 6 | *Far cenno con lo sguardo* (to beckon with gaze) | I want to attract your attention. | | |
| 7 | *Fissare* (to stare) | I address you (and you cannot escape my request for attention). | | |
| 8 | *Occhieggiare* (to peep) | I peep sometimes, shyly asking for your attention. | | |
| 9 | *Ricambiare lo sguardo* (to return another's gaze) | I accept your request for attention/ communication. | Reply | |
| 10 | *Distogliere lo sguardo* (to avert gaze) | I do not want to see/communicate with you. | | |
| 11 | *Aggrottare le sopracciglia 2* (frowning eyebrows) | I don't agree/ I don't trust. | Incomprehension Distrust | |
| 12 | *Ammiccare* (to blink) | I call your attention/I am in agreement with you. | Agreement, complicity | |

*(Continued)*

**TABLE 4.3**  (Continued)

| 1. Word or expression | 2. Meaning | 3. Subclass of meanings | 4. Class of meanings |
|---|---|---|---|
| 13 *Fare l'occhiolino* (to wink) | We are accomplices (we somewhat agree on illicit things). | | |
| 14 *Guardare di traverso* (to look at someone sideways) | I don't trust you/ I disapprove. | Disapproval | |
| 15 *Occhiataccia* (dirty look) | I am angry at you, I strongly disapprove. | | |
| 16 *Occhi cattivi* (bad eyes) | I want to hurt you. | Threat | |
| 17 *Sguardo severo* (stern gaze) | I reproach you. | Reproach | |
| 18 *Guardare dritto negli occhi* (look someone straight in the eye) | I address you, just you, you cannot escape. | Accusation | |
| 19 *Occhi al cielo 1* (look up) | I ask God for help. | Prayer | |
| 20 *Sguardo di sfida* (stare of defiance) | I am not afraid of you, I challenge you. | Sfida | |
| 21 *Guardare in faccia* (look in the face) | I am not afraid of you, I am at your level. | | |
| 22 *Guardare di sottecchi* (to look stealthily) | Careful, I check you out (unnoticingly). | | |
| 23 *Guardare di sotto in su* (look up at someone) | I am your servant (ironic); I judge you. | | |
| 24 *Guardare dall'alto in basso* (look down to another) | I am superior to you. | | |
| 25 *Occhi spalancati* (wide open eyes) | I am surprised. | Surprise | Emotions |
| 26 *Sbarrare gli occhi* (barred eyes) | I am surprised. | | |
| 27 *Sgranare gli occhi* (widen your eyes) | I am surprised and I want to understand this better. | | |

*(Continued)*

**TABLE 4.3** (Continued)

| 1. Word or expression | 2. Meaning | 3. Subclass of meanings | 4. Class of meanings |
|---|---|---|---|
| 28 *Fare tanto d'occhi* (do so much of eyes) | I am surprised. | | |
| 29 *Occhi sbarrati 1* (eyes wide open (with terror)) | I feel terror. | Terror | |
| 30 *Occhi sbarrati 2* (eyes wide open [with anguish]) | I feel anguish. | Sorrow | |
| 31 *Occhi fuori dalle orbite* (lit. eyes out of their sockets) | I'm out of my mind. | | |
| 32 *Occhi stralunati* (dazed eyes) | I am very disturbed. | | |
| 33 *Occhi tristi* (sad eyes) | I am sad. | Sadness | |
| 34 *Sguardo perso nel vuoto* (staring out into space) | I am concentrating on my sad thoughts. | | |
| 35 *Sguardo fisso* (fixed gaze) | I am concentrating on my thoughts (of anger or anguish). | | |
| 36 *Occhi lucidi* (shiny eyes) | I am about to cry. | | |
| 37 *Occhi rossi* (reddened eyes) | I have cried, I am very sad. | | |
| 38 *Chiudere gli occhi* (close eyes) | I am tired, I want to be alone with myself. | | |
| 39 *Occhi bassi* (downcast eyes) | I am ashamed. | Shame | |
| 40 *Occhi iniettati di sangue* (bloodshot eyes) | I am furious. | Fury | |
| 41 *Aggrottare le sopracciglia 3* (frowning eyebrows) | I am angry at you. | Anger | |
| 42 *Accigliato* (frowny) | I am angry. | | |
| 43 *Corrucciato* (frowned) | I am in a bad mood. | | |
| 44 *Fulminare con lo sguardo* (glare; lit. fulminating by gaze) | I am very angry at you. | | |

*(Continued)*

**TABLE 4.3** (Continued)

| 1. Word or expression | 2. Meaning | 3. Subclass of meanings | 4. Class of meanings |
|---|---|---|---|
| 45 *Fare gli occhiacci* (giving someone the stink eye) | I am very angry at you. | | |
| 46 *Sguardo duro* (hard gaze) | I will have no mercy. | | |
| 47 *Sguardo gelido* (icy stare) | I feel a cold anger at you. | | |
| 48 *Occhi al cielo 2* (rolling eyes 2) | I ask the sky for help because I can't bear this anymore. | Impatience | |
| 49 *Occhi che brillano* (shining eyes) | I feel happiness, I feel enthusiasm. | Happiness, Enthusiasm | |
| 50 *Occhi che luccicano* (sparkling eyes) | I strongly want (something to happen or to make some action myself). | Desire | |
| 51 *Mangiare con gli occhi* (lit. to eat someone/ something with eyes) | I strongly long for something or someone. | | |
| 52 *Fare gli occhi dolci* (making sheep eye, going googly-eyed) | I am in love with you. | Love | |
| 53 *Sguardo sognante* (dreamy gaze) | I am dreaming (of someone I love). | | |
| 54 *Occhio languido* (languid eye) | I'm consumed with love for you. | | |
| 55 *Occhio di triglia* (lit. mullet eye) | I'm bamboozled, I don't understand anything anymore when I'm with you. | | |
| 56 *Occhi negli occhi* (eyes in your eyes) | I love you, I could spend hours looking at you, I like you. | | |
| 57 *Sguardo assassino* (lit. murderous glance) | I am trying to impress you, trying to seduce you. | | |

*(Continued)*

**TABLE 4.3** (Continued)

| 1. Word or expression | 2. Meaning | 3. Subclass of meanings | 4. Class of meanings |
|---|---|---|---|
| 58 *Mangiarsi con gli occhi* (lit. to eat someone/ something with eyes) | I long, I admire, I like you/I want to be delighted by the sight of you. | | |
| 59 *Spogliare con gli occhi* (undress with eyes) | I sexually desire you. | | |
| 60 *Occhi a mandorla* (almond-shaped eyes) | I am of Eastern ethnicity. | Ethnicity | Identity |
| 61 *Cipiglio* (frown) | I am strict, not lenient. | Strictness | Personality |
| 62 *Occhi di ghiaccio* (icy eyes) | I am inflexible with you. | | |
| 63 *Sguardo altero* (haughty look) | I am superior, so much so that I don't even need to control you. | Pride | |
| 64 *Sguardo altezzoso* (haughty look) | I am superior to you, so I do not even need to look at you. | | |
| 65 *Guardare dall'alto in basso* (look down to someone) | I am superior to you. | | |
| 66 *Occhi da pesce morto* (lit. rotten fish eye) | I am tired, stupid (I ironically pretend to be stupid). | Inability, stupidity | |

about. In Chapter 6 we will call it a "deictic gaze": it is the equivalent – made by eyes – of "deictic gestures", such as *pointing at something by the index finger*, to solicit the addressee's attention indicating something or someone in the surrounding physical context. This is then a type of gaze that provides information about the World.

Among the Italian words and idioms, this seems to be the only one of this type; a fair amount are referred to information about the sender's mind: sender's beliefs, goals, and emotions. A *sguardo serio* (serious gaze, line 2), tells the interlocutor you are talking seriously, you take responsibility about what you are saying, thus informing about the degree of certainty of the conveyed information. *Aggrottare le sopracciglia* (frowning eyebrows, line 3) communicates that one is concentrating and provides metacognitive information on the cognitive processes at work in the sender's mind. Several words about gaze mention the sender's goals: requests for attention (*occhiata* = glance, *fissare* = stare), positive or negative replies (*ricambiare lo sguardo* = to return the other's gaze, *distogliere lo sguardo* = to avert gaze), and expressions of agreement or complicity (*ammiccare* = to wink), defiance, threat or reproach (*sguardo di sfida* = defiant gaze, *occhi cattivi* = bad eyes, *occhiataccia* = dirty look). Several words about gaze express emotions: surprise, terror, various degrees of sadness (*occhi tristi* = sad eyes, *occhi lucidi* – lit. shiny eyes but to mean someone who has just cried or is about to cry; *sguardo perso nel vuoto* = staring out into space – as one is concentrated on sad thoughts), anger and fury (*accigliato* = frowny, *fulminare con lo sguardo* = to glare, *occhi iniettati di sangue* = bloodshot eyes), love (*fare gli occhi dolci* = to make sheep's eye, *occhio languido* = languid eye).

Further expressions mention gazes informing about the sender's identity: some concern physical identity (*occhi a mandorla* = almond-shaped eyes), others, personality traits such as strictness (*occhi di ghiaccio* = icy eyes; *accigliato* = frowny) or pride and conceit (*guardare dall'alto in basso* = looking down on others).

Among the expressions listed in Table 4.3, some are polysemic, so their different readings are distinguished from one another by a number. *Aggrottare le sopracciglia* (frowning one's eyebrows) may convey anger (line 41) but also metacognitive information, namely concentration when trying to understand something (line 3), or may communicate disagreement or distrust (line 11). Furthermore, sometimes the meaning of a noun or adjective is different from one of the corresponding verb: in Italian *sbarrare gli occhi* (opening eyes wide) is generally interpreted as surprise, while *occhi sbarrati* (eyes wide open) more as terror or anguish.

These are not all the meanings our gaze can communicate, but only the ones we may discover in the words of the Italian language. Yet even from this bare overview, we can see how the gaze is a rich and sophisticated communication system: in my hypothesis, it is a lexicon proper, i.e. a list of correspondences between signals and meanings that are codified, stored in our long-term memory, in which a specific configuration of traits and behaviours of organs in the eye region is connected in memory to a set of simple or complex beliefs, i.e. to a meaning.

In order to discover all the lexical entries of this communication system, we must hypothesise that there are more entries than those we have listed here and more than those that are expressed only by a verbal language.

In Chapter 6, again adopting the deductive method, we will see which semantic areas have meanings that can be conveyed by "gaze words": for each type of meaning, we will wonder if at least one signal exists, and which one communicates that meaning by traits or movements of the eye region, thus finally analysing in detail the semantic side of this lexicon. Further, we also must wonder if the side of the signal is as rich, complex, and systematic as the side of the meaning is. As well as a lexicon of our gaze, is there also an "alphabet" of our eyes? Could there be a small set of elements that, in various possible combinations, give rise to all the signals of gaze constituting that lexicon? This is what we are going to investigate in Chapter 5.

# 5

# OPTOLOGY

## The phonology of gaze

Is there an alphabet of the eyes? Can we find a set of elements that, combined in different ways, may give rise to the whole range of possible ways of looking that our languages express?

In 1960 William Stokoe, a pioneer in sign language research, set out to demonstrate that, unlike many would argue, a sign language is not simply a sort of pantomime, a rudimentary mimic language devoid of the systematicity of a verbal language; to the opposite, it is a full-fledged language in its own right, governed by precise and systematic semantic, syntactic, and even phonological rules (Stokoe, 1978).

But how can we find a phonology in a gestural language? How can phonemes exist in a system that does not work in an acoustic but in a visual modality?

As a matter of fact, Stokoe succeeded in his enterprise: by analysing the gestures used by the deaf in America – the American Sign Language – he found an equivalent of the phonemes of a vocal language and called them cheremes (from Greek, *cheir* = hand).

Here we will try to find out the "phonemes" of gaze, which we will call optemes so as to found a "phonology" of the gaze, that we call "optology".

## 5.1 Cheremes, phonemes and parameters

To explain what a chereme is, even for people who cannot sign a sign language, you may simply think of the so called symbolic gestures: those gestures that in a given culture have a shared meaning, which can generally be translated into a word or sentence. Take two symbolic gestures quite widespread in the Western world: the gesture for "Victory", used to celebrate

DOI: 10.4324/9781032678344-5

some accomplishment, and the one for "crossing fingers", intended to wish oneself or others to succeed in something. The two gestures are similar in various aspects of their performance: both are made at medium height in front of the Sender, with palm facing the addressee, but they differ in one respect: the shape of the hand, with *index and medium finger separated to form a V* in the former gesture and *crossed* in the latter. These two different handshapes can be viewed as cheremes – having a "phonemic" value – because they distinguish two gestures with two different meanings; just like the phonemes /f/, /p/, /g/, /s/ distinguish the words *fun, pun, gun, sun* from one another, and all of them from a non-word like *lun*.

A chereme – for instance, a specific handshape – is like a phoneme in that switching from one to another you have another meaning or something with no meaning.

As shown by Stokoe (1978) and confirmed by subsequent scholars (e.g. Sparhawk, 1978; Kendon, 1988; Calbris, 1990), any gesture can be described in terms of various criteria, or parameters. For example, as to the manual part of signs of the Italian Sign Language (LIS), four parameters were proposed: (1) handshape, (2) location, (3) palm orientation and metacarp direction, and (4) movement (Volterra, 1987; Volterra et al., 2019). By applying these four parameters to the "symbolic" gestures of Italian hearing people, Poggi (2002a, 2007) showed that, with respect to each parameter, a symbolic gesture may assume a small number of possible values. For the gesture "Victory", the handshape parameter takes the value *closed fist with extended index and middle finger, in V shape*; as to location, the value *neutral space* – the portion of space, a quarter of a sphere, in front of the sender; as to palm orientation, *palm to addressee*; and as to movement, *still*, or *shortly back and forth*.

As to the parameter handshape, a chereme, such as *extended index and middle finger*, is a specific value taken by the hand.

In general, each gesture is defined by the combination of values it assumes in all four parameters, and the "phonology" of each system of gestures (its "cherology") consists of the specific values that each gesture may assume about the four parameters. For example, in Italy, which has a "gesture prominent culture" (Kendon, 2004), the cherology of the symbolic gestures of Italian hearing people (Poggi, 2007) is almost as rich as one of LIS because it has 39 handshapes, 6 orientations and 35 locations.

## 5.2 Parameters and values of gaze

If research has been able to write down the cherology of whole systems of signs of the deaf and other symbolic gestures by identifying their parameters and values, our challenge is to write down the "optology", i.e. to identify the parameters and values of the gaze.

Several studies carried on at Roma Tre University, by adopting the observational method, have analysed more than 500 cases of gaze in videorecorded data: TV talk shows, classroom interaction, rehearsals and concerts of choirs and orchestras. This has allowed us to find out the parameters of gaze, each with a number of possible values (Table 5.1), which, when combined, make up the thousands of gaze items that populate our day (Pezzato, 1998; Pezzato & Poggi, 1999; Poggi, Pezzato & Pelachaud, 1999; Dal Monte, 2001; Poggi & Pelachaud, 2002; Liberati, 2002; Bonsignore, 2002; Poggi, Merola & Liberati, 2003, De Paolis, 2005; Poggi & Ansani, 2018a, 2018b, 2022).

The region of our face relevant for gaze communication – the eye region – includes eyebrows, upper and lower eyelids, eyes, and eye sockets. For each of these parts or subparts, one may consider some aspects, movements, or morphological traits: as for eyes, for example, their

**TABLE 5.1** Parameters and Values of Gaze

| *Parameter* | | *Sub-parameter* | | *Values* |
|---|---|---|---|---|
| Eyebrows | right/left | Inner part | | default/up/down |
| | | Central part | | default/up/down |
| | | Outer part | | default/up/down |
| Eyelids | right/left | Upper | position | default/raised/lowered/closed |
| | | | tension | default/tense/corrugated |
| | | | movement | winks/blinks/vibrates |
| | | Lower | position | default/raised/lowered |
| | | | tension | default/tense/corrugated |
| | | Corner | position | default/up/down |
| | | | tension | default/tense/corrugated (crow's feet) |
| | | | aperture | open/narrowed/closed |
| Eyes | right/left | humidity | | dry/humid/tears |
| | | reddening | | no/reddened/bloodshot |
| | | pupil dilation | | default/dilated/narrow |
| | | focusing | | yes/no |
| | | iris position | | centre/left/right/up/down |
| | | | | right corner/left corner/combinations |
| | | iris direction | | forward/up/down/left/right/unfocused/ combinations |
| | | head direction | | forward/up/down/left/right/ combinations |
| | | trunk direction | | forward/up/down/left/right/combinations |
| | | interlocutor | | forward/behind/over/under/left/right/ combinations |
| Eye sockets | right/left | | | default/hollowed |
| Duration | | | | short/medium/long |

position, direction, humidity, focusing, pupil dilation are pertinent; eyelids may open, close, vibrate, blink, wink. And duration is relevant too (Table 5.1.).

Not always have the studies on the gaze recognised such a richness of its "phonology": they have most often tried to state where the eyes look at or have examined some movements of the eyebrows or cases of pupil dilation, disregarding several aspects of the position and movements of eyelids and eyelashes, while all of these aspects of gaze may have a phonological (optological!) value, i.e. their variation determines changes in meaning.

But how can we decide if a given parameter is relevant or not? This is where the method of the speaker's (gazer's) judgements comes into play: a parameter is relevant if changing its value changes the meaning of a gaze. Here, then, is where the reflection on the signals necessarily becomes intertwined with one on the meanings.

The eyebrows, for example, are very important (Eibl-Eibesfeldt, 1972; Ekman, 1979; Costa & Ricci Bitti, 2003; Fornés Pallicer & Puig Rodríguez-Escalona, 2024), not only because they express emotions such as anger, surprise, concern but also because they emphasise what you are saying (they tell the interlocutor which is the topic and which is the comment, i.e. the most important part of a sentence), as well as whether or not your interlocutor agrees with what you are saying. The eyelids determine the closure of the eyes, which is often meaningful: they are *closed* when one is concentrating or wants to refrain from interaction; they are *half-open* in the *lazy eye* of the lover or when one makes the *rotten fish eye*, i.e. when one wants to appear a little stupid; finally, they are *half-closed* when one makes the eyes small in a look of hatred. The eye sockets also have, if not a communicative, at least an informative, involuntary expressive value: *dark circles* indicate fatigue or physical exhaustion.

As to the eyes, further, their humidity may reveal joy or enthusiasm (*sparkling eyes*) or else sorrow (*tears*); the *reddening of the sclera* may reveal you have cried, hence a great sadness or, to the opposite, an intense anger (*bloodshot eyes*). *Dilated pupils* reveal sexual or other kind of excitation; and a *non-focused eye, staring out into space*, shows you are lost in your thoughts.

As to the eyes' spatial behaviour, the direction of the iris is important not merely by itself but especially depending on the direction of head and trunk, and on the interlocutor's position. The default case is when *eye, head, and trunk are all turned towards the interlocutor*, and every gaze that deviates from this position becomes meaningful.

In a famous video by Eibl-Eibesfeldt, showing a flirt between a boy and a girl in New Guinea, the girl's *head is turned away*, but her *eyes stealthily look* at the boy with a seducing shyness.

Yet, also when I *look at you sideways* to show distrust, even in this case it is exactly the incongruence in the direction of eyes, head, and trunk that seems to reveal a conflict about whether to trust you or not.

The duration of gaze is relevant too. How long can you stare at someone or sustain a gaze? The answer is determined by strict biological rules (Argyle & Cook, 1976; Morris, 1977; Clift, 2024): if you *stare into my eyes for more than a few seconds*, you either love me (the gaze of a mother with child, of lovers, of a seducer) or you're about to beat me up (the defiant gaze of two bullies in the alley).

## 5.3  Analysing gaze: the signal and the meaning

Singling out the parameters and values of gaze allows us to analyse videorecorded cases of it in detail.

1. During an interview, the actor Diego Abatantuono speaks of his friend Simona Izzo with admiration, and to describe her tightrope walking skills as woman, mother, and matriarch of her family, he says: "*E' la trapezista dei Tognizzo cioè riesce aaa . . . parlare anche vol . . . in aria, mentre volteggia da un . . . da un paletto a un bilanciere*" ("she is the trapeze artist of the Tognizzos, that is, she can . . . speak even vault . . . in the air, while vaulting from . . . from a pole to a barbell").

While uttering the vocalisation *aaa . . .*, Abatantuono *raises his head*, he *bends his neck back*, and he *moves his eyes from high left to high right*, as if mimicking a person who looks up in the air to follow the vaulting of an acrobat.

In Chapter 6, we will better see the meaning of this gaze; here we just show how the signal is annotated in Table 5.2.

Line 1 contains the verbal context: here, a whole sentence with, in bold, the word or vocalisation parallel to the gaze analysed (the lengthened vowel **aaa**), which Line 2 segments into three times, t1, t2, t3, giving, at Line 3, the three fragments a-, a-, a. Lines 4–7 analyse the gaze items produced while uttering those three vowels in terms of their parameters and values. As to the parameter at Line 6, "eyes", the sub-parameters are distinguished of humidity, reddening, iris direction, position of the iris in the sclera, and so on. Line 8, for each of the three subsequent times, contains the meaning attributed to the whole configuration of gaze analysed, with all its values, and Line 9 classifies that meaning in terms of the semantic typology adopted (see chapters 2 and 6).

**TABLE 5.2** Analysing a Real Gaze

| 1. Verbal context | | | | *E' la trapezista dei Tognizzo cioè riesce <u>aaa</u>. . . parlare anche vol . . . in aria, mentre volteggia da un . . . da un paletto a un bilanciere* (she is the trapeze artist of the Tognizzos, that is, she can . . . speak even vault . . . in the air, while vaulting from . . . from a pole to a barbell) | | |
|---|---|---|---|---|---|---|
| 2. Timeline | | | | t1 | t2 | t3 |
| 3. Verbal modality | | | | a- | a- | a |
| 4. Eyebrows | right/ left | inner | | up | up | up |
| | | central | | up | up | up |
| | | outer | | up | up | up |
| 5. Eyelids | right/ left | upper | position | raised | lowered | raised |
| | | | tension | tense | tense | tense |
| | | | movement | | closes and immediately opens | |
| | | lower | position | raised | raised | raised |
| | | | tension | tense | tense | tense |
| | | external corner | direction | up | down | up |
| | | | tension | tense | tense | tense |
| | | | aperture | open | closed | open |
| 6. Eyes | right/ left | humidity | | medium | | medium |
| | | reddening | | default | | default |
| | | pupil dilation | | – | | – |
| | | focusing | | no | | no |
| | | iris position | | up left corner | | right corner |
| | | iris direction | | up left | | up right |
| | | head direction | | up left | up forward | up left |
| | | trunk direction | | up | up | up |
| | | interlocutor | | in front | in front | in front |
| 7. Dark circles | right/left | | | yes | yes | yes |
| 8. Meaning | | | I | I refer to something up there on the left. | I am surprised. | I refer to something up there on the right. |
| | | | II | pole | | barbell |
| 9. Type of meaning | | | I | entity | emotion | entity |
| | | | II | | | |

## 5.4   Optemes: phonology or morphology?

While observational qualitative analyses and the speaker's (gazer's!) judgements allow us to find out the parameters and values of gaze, to demonstrate that some values in certain parameters are really comparable to phonemes, hence that optology really has a status similar to the phonology of verbal languages, for gaze too we should single out "minimal pairs": pairs of gaze items in which the variation of a single value in one parameter corresponds to a difference in meaning, just like varying from the value (in terms of Prague's school and Jakobson & Halle, 1971, the "distinctive feature") "voiced" to "voiceless" determines the switching from *van* to *fan*.

In a study on 100 students, 88 females and 12 males aged 16–20 (Poggi & Roberto, 2007), the hypotheses were (1) that a certain value in a parameter determines the same nuance of meaning in gaze items that differ in other respects, and (2) that varying a single value in one parameter, while keeping the same values in all other parameters, may change the meaning of a gaze item.

To test these hypotheses, an empirical study was conducted exploiting the simulation in Virtual Agents. To construct stimuli – gaze items – that differ from one another in a controlled and systematic way, instead of pictures or videos we used the software Greta Face Library (Poggi & Pelachaud, 2000; Bevacqua et al., 2007). Greta is an "Embodied Conversational Agent", built by computer graphics techniques, that runs as a 3D interface on a computer that generates a multimodal communicative behaviour similar to a human's. Of course, nowadays the most recent AI techniques would make the simulation of gaze stimuli even easier; Greta, the software we used at the time, is actually a precursor of today's more sophisticated devices.

The library of Facial Actions of this software allows one to perform all the muscular actions that give rise to facial expression, letting one move the muscles of the mouth, the forehead, and also other parts of the face, namely, eyebrows, eyelids, iris position, so as to allow the user to vary the values of all gaze parameters at will. Further, in some cases, the software even allows one to see the threshold where a variation switches from one meaning of a gaze to another different meaning: a very subtle change in the values of a parameter sometimes causes a semantic change. For example, when combining *half-closed upper eyelids* with *lower eyelids more and more lowered*, if Greta's FAPs (facial animation parameters) decrease from 540.00 to 400.00, the meaning still is "I am trying to remember", but as soon as they reach 340.00, the meaning becomes "I am sad".

In the study, to assess if some gaze items that differ only for a value in the parameter "eyelids position" have different meanings, by exploiting the Greta Face Library, 15 gaze items were constructed; for each of them, an open question asked participants to attribute it a meaning; then a multiple-choice question was posed to choose the most acceptable among four possible meanings. The results confirmed both hypotheses. As to hypothesis 1, when a value in a certain parameter is the same in various items, even if the meanings attributed by subjects to those items are not exactly the ones posited by the hypothesis, among the hypothesised meanings and the chosen distractors there is always a shared semantic element: for example, in all of the items with *inner parts of the eyebrows raised* (A-shape eyebrows), whatever the position of the iris in the sclera (up, down, or in the middle) that gaze always communicates an emotion of low attivation, such as sorrow, displeasure, disappointment, resignation, sadness. As to hypothesis 2 – that changing a single value changes the whole meaning of an item – it was found, for instance, that in a gaze item with *eyes centred in the sclera, direction to the interlocutor*, and *raised eyebrows*, simply varying, in the parameter "eyelids aperture", from the value *wide open* (Figure 5.1a) to *medium aperture* (Figure 5.1b) to *half-closed eyelids* (Figure 5.1c) changes the respective meanings from "surprise" to "perplexity" to "haughtiness".

So even single values in a parameter have a distinctive function; that is, they distinguish minimal pairs of gaze items, having therefore a phonemic value: we will call them optemes.

Yet are these optemes totally equivalent to phonemes of a verbal language, or are they rather more similar to morphemes?

As a matter of fact, there is an important difference between words and gazes: in words, the phonemes are sound segments that determine a change of meaning, but they are not meaningful per se. In gaze items, instead, a certain position of the eyebrows or of the eyelids is not totally devoid of meaning. This seems to assimilate the values in the parameters of gaze, more than to phonemes (sounds without meaning) to morphemes (meaningful sound sequences): just like an *s* added to the word *cat*, where *s* adds a semantic element "PLURAL", "MORE THAN ONE", to one of the root *cat*, "PET FELINE").

Some authors have already attributed a morphemic – not only phonemic – value to signs of the deaf and gestures of hearing people, where

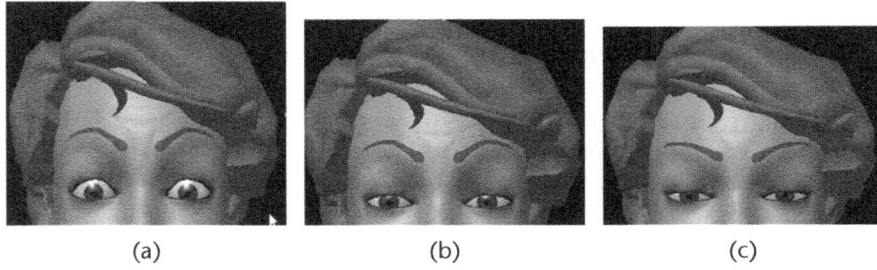

| (a) | (b) | (c) |

**FIGURE 5.1** Greta's eyelids: (a) surprise; (b) perplexity; (c) haughtiness.

sometimes even a single value of a parameter bears a specific meaning. For example, in various signs of LIS (Italian Sign Language) the *extended index finger* bears a meaning of uniqueness (Boyes-Braem, 1981; Volterra, 1987); in the parameter "movement", *moving the hand repeatedly from left to right* conveys the idea of COUNTING (Calbris, 2003, 2011); in the parameter "location" the gestures that touch or indicate the head generally refer to MENTAL FUNCTIONS (Kendon, 1992). In all of these cases a certain feature of the signal systematically corresponds to a semantic feature, just as with morphemes (Poggi & Roberto, 2007).

Based on this hypothesis, an empirical study has been carried on (Poggi, Spagnolo & D'Errico, 2010; Poggi, D'Errico & Spagnolo, 2010) to test whether the different values of a single parameter can have a morphemic value, that is, if they convey a specific meaning: not the global meaning attributed to a gaze item as a whole but an idea, possibly a very general and abstract element of meaning (like a "theme" of ancient languages such as Greek) that is shared by all the gaze items characterised by that particular value.

The working hypothesis was that, in the parameter "position of the upper eyelids", different values (*wide open, half-open, half closed eyelids*) correspond to (hence they mean) different levels of physiological, emotional, or cognitive activation.

In a survey with stimuli, once again, constructed by exploiting Greta Face Library, submitted to 360 participants (208 females and 152 males, aged 7–86, mean 36.8), the subjects were presented with open and multiple-choice questions and asked to attribute meanings to 9 gaze items that combined the value *wide open* of the parameter "upper eyelids position" with the values *default* vs. *raised* of the parameter "lower eyelids". The results show that the meanings attributed by participants to gaze items with *wide open eyelids* generally concern emotions, such as "I am astonished", "I am surprised", "I fear", all sharing a semantic element of HIGH ACTIVATION and alert (Figure 5.2).

The gaze items with *half-closed upper eyelids*, on the contrary, convey a meaning of DEACTIVATION, caused by a physical state, such as "sleepy" or

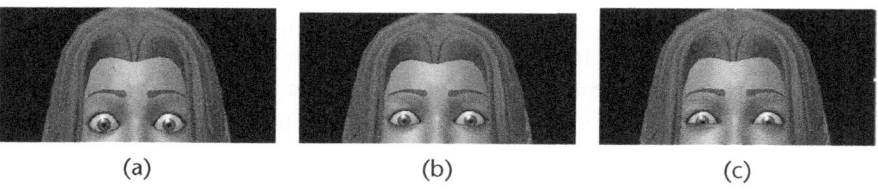

|           |           |           |
| :-------: | :-------: | :-------: |
|    (a)    |    (b)    |    (c)    |

FIGURE 5.2   (a) Wide open upper eyelids + wide open lower eyelids; (b) default lower eyelids; (c) raised lower eyelids.

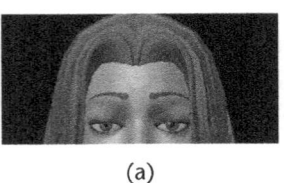 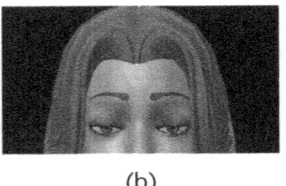 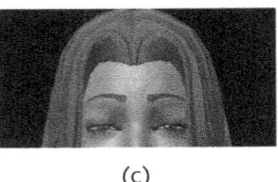

(a)                                    (b)                                    (c)

**FIGURE 5.3**    (a) Half-closed upper eyelids; (b) Half-closed upper eyelids + default lower eyelids; (c) Half-closed upper eyelids + raised lower eyelids.

"exhausted", or by a cognitive ("bored") or emotional state ("sad", "I am sorry") (Figure 5.3).

Therefore, the aperture of our eyelids seems to have a morphemic role.

Setting analogies between the structures of verbal languages and those of hands' and eyes' communication systems is not trivial. In a verbal language, we can count five levels of analysis: distinctive features (Jakobson & Halle, 1971), phonemes, morphemes, words, and sentences.

In the gaze, a lexical entry of gaze (a word of the eyes), with its combination of values in the various parameters, generally corresponds to a whole sentence because its meaning includes the performative too. A gaze with *raised eyebrows* and *wide open eyelids* can be paraphrased by a whole informative sentence, "I inform you that I am surprised".

The values of gaze parameters, e.g., the values *"wide open"* or *"half-open"* of the parameter "eyelids aperture", might be viewed as corresponding to distinctive features of a verbal language, which distinguish one phoneme from another, with phonemes in their turn distinguishing a word from another. For example, in a verbal language, in the parameter "voicing", the feature (value) *voiced* of the consonant /v/ in the word *van* is in opposition with the feature "voiceless" of /f/ in *fan*; in the parameter "way of articulation", the feature "fricative" of /f/ in *fan* is in opposition with the feature "stop" of /p/ in *pan*; and in the parameter "place of articulation", the feature "bilabial" of /p/ in pan is in opposition to the feature "velar" of /k/ in *can*. But the analogy stops here: distinctive features and phonemes distinguish the meanings of words, but do *not* have a meaning by themselves. In our gaze, instead, even a single value of one parameter, such as *half-closed upper eyelids* by itself bears a meaning: it does not have a barely phonemic function but a morphemic one. The morphemes of communication systems like those of gestures or gaze are better comparable to roots or themes, like those of languages such as ancient Greek, or as those found by Kendon (2004): they bear meanings that combine with other meanings, but they are also very general, for instance, activation, deactivation, effort. Further, they are meanings tightly linked to the body because they concern physiological reactions caused by or connected to universal cognitive or affective states. In this sense, the values of gaze parameters can be seen as "embodied morphemes".

# 6
# THE GAZEIONARY

In Chapter 5, we dealt with Optology, the phonology of gaze: the set of parameters and values of traits and behaviours in the eye region that, combined, make up all the possible meanings of our gaze. But to analyse these signals only makes sense if they correspond to meanings.

## 6.1 Codified and creative gaze items

As mentioned in chapters 2 and 4, two types of communication systems exist: codified and creative. A codified system includes a mental "lexicon" in which each signal (a word, a gesture, a gaze . . .) is permanently connected to a particular meaning: for example, the meaning "I am surprised" is expressed by a *raising of the eyebrows*. In a creative system, instead, the sender creates a new signal on the spot by producing a movement or displaying a trait which by resemblance recalls the intended meaning: to refer to quite a dumb person, I may *open eyes wide* to imitate its dumbfounded expression.

In the system of gaze, the codified signals constitute a lexicon, i.e. a set of correspondences between traits displayed or behaviours performed by the eye region and meanings that the sender may have the goal to communicate. To describe this lexicon, we may write down a "gazeionary", i.e. a dictionary of eyes.

## 6.2 Towards the gazeionary

What are the "words" of our gaze? In Chapter 4, we found out a fair number of lexical entries of gaze, by adopting an ethno-semantic method, that is, starting from the words that name acts of gaze in the Italian language. But not necessarily are all the "words of" gaze named by "words about" gaze.

DOI: 10.4324/9781032678344-6

Probably many more of them exist, and to discover them, we can take a top-down approach, i.e. adopt a deductive method.

Here I start from a taxonomy of meanings that the human being may have the (conscious, unconscious, tacit, social or biological) goal of communicating, and for each type of meaning I wonder if there is a type of gaze to communicate it; I may do so also by exploiting the speaker's judgements and/or observational data.

A well-known saying goes: "The eyes are the mirror of the soul", and even famous philosophers such as Descartes (1649) have argued that our gaze faithfully reflects our emotions. But does it only tell us about emotions? Only about our soul? As we shall see, our eyes can also tell us about the external world, about what we want, what we think and who we are. As mentioned previously, the meanings we communicate can be about the external world, about our identity, or about the content of our mind in relation to what we are communicating.

Information about the world includes our beliefs about concrete and abstract objects and events, as well as the times and places in which they occur or exist; information about identity concerns gender, age, ethnic and cultural roots; personalities and other internal traits of the sender; and information about the sender's mind concern the beliefs, goals and emotions regarding what she or he is communicating. What are, then, the items of gaze that communicate these three types of meanings?

### 6.2.1 Gaze items about the world

In our everyday interactions, we communicate about events, with their place and time, and we refer to concrete and abstract properties of objects, persons, animal, facts, discourses, and their relationships. With eyes too can we communicate some of these meanings, particularly by deictic gaze items, which indicate what one refers to in the surrounding context, and attributive gaze items, which inform about physical properties of objects.

#### 6.2.1.1 The deictic gaze: pointing at a referent

A deictic signal (from Greek *dèicnumi*, which means "to point") is one used to indicate something or someone, thus constructing a referent, something to communicate about with our interlocutor. Adverbs like *here* or *there*, pronouns like *this* and *that*, gestures like *pointing* at some person or object with the whole hand or the index finger, are deictic signals: they indicate to the addressee what we want to refer to in our discourse. A "deictic gaze", therefore, is a way to look toward some point, in the surrounding physical context, where an object or person or occurring event is located, in order to let the addressee understand "I refer to what is/is occurring in that place". In all cases – pronouns, gestures, gaze items – the deictic signal asks the addressee to complete the received information by other beliefs drawn from context: if while saying *that* I point at a book, this means I am referring to the book, but if I point at a boy instead, I refer to the boy.

A deictic gaze from my corpus is produced by Achille Occhetto, the chief of the Leftist Democrats, during a pre-electoral debate in 1994 against Silvio Berlusconi, the chief of the right-wing party.

> Occhetto reminds of a case in which he did not take advantage of an accusation against Berlusconi's brother. While saying *"Quando è venuta fuori la vicenda del fratèllo di Berlusconi"* (When the story of Berlusconi's brother came out), in uttering the word *"fratèllo"* (brother), Occhetto makes a deictic gesture, *pointing at right* (where Berlusconi is sitting) *with his index finger*, and for one second he *turns his head and eyes* in the same direction, to communicate "I refer to an event connected with the person there".

While in this case a specific person is pointed at, sometimes the deictic gaze – just like a deictic gesture – may generally indicate a fact, an occurring event. For example, while talking to B, A may *look at C and D* who are arguing with each other, and then *look at B* as if saying: "Let's go, they are arguing". Here the gaze to C and D only means "I refer to what is happening there", it can only point at some place; it is up to interlocutor B to understand that the warning to get away is motivated by C's and D's argument.

The deictic use of eyes is often exploited when it is better not to have someone else understand we are pointing at someone or something. Less visible than a deictic gesture, a deictic gaze is a more furtive, concealed way to point at someone. In fact, often the iris direction is not the same as that of the face: my face addresses the interlocutor, but this already bears the meaning "I am addressing you, please pay attention to me". My eyes instead are directed towards the object or person I want to point at: "that is the one I want to refer to"; but, if possible, I do not want other people to know that it is right there that I direct my and my interlocutor's attention: a somewhat oblique gaze, with respect to my head and trunk's direction, so as to appear somewhat furtive, stealthy. Actually, if I want my pointing to be overt, I will tend to make a gesture, while I generally use gaze to make my indication less visible: that is why I only move my eyes but not my head.

### 6.2.1.2 Attributive gaze

In addition to constructing a referent, our gaze can also have an "adjectival", "attributive" function: to inform about physical properties of the referent and further, metaphorically, about abstract or mental properties. For example, we may *squint our eyes till almost closed* as we talk about very small things or *open eyes wide* when talking about huge objects. In these cases, eyes even exploit a form of communication that is, if not iconic, at least motivated: there is a natural, non-arbitrary connection between small eyes and small things, since when we look at a small thing or one small because it is far away, we "sharpen" our eyes, we squint our eyes more to see better. These are the gazes our grandmas would perform when telling stories to kids, *squint eyes* when saying "she saw a teeny tiny chair", *open them wide* when saying "the ogre had huge huge boots".

*Squinting* or *opening eyes wide* also indicates (small or big) quantities: these kinds of gaze can be paraphrased as "little", "much", "many": the device at work can be either the one of iconicity (big eyes = big quantity) or one of a natural motivatedness where a high quantity makes you open eyes wide out of surprise or coming across a big object in one's visual field.

Yet *opening wide* or *squinting eyes*, besides indicating a physical big or small size, may also indicate abstract or mental qualities: for example, when talking of something which is not physically small but conceptually subtle. A teacher may *squint her eyes* when going to outline a subtler distinction or when transitioning from a general case to a particular subcase, or when explaining a particularly sophisticated nuance of a concept. And even in this case, we do not know if it is iconicity, i.e. the imitation of something mentally small, or a natural motivatedness because one *half-closes eyes* to see better – a metaphor of focusing with the mind's eyes.

But the potential of gaze in providing information about the world is not only here. Sometimes even a deictic gaze (one pointing at a referent) may be used in description and narration to communicate properties or relations: as we have seen in Chapter 5 in the example of the man mimicking the act of *looking up in the air* to follow a trapeze artist's vaulting, *pointing by eyes up there on the left and then on the right* is a deictic gaze, but it is used to describe an action by enacting it, hence becoming an iconic gaze. The meaning conveyed by the two deictic gaze items, "I refer to someone up there on the left" and "I refer to someone up there on the right" makes one infer "I refer to someone moving speedily in the air from one to the other side": i.e. someone so agile (an attributive meaning) as to be (metaphorically, in that case) an acrobatic trapeze artist.

### 6.2.2   Gaze items about the sender's identity

Communication about one's identity is generally governed by biological, tacit or unconscious goals, and it is more typically performed by morphological traits than by actions or movements. A person's age, for instance, is made clear by *wrinkles around the eyes*, while the *shape of the eyes*, namely the *eyelids fold*, reveals the ethnicity. But concerning our identity, with our gaze we also produce other deliberate and conscious communicative acts. Our personality, intellectual gifts and social attitude also shine through our eyes. If you *look down to others*, I can understand you do not want to mix to other people, and you see all of them as inferior: your *chin is raised*, and your *eyes do not stare in the same direction as your face: face looks up, eyes look down*, so that your *eyelids are half-closed*. The *raised chin* might derive, in evolution, from the face and mouth refraining from something disgusting, and *looking at the other with half-closed eyes* might stem, ethologically, from the difference between dominant and submissive animals (Argyle & Cook, 1976): the lower status one must *keep one's eyes open* to steadily check out the dominant's behaviour so as to readily do his will, whereas the dominant one may display inattention because his position shields him from aggression. This combination of optemes – different directions of head and eyes + half-closed eyelids – seems to communicate "I am disgusted at you" + "I do not need to look at you, I am dominant", hence making you infer a permanent personality trait such as "I am one who does not care about this kind of things".

It is the prerogative of physiognomy (Lavater, 1819; Magli, 1995; Gullotta & Tuosto, 2017) to study how cognitive traits (such as in a "smart gaze") or other personality characteristics (see "good eyes," "stern look") shine through the eyes as well as the rest of the face.

### 6.2.3   Gaze items about the sender's mind

From our communication, our interlocutor understands not only the information we want to transmit but also beliefs about what we believe, think, want and feel in that regard. All verbal and bodily communication systems – words, intonation, facial expression, posture, gesture and gaze – very often communicate right about our communication, that is, they are a means of that meta-communication we call information about the sender's mind. We may call all of these signals "mind markers" (Poggi, 2007); they include those that Pragmatics calls "discourse markers" (Schiffrin, 1987) – such as words or interjections like *well, so, anyway* – but they encompass much more than this, since they provide information also about units that are smaller than a discourse. And some gaze items also belong to this category. Let us see some frequent "gaze mind markers" (Table 6.1).

#### 6.2.3.1   Gaze items about beliefs

Like with other body communication systems, by gaze the sender can also provide two types of information concerning the beliefs mentioned in his/her communication with the interlocutor: information about the level of certainty of the beliefs conveyed, as well as about their source: what linguistics calls epistemic and evidential information, respectively (Zuczkowski, Bongelli & Riccioni, 2017).

*Epistemic gaze.   The eyes of certainty*. The degree of certainty of a belief (Castelfranchi & Poggi, 1998) is a meta-belief. For all the beliefs that we hold

**TABLE 6.1** Gaze Mind Markers

| Type | Subtype | Signal | Meaning |
|---|---|---|---|
| BELIEFS | degree of certainty | *slight eyebrow frowning* | I am serious, I am certain of this. |
| | | *raised eyebrows with normal aperture eyes* | I have some doubts about this. |
| | metacognitive | *eyes downward leftward* | I am trying to remember. |
| | | *eyes upward* | I am trying to make inferences or to plan. |
| | | *closed eyes* | I am concentrating, I am thinking. |
| | | *staring out into space* | I am lost in my thoughts. |
| GOALS | performative | *standing stare to interlocutor* | I defy you. |
| | topic-comment | *gaze averted from interlocutor* | This is the topic of the sentence. |
| | | *gaze to interlocutor, raised eyebrows* | This is the comment of the sentence. |
| | metadiscursive | *raised eyebrows* | but, on the contrary (a contrast between two beliefs) |
| | | *open and close eyelids slowly* | I pass over this topic. |
| | metaconversational: turn-taking | *opening eyes wider, look at interlocutor* | I ask for a speaking turn. |
| | metaconversational: backchannel | *closing the eyes* | Yes, I see, I'm following you. |
| | | *frowning the eyebrows* | I don't understand. (Or I don't agree.) |
| EMOTIONS | | *Inner parts of the eyebrows raised* | I am sad. |
| | | *fully raised eyebrows and sparkling eyes* | I feel enthusiasm. |
| | | *downcast eyes* | I am ashamed. |

in our minds, there is another piece of information that we know: how certain we are of them. This information is conveyed, in a verbal language, by verbal modes such as indicative or conditional, which qualify the knowledge of the event we are talking about as certain or uncertain; but also by adverbs such as *certainly, probably, perhaps, not*; by verbs such as *believe, affirm, state*; by adjectives such as *certain, convinced*; by nouns such as *doubt, suspicion, certainty*. But a speaker's body also tells us the degree of certainty he attaches

**FIGURE 6.1**  Perplexity (The Italian comedian Gigi Proietti).

to what he is saying, for example by *shrugging his shoulders* or a *direct stare to the interlocutor*. So we have gaze items of certainty, such as *looking at the interlocutor with a slight frowning of the eyebrows*, which means "I'm sure of what I'm saying", or "I'm serious", "I'm not joking". There are also glances of uncertainty, such as *raising the eyebrows without opening the eyes wide*, which expresses perplexity, i.e. a mental state of suspension between believing and disbelieving (Figure 6.1).

*Metacognitive eyes. The gaze of thought.*  For humans, like for many other animals, sight is the high road to knowledge, not only as we look at the world around us, but also as we look at the eyes and face of our interlocutor, since this gives us important information on his/her thoughts and communicative intentions. This is why we look at the speaker as we are the listener; but as we are the speaker, we have to elaborate our thought before putting it into sentences, plan our discourse, retrieve concepts and words from long-term memory. We must then focus our attention on our internal thoughts, and prevent the cognitive overload of beliefs coming from outside. This is why, as we start speaking (Kendon & Cook, 1969; Goodwin, 1981; Rossano, 2013), our gaze shifts from a function of "eyes to see" or "eyes to look" to one of "thinking eyes".

Therefore, not to be distracted in talking we *close our eyes completely*, or we do not *look* at the interlocutor or the surrounding context, but *away*: upward, or downward, or even forward, but looking *somewhere* far away and without focusing. These types of gazing serve first and foremost to avoid attentional overload and to help us focus; and on the other hand we can look in different directions depending on the specific purposes for which we need to focus: *upward* for reasoning, making inferences, planning; *downward laterally* for remembering; *at a distant point ahead*, but *without focusing*, for thinking as if we were alone with ourselves, and retracting from the interaction.

These various ways of seeking concentration, initially functional for individual goals only, from an initial expressive goal of internal need, may have progressively acquired specific meanings, becoming communicative looks of different kinds (Poggi, 2007): *closing one's eyes* means "I am concentrating", *looking away*, "I want to be alone with my thoughts", *looking down*, "I am trying to remember", *looking up* can mean either "I am searching memory" or more specifically "I am looking in memory how to connect beliefs", i.e. "I am trying to make inferences"; and since inferences are very often necessary in planning, because we need them to predict the possible consequences of our actions, *looking up* can finally mean "let's see how I can do it".

These are "metacognitive gaze items" because they tell us about the sender's cognitive actions and about the type of cognitive source from which they draw the beliefs they talk about.

We communicate the same types of information even by other signals in the verbal modality, among which interjections (Poggi, 1981, 2022b). For example, *ah* in Italian (corresponding to *oh* in English) signals a process of acquisition of belief, it means "I did not know this belief so far, it is new to me, and I take note of it; I accept it and believe it as true (and interesting)". *Bèh* (= well) expresses a decision-making process still in progress: "I am still deciding on whether and what to say or do".

A sub-case of metacognitive information often expressed by gaze is about the source of our beliefs. Information about the source of beliefs is a meta-belief concerning the source of the belief the sender is talking about. Some Amerindian languages have "evidential" verb modes which, concerning a mentioned event, tell you if the speaker has seen it with his own eyes, only heard about it, or retrieved it from memory. This is why linguistics calls the information on the source "evidentiality". But some signals also in languages provide this information without evidential modes, whether in text or speech: saying or writing "*according to X,...*" or putting a sentence in *quotation marks* is like saying "This information has been provided by X, not primarily by me": in this way, we take away some of the responsibility for what we are saying or writing.

In the lexicon of gaze, my eyes *downward sideways* tell you that a belief I am going to communicate is one I am retrieving from my memory, if I *look downward leftward*, from my autobiographical memory, while if *downward rightward*, I am trying to retrieve numbers or abstract concepts (Bandler & Grinder, 1979). If I *look up*, I am reasoning, so the information I am going to utter comes from my inferences; if I am a student at an oral examination, such a gaze means I cannot immediately find the answer in memory, but I have to think about it.

Let us see some real cases of metacognitive gaze items. The *closed eyes* are considered by Morris (1977) a case of "cutoff", a way to refrain from interaction while talking. An orchestra conductor, instead, by closing his eyes expresses concentration but also solicits the orchestra members to concentrate, thus preparing to start.

*Looking up* is a typical movement of a student who gathers ideas – explores his own mind – before answering the professor's question. One who generally *looks up* longer than usual is a character by the Italian comedian Carlo Verdone (Figure 6.2).

The comedy of the character, a rather naïve boy, lies in the frequency – and duration – of this upward gaze, exhibited every time he is asked a question: it just seems that, for him more than for others, inferences are particularly slow and difficult.

One more "gaze of thought" can be found in two fragments of "Donne al bivio" (Women at the Crossroad), an Italian talk show where a journalist

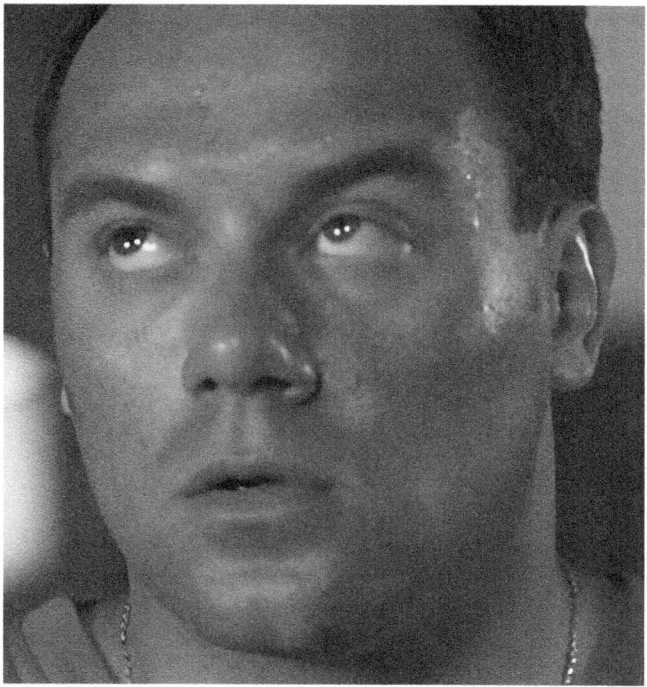

**FIGURE 6.2**   I am thinking.

interviews women who had a complex or dramatic past: here, both a former drug addict and a famous terrorist, before and while talking of dramatic aspects or times in their lives, *look down to the left*. This type of gaze means "I am trying to remember, to retrieve from memory". More than that, since the contents found are particularly painful, in both interviewees *looking down*, avoiding the interlocutor's gaze, expresses shame and a desire to escape the interaction (Castelfranchi, 1988; Castelfranchi & Poggi, 1990; Poggi, 2007).

These "gaze items of thought" can be interpreted in three ways:

1. As simple noncommunicative uses of the eyes. *Looking away from the face of the interlocutor* helps us to concentrate, which is why we are not looking at him or her. In this case, we are not communicating with the eyes, we are just trying not to distract ourselves.
2. Since whenever we need to concentrate, we tend to look away from the interlocutor, the other person may begin to connect it with concentration, and attribute this meaning to it: from a noncommunicative action a communicative signal has arisen.
3. We often concentrate to look for the right words to say, but this takes time, risking losing our turn to speak; so as often as we concentrate, we must also keep our turn. So communicating "I am concentrating" ends up communicating "I have not finished my speech, let me finish expressing my thought": from the first meaning comes another inferable from the first (Table 6.2).

In conclusion, each "gaze of thought" may be either a noncommunicative (thinking eyes) or a communicative one, and sometimes may even communicate, besides a literal meaning, an indirect one.

### 6.2.3.2 Gaze items communicating goals

By eyes, we can communicate the goal of a single communicative act (the performative of the sentence), of a whole hierarchy of goals (the plan of a sentence or discourse) or of the conversation management.

**TABLE 6.2** Origin of Communicative Gaze Items

|  | Noncommunicative | I meaning: gaze of thought | II meaning: gaze of turn-taking |
|---|---|---|---|
| Look away | avoid distraction; help concentrating | I have to concentrate. | Leave me the speaking turn. |

**FIGURE 6.3**   I order you.

*Performative eyes.*   Several gaze items communicate the performative of a communicative act. A peremptory order is communicated by a serious and strict gaze, with *inner parts of the eyebrows slightly closer*, like in an angry gaze (Figure 6.3).

An interesting case of a defiant gaze is displayed by the politician Paolo Cirino Pomicino during the so-called Clean Hands trial (see Figures 6.4a and 6.4b below). This trial in 1994 changed the fate of Italy: an entire ruling class tried for corruption faced a reversal of power relations in Italian politics. In one session of this trial, Paolo Cirino Pomicino, a very powerful mayor of the Christian Democrats, is questioned in the courtroom by Antonio Di Pietro, at this time an obscure prosecutor, but to show him that he does not fear him and that, in spite of appearances, he is even more powerful than Di Pietro, Cirino Pomicino almost throughout the interrogation *sustains his gaze* and *stares at him defiantly*, with his *chin raised* (an expression of pride) and his *gaze fixed in Di Pietro's eyes* (Figure 6.4a). By *sustaining his gaze* he communicates "I do not fear you, I do not acknowledge your power over me". Indeed, the one who *lowers his gaze* when *looked at fixedly* acknowledges the dominance of the other and submits; while the one who *sustains his gaze* communicates that he does not give up to his control – hence his power – over the other. This is the extent to which even a glance can constitute a relevant move in interaction, socially and even politically.

Let us compare this type of gaze with the haughty gaze of snootiness and superiority seen in Chapter 5: both proclaim greater power than the other, but the gaze of haughtiness denotes a stable, already proclaimed state of greater power, which is even part of the sender's identity. Defying another, on the other hand, is a communicative act perpetrated by someone who is currently at a disadvantage to the other, who currently has more power than him, but by refusing to acknowledge this disadvantage and to submit, the sender of the *defiant gaze* makes it clear that he has the potential to win over the other and to acquire more power than him, by flaunting the refusal to submit.

*The informational structure of the sentence: eyes for the topic and for the comment.* In our mind, our beliefs are connected to each other in networks, in such a way as to be easily retrieved; therefore, in every act of communication we, besides providing new beliefs, also have to make it clear which is the topic, i.e. to which beliefs already present in the other's cognitive networks and shared with ours do the new beliefs refer and must be connected. This is why in every communicative act a *topic* and a *comment* can be distinguished. The *comment* is the new belief conveyed by the sender, and the *topic* is the fragment in the addressee's cognitive networks to which the new belief must be connected. And it must be clear what in the act is the "given" belief, taken for granted and already shared, and which is instead the "new" one, to which the addressee must pay most of the attention. Thus every sentence has a specific "informational structure", a division of labour, where a part contains the given and the other the new information; also, for this very reason, a particular prominence must be attributed to the new information: this is what we do by "emphasis". To emphasise means to stress that a particular part of the sentence structure (the comment), being the new piece of information, is the part to which the sender asks the addressee to pay more attention. Various means can be used to give emphasis to a part of the sentence: syntactic ones, e.g. the left dislocation (*The wine, Mary has already bought it*); lexical (Mary *did* buy the wine); phonetic (*Mary* bought the wine – with *Mary* stressed); gestural means (making a batonic gesture while uttering *Mary*). But emphasis may be given by our gaze too. While uttering the topic, our *gaze is not directed to the interlocutor*, while we *stare at him* during the comment (Guaïtella, Cavé & Santi, 1993; Torres, Cassell & Prevost, 1997). Again, to emphasise the comment – conveying that is the word or part of sentence we are more concerned to transmit – we *raise our eyebrows*, possibly even *opening our eyes wide*. In fact, this is the expression of surprise, and communicating "I am surprised", through mirror neurons, solicits surprise in the other, but surprise awakens attention.

*Metadiscursive eyes.*   A discourse is a sequence of sentences connected by logical links, and, as we make a discourse, the other must understand not only our sentences but their connecting links. This is why we use several signals that open a window into our communicative plan, e.g. topic-to-topic transitions and causal, final, conditional, adversative links. They are "meta-discursive" markers, because they communicate about our discourse: by saying *concluding*, or *coming to the second point*, the speaker makes explicit where she is in her discourse; using conjunctions such as *because, if, but, on the other hand* makes explicit the logical relations between sentences or paragraphs.

Some of these tasks are also performed by the gaze. For example, an adversative adverb such as *nevertheless* or *but* is often accompanied by a *raising of eyebrows*, which signals an adversative link, i.e. blocks an inference: it means "do not draw from the following sentence the inferences you would make on the basis of the preceding one; rather, know that just the opposite  is the case".

Another metadiscursive gaze is a rapid *closing and reopening of the* eyes, often accompanied by a *slight turn of the head*, which refers to a subtopic of the discourse and communicates "I pass over this topic".

*Metaconversational eyes.*   One more important function of our gaze is conversation management. Conversation is a sequence of discourses by two or more people who take turns speaking, and whose sentences "respond" to each other, that is, they adopt each other's communicative goals. Two important activities in conversation are turn-taking and backchannel. First, since conversationalists cannot speak at the same time, there are cogent rules for asking for and giving turns to speak. If you want to speak while the other person is speaking, you can both ask and give the speaking turn with verbal (*may I speak?*; *please*), gestural (*raise your hand or index finger; point* to the other person with your *hand palm up*), postural signals (*leaning toward the other* person by *slightly opening your mouth*), but also with your gaze (Jokinen, 2011). To give the turn to one of the listeners just *look at him*; to ask for it, *lean toward the speaker* while *opening your eyes wider*.

The interlocutor, on the other hand, must often give a backchannel, or feedback, to the speaker (Allwood, Nivre & Ahlsén, 1992; Cerrato, 2005), that is, let him know if he is following, if he understands, if he is interested, if he agrees (Poggi, 2007, 2022a). So, *frowning* signals that I don't understand and you have to explain more, but the indirect meaning can also be that I don't believe you or that I disagree. Instead if I understand and agree, I may communicate this by *nodding* but also simply by *closing my eyes* – which is almost a *yes*. To convey I am interested, I can *raise my eyebrows*: a sign of surprise for something unexpected that therefore elicits curiosity.

### 6.2.3.3 The eyes of emotions

And here we finally come to the eyes as the mirror of the soul, that is, of our emotions. The gaze can communicate individual emotions, those that are not directed at another – such as fear, terror, joy, sadness, surprise, excitement, worry, dismay – but also social emotions, those that we feel toward another person or that concern our relationships with others: love, admiration, contempt, anger toward someone.

Some of these emotions are present in the corpus of looks analysed.

In a TV talk show dealing with a law proposed in the Italian Parliament concerning a "temporary wedding contract", Alessandra Mussolini, a member of the fascist party Movimento Sociale Italiano (Italian Social Movement), to show her scandal about such a proposal, displays an intense anger, with *wide open eyes* and *frowning eyebrows*.

In a fragment of the talk show "Women at the Crossroads", Adriana Faranda, a former Red Brigades terrorist interviewed about her experience in prison, at certain moments in her reenactment, with her *eyes wide open* expresses terror.

Cirino Pomicino, during the interrogation by Di Pietro, who is hounding him with the insistence of his questions, unexpectedly interrupts his *defiant stare* at the prosecutor, supported by the continuous *sneer* aimed at not showing that he feels hounded (Figure 6.4a), with a *gaze staring into space*, which for a moment reveals his own dismay at the insistent questions (Figure 6.4b).

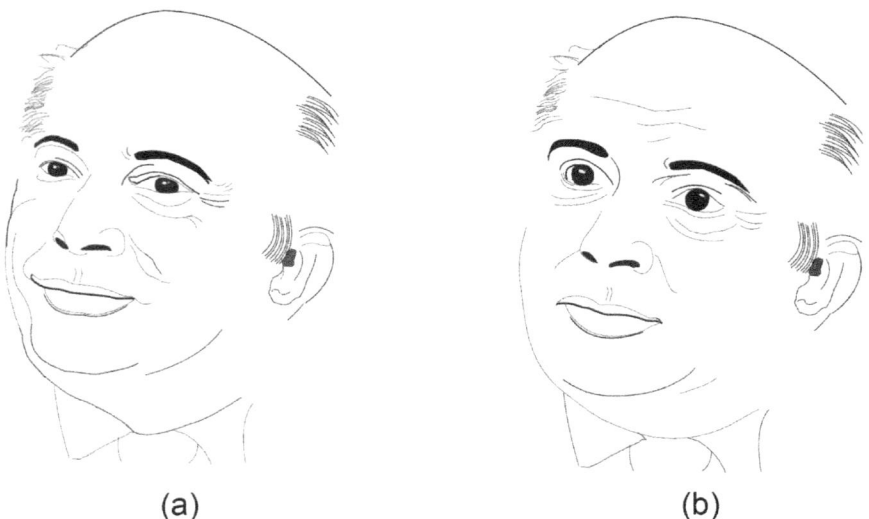

(a)                                           (b)

**FIGURE 6.4** (a) I defy you; (b) I am dismayed.

## 6.3 The gazeionary: a lexicon of gaze

Table 6.3 presents a fragment of the lexicon of gaze, where the lexical entries – the signal–meaning pairs – are drawn partly by videorecorded data analysed by a qualitative observational method and partly by the deductive method combined with the speaker's judgements.

The list of entries has the form of a *Thesaurus* (Roget, 1962), that is, it starts from the types and subtypes of meanings and matches them to signals of gaze. Yet it is not a complete list, both because it only encompasses information on the world and information on the sender's mind and because, even within these types, not all possible items are mentioned. But I hope, nonetheless, this is enough to display the richness of the communicative repertoire of our eyes, and to encourage going on in the endeavour of finding more "gaze words".

**TABLE 6.3** Lexical Entries of the Lexicon of Gaze

| *Type of meaning* | | | *Meaning* | *Gaze* |
|---|---|---|---|---|
| **Information about the world** | *Reference* | Entity | I refer to the object/person/ event there. | *Eyes directed to the referent* <br> *Head directed to the interlocutor* |
| | *Predication* | Property | small difficult to see, understand, remember subtle (physically or conceptually) | *Squeeze eyes* |
| | | | Big, huge (also morally) very (superlative) | *Wide open eyes* |
| **Information about the sender's mind** | *Beliefs* | Certainty | I am serious, I'm not kidding. | *Slightly frowning eyebrows* |
| | | Metacognitive | I am doubtful. I am perplexed. | *Raised eyebrows with normal eyes aperture* |
| | | Attention | I am concentrating. | *Frowning eyebrows* |
| | | | I am concentrating on my thoughts. | *Closed eyes* <br> *Staring out into space* |

*(Continued)*

**TABLE 6.3** (Continued)

| Type of meaning | | | Meaning | Gaze |
|---|---|---|---|---|
| | | Memory | I am trying to retrieve this belief from my long-term memory. | Eyes downward leftward |
| | | Inference | I am making inferences/I am planning. | Eyes looking up |
| Information about the sender's mind | Goals | **Performative** | | |
| | | Request for attention | I address you. | Looking at the interlocutor |
| | | | I am trying to attract your attention. | Raising eyebrows with head tilted back |
| | | | I address you in a peremptory way. | Direct gaze |
| | | | I am trying to attract your attention, but I do not want others to realise it. | Oblique glance |
| | | | I want you to know I am here, but with a discreet presence. Sometimes I show, sometimes not, shyly trying to solicit your attention. | Peeping: brief repeated glances |
| | | Question | I ask you. | Frowning the eyebrows Raising the eyebrows |
| | | Answer | I accept your request for attention. | Returning the gaze |
| | | | I do not want to look at you. | Looking away |

*(Continued)*

**TABLE 6.3** (Continued)

| Type of meaning | | | Meaning | Gaze |
|---|---|---|---|---|
| | | Agreement Complicity | I am on your side. I ask for your complicity. | Wink |
| | | | We are accomplices (allies on somewhat illicit things). | Wink |
| | | Distrust Disapproval | I do not trust you. I disapprove. | Oblique gaze with head canting and half-open eyes |
| | | | I don't believe it. | Frowning the eyebrows |
| | | Defiance | I defy you. | Staring the interlocutor in the eye without averting gaze |
| | | Threat | I threaten you. | Stare fixedly with half-open eyes and tense eyelids |
| Information about the sender's mind | Goal | **Sentence** | This is the topic. | Avert gaze from the interlocutor |
| | | | This is the comment. | Look at the interlocutor Raise the eyebrows, with wide open eyes |
| | | **Metadiscursive** | What I am about to say is in contrast with the preceding beliefs. | Raise the eyebrows |
| | | | I pass over this topic. | Shortly squint the eyelids |
| | | **Metaconversational** Turn-taking | I ask for the speaking turn. | Open eyes, gaze to the speaker |

*(Continued)*

**TABLE 6.3** (Continued)

| Type of meaning | | | Meaning | Gaze |
|---|---|---|---|---|
| | | Backchannel | I am following you (and I understand). | Short eye closure |
| | | | I don't believe you. | Raise the eyebrows with not very open eyes |
| | | | | Raise the eyebrows; oblique gaze with head canting and half-closed eyes |
| | | | I don't understand/I don't agree. | Frowning eyebrows |
| | | | This is surprising. | Look at the speaker with raised eyebrows |
| Information about the sender's mind | *Emotion* | I am happy. | | Sparkling eyes |
| | | I am sad. | | Inner parts of the eyebrows raised |
| | | I am afraid. | | Wide open eyes with frowning eyebrows |
| | | I am surprised. | | Wide open eyes with raised eyebrows |
| | | I am worried. | | Inner parts of eyebrows raised and closer |
| | | I am dismayed. | | Eyes not focusing and looking far away |
| | | I am excited. | | Dilated pupils |
| | | I love you. | | Sparkling eyes, half-closed eyelids |
| | | | | Eyes into the other's eyes |
| | | I contemn you. | | Oblique gaze, raised eyebrows, half-closed eyelids |
| | | I am ashamed. | | Eyes downcast |

# 7
## GAZE AS A LEXICON

Our looks, gazes, stares, glances, in a way not so different from our words and symbolic gestures, seem to constitute a lexicon. So much so that in the previous chapter we have even tried to do what linguists have been doing for centuries with the verbal languages (and more recently with the sign languages) of the world: to construct a fragment of a gazeionary: a dictionary of the eyes.

### 7.1 A lexicon, really?

Some might consider this too bold a hypothesis: could it really be that our eye language, or one of our everyday gestures, is so similar to a verbal lexicon? Are they not, these languages, more evanescent, elusive, context-bound than our much more solid languages?

In fact, linguistic speculation has advanced provocative and extreme hypotheses regarding the meaning, not to mention these strange body signals – gestures, glances, postures – but even of words. There are even some who say that meaning does not exist (distinguished people, a certain Wittgenstein, for example), they speak of indeterminacy of meaning. That would be to say that a word now means this, but in another context something else, without a rule, without a systematicity. I simply think that this is not so: that if it were so, communication would not exist, we could not understand one another in all the exchanges of our daily life, and in the rituals of public life. Obviously, every now and then there are misunderstandings, so-called "communication failures" (Tirassa, 1991; Zani, Selleri & David, 1994; Anolli, 2011), because, in communication as in any human

DOI: 10.4324/9781032678344-7

activity, one can make mistakes, explain oneself wrongly, or get the wrong end of the stick, but they are mistakes that confirm the rule, precisely because they arise from its violation.

I would say, if anything, that in most cases we understand one another quite fine, and when this is not the case, it is because someone actually either does not want or is not able to understand or be understood, and that communication is a very efficient and cost-effective tool, one in which each signal has its own distinct meaning, since it would be useless to have several signals for the same meaning, and confusing to have several meanings for one signal.

Of course, something would seem to crack this limpid symmetry. Communication systems are – all of them, whether words or all other body signals – subject to the disfiguring diseases of synonymy (multiple signals for one meaning) as well as homonymy and polysemy (one signal for multiple meanings). And it cannot be said at all that body signals – unlike words – are the realm of polysemy and vagueness. Such diseases also flourish in languages. Each word generally has more than one meaning: if you open a dictionary, for each entry you see many little numbers (a., b., c., . . .) that distinguish its various "meanings" or "readings". And reciprocally, a particular dictionary – the dictionary of synonyms – owes its name and its very existence to the fact that very often one meaning (or rather almost the same meaning) can be conveyed by several different signals. So synonymy (two or more signals for one meaning) and homonymy and polysemy (one signal for two or more meanings), far from being exceptions, are indeed a typical feature of lexical systems, both verbal and nonverbal ones.

These characteristics of lexicons are thus the greatest challenge to the researcher who wants to compile a lexicon: a list of verbal or bodily "words" in which each signal has one, two, ten, but not an indeterminate number of meanings.

## 7.2 Polysemy

To show that even a signal other than a word, even if polysemic, has its own precise meaning and that this does not vary infinitely even in the possible infinite contexts, it is useful to show that in all those meanings there is a common semantic core, a part of meaning that recurs in all contexts or that at any rate there is a semantic link between the meanings that in those contexts the signal acquires (Allwood, 2003). This has often been demonstrated for words (Castelfranchi, 1975; Parisi, 1975; Antinucci, 1975; Poggi, 1981), but it can also be shown for other types of signals.

The link between two meanings of a polysemic signal can be of two types: either componential or inferential.

### 7.2.1 A componential link

In some cases, the meanings *a, b, c* share one and the same semantic component (i.e. a part or a "piece" of meaning) *x*, to which each of them adds different components: *a* means *x + y*, *b* means *x + z*, *c* means *x + k*.

For example, we *raise our eyebrows* when we want to communicate surprise or incredulity or as we emphasise a word, or as we say *but* to express an adversative link. Actually, surprise is an emotion caused by the violation of an expectation; incredulity is a mental state in which we do not accept some belief as true uncritically; emphasis is the communicative intention of stressing as important the information one is providing. In all of these cases there is some NEW AND UNEXPECTED INFORMATION, which in one case is considered for the emotion or mental state it causes, in others for the alert the sender communicates to the addressee. Therefore this type of gaze is polysemic, since it has four partly different meanings, but in all of them, besides the additional pieces of meaning that distinguish them from one another, a common semantic component is shared of NEW AND UNEXPECTED INFORMATION.

### 7.2.2 An inferential link: indirect, literal and originary meanings

In other cases, the different meanings of the same polysemic signal are connected by an inferential link: from meaning *a* one can infer meaning *b*, from *b*, *c*, and so on. This is the case for indirect meanings.

The words and sentences of a language, but in the same vein other signals too – gestures, gaze items, acts of physical contact – besides their literal meaning may also have one or more indirect meanings (Castelfranchi & Parisi, 1980; Parisi, 1979; Poggi, 2007, 2022a). The literal meaning of a signal or combination of signals is the one you can attribute to it on the basis of the rules of its communication system. For example, in verbal languages the literal meaning of a sentence or part of a sentence is determined by the meanings of the words and of their syntactic construction, while a possible indirect meaning must be inferred: it cannot, by definition, be understood simply thanks to the knowledge of the lexical and syntactic rules. The word *sea* literally means "an expanse of salt water in unlimited quantities", but if I say *a sea of troubles* you can infer "a lot of troubles". The sentence *can you pass the salt?* is literally a question aimed to know whether you have the physical capacity of passing me the salt, but you can infer (indirect meaning) that I am asking for the salt.

Also, signals other than words or sentences – gestures, gaze items, facial expressions – have indirect meanings, inferable from their literal meanings, and the divergence between the literal and indirect meanings, when generating two both frequent uses, gives rise to a case of polysemy. For example, the word *bravo!* and the gesture of *applause* can be used with their literal meaning of approval and praise or else ironically, in which case you can infer an opposite meaning, a criticism or reproach. Actually, since these two readings – very different, even opposite – are finally codified in memory as two distinct meanings of the same word or gesture, they are a case of polysemy: the same signal has two meanings, praise and reproach. But there is an inferential link between them: to draw the former from the latter, you simply have to apply the typical rule of irony, turning a meaning into its opposite (Bara, 1999; Attardo et al., 2003; Cavicchio, Magno Caldognetto & Poggi, 2005; Poggi, Cavicchio & Magno Caldognetto, 2005): "I praise you (ironically) = I reproach you".

Besides connecting a literal meaning with a corresponding indirect meaning, other inferences also connect it to its "originary meaning": the one from which the literal meaning derives. The literal meaning of a body signal, in fact, often stems out of a physical action that previously did not have a communicative value (Posner & Serenari, 2001; Serenari, 2003; Posner, 2003). For instance, among the acts of physical contact, the *kiss* ethologically evolves from the mother's act of feeding the baby with prechewed and softened food: an act of caregiving, which then becomes a symbol of affection (Eibl-Eibesfeldt, 1972).

Similarly, in the gaze language the *raising of the eyebrows*, which communicates a meaning of surprise (Ekman, 1979), probably derives from the physical action of *opening the eyes wide* to see more, to acquire more information. This action aimed at a wider comprehension lets you infer there is something surprising, something one cannot account for but that needs to be accounted for. Thus the noncommunicative action of trying to see better gets ritualised – it becomes non-practical but communicative action (Eibl-Eibesfeldt, 1972) – and acquires the meaning of showing surprise. Likewise, the *frowning of the eyebrows* is originally a movement that cooperates with the action of focusing to see something more sharply, but then it is interpreted as a signal of concentration, of focusing attention to understand better, and this is its literal meaning. But if I try to understand, this means I do not understand, hence this signal acquires the indirect meaning of incomprehension. Finally, as we will see, the signal may be used rhetorically as a euphemistic way to convey disagreement.

Actually, many body signals have three meanings that are different but inferentially connected: the literal meaning, the indirect one that can be inferred from it, and a sort of primitive, originary meaning, often a noncommunicative action, from which the literal meaning has stemmed (Table 7.1).

What can we conclude, based on these devices singled out in polysemy? That if all the meanings of a polysemic signal may be traced back to a shared semantic core, connected by way of semantic components or inferences, the semantic coherence among the various meanings of a (verbal or bodily) signal, and

**TABLE 7.1** Originary, Literal and Indirect Meanings

| Modality | Signal | Originary meaning | Literal meanings | Indirect meaning |
|---|---|---|---|---|
| Gesture | *applause* | | I praise you. | I blame you. |
| Physical contact | *kiss* | I feed you. | I love you. | |
| Gaze | *eyebrows raising* | I try to see more. | Surprise/ incomprehension: there is something I don't understand. I am surprised. | Emphasis: I want you to be surprised too: this is new and important information. |
| Gaze | *eyebrows frown* | I try to see things more sharply/ precisely. | Concentration: I concentrate to solve a problem. | Incomprehension: There is something I don't understand. → Disagreement: It is not that I don't understand: I don't agree. |

along with it the systematicity of relations between signals and meanings, are saved. And if even in the actions of our eyes we can find such recurrences and systematicities, then indeed our gaze is a lexicon. And the enterprise of writing it down is possible and not pointless.

## 7.3 Synonymy

The existence of indirect meanings and consideration of the inferences through which they are understood also make it possible to explain sometimes bizarre phenomena of synonymy in body signals.

For example, to express perplexity, incredulity or disagreement, we can use opposite behaviours of the eyebrows, both *frowning* and *raising* them. Literally, *frowning* means incomprehension, while *raising the eyebrows* means surprise; but if we look at the inferences that can be drawn from these meanings, the outcome may be the same: both signals indirectly communicate "I do not completely accept what you say". In fact, if I am surprised (I *raise my eyebrows*), what you say is odd, unexpected, almost incredible; therefore I am indirectly communicating that I don't believe what you say. On the other hand, showing I don't understand (by *frowning my eyebrows* as if I were trying to see things better) is at times a polite way to let you understand I don't agree in fact. This is why these two signals of the eyebrows, seemingly opposite, may both mean non-total acceptance of what the other is saying: at the level of their indirect meaning, they may even be synonyms.

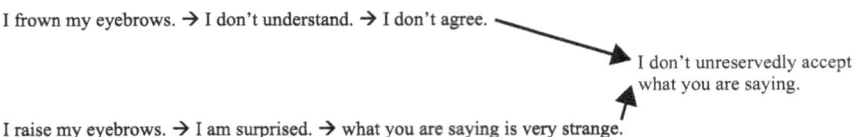

I frown my eyebrows. → I don't understand. → I don't agree.

I don't unreservedly accept what you are saying.

I raise my eyebrows. → I am surprised. → what you are saying is very strange.

In this case too, by considering indirect meanings, we can account for the synonymity of bodily signals and at the same time maintain the idea that, even in these apparently evanescent systems of communication, there are precise and systematic correspondences between signals and meanings.

## 7.4   Universal or cultural?

But are these correspondences between signals and meanings universal or cultural? Innate, i.e. inscribed in our genetic heritage, or conventional and acquired through learning from our culture? And so will our gaze, our gestures and postures, our facial expressions also be understandable in another culture, or will our body in another country have to learn other "words" to communicate with others and to avoid misunderstandings?

The answer to such questions are not straightforward. Some of these signals are biologically codified, others are culturally learned. If you make the "vertical ring" gesture, *thumb and index finger touching to make a circle*, this means approval (okay) in the USA and other Western countries, but it is an insult in Greece; therefore, it is a culturally codified gesture. But if you show jubilation by *shaking your fist up in the air* people will understand you across all countries because it is biologically determined and therefore universal for a gesture of expansion to be connected with the high physiological activation brought about by an emotion such as jubilation.

For many gestural systems, the correspondences between signals and meanings differ across cultures, as shown by the existence of different gestural lexicons in different countries: Japan, Italy, Germany, Russia, Portugal, Catalunya (Rector, Poggi & Trigo, 2003); but for many other communication systems, especially the phylogenetically older ones, such as facial expressions, gaze and physical contact, these correspondences are probably largely innate and therefore universal. Let us see why.

*Meanings vs. norms of use.*   In any communication system, we can distinguish two types of rules: SEMANTIC RULES and NORMS OF USE (or interactional rules). Semantic rules establish the correspondence between signals and meanings, leading to instructions of this kind:

If you want to communicate the meaning "I greet you", say *hello*.

A verbal language comprises many rules of this kind: lexical and syntactic rules. But even a communication system of gestures or gaze can have lexical rules, such as:

If you want to communicate the meaning "I greet you", *shake your hand, palm towards the interlocutor, from right to left.*
If you want to communicate the meaning "I greet you", *raise and lower your eyebrows* (Eibl-Eibesfeldt, 1972).

In addition to the SEMANTIC RULES, we have NORMS OF USE, which establish not how to communicate a certain meaning but whether a certain meaning can or cannot, should or should not be communicated in a given situation. Norms such as:

If you meet a person you know, apply the rule for the meaning "I greet you".
If you meet a person you do not know, do not apply the rule for the meaning "I greet you".

In other words: a communication system tells you not only what to do if you want to communicate a certain meaning but also whether and when communicating it is prescribed, forbidden or permitted. These are the NORMS OF USE of communicative signals; actually, they are the rules of appropriateness studied by sociolinguistics (Wardhaugh & Fuller, 2021), also very close to the so-called display rules identified, with regard to the expression of emotions, by Ekman and Friesen (1971): those that advise us not to *laugh loudly* at a funeral, to *smile cordially* when we are introduced to a person, or not to *stare into a person's eyes* in a lift.

It is important to distinguish between these two types of rules because they behave differently with respect to the nature–culture issue, depending on the communication system. For example, the facial expression of emotions might be universal as far as semantic rules are concerned but culturally determined as to their norms of use; on the other hand, in the verbal expression of emotions, both semantic rules and norms of use vary among cultures.

But how do these norms of use work? Some of them are very general: for example, in some cultures making gestures tends to be sanctioned, since gestures are considered an informal way of communicating, a too emotional or "primitive" one, and this leads to inhibiting gesturing in general. Typically, for instance, the British gesture less than the Neapolitans, they have fewer gestures in their lexicon, with fewer gesture handshapes and less amplitude (Kendon, 2004). Moreover, in addition to these general ones, there are the norms of linguistic taboo and interdiction (Galli de' Paratesi, 1969; Kita & Essegbey, 2001): those that prohibit the use of a communicative signal because its form or meaning is impure, obscene or improper. From this point of view, even among words those that are insulting or obscene (swear words and "bad words") will more often be tabooed in a "prudish" or traditionalist culture than in an uninhibited culture.

Yet in communication systems different from words, cultural variation will apply more to norms of use than to semantic rules. My hypothesis is that a *languid eye*, a *seductive glance*, or *looking down on someone* all over the world are produced in the same way and have the same meaning. But if in one culture treating someone with condescension is very insulting and in another showing oneself too openly in love is considered improper or obscene, then in those cultures those types of glances will be strongly disapproved of and will be much rarer to see.

### 7.4.1 Nature and culture in the lexicon of gaze

Thus even if cultures differ greatly in the norms they impose on the use of gaze (Argyle & Cook, 1976; Duranti, 1992), it is nevertheless plausible that a universal lexicon of gaze exists from a semantic point of view; indeed, it is precisely because a fixed gaze has a defiant meaning, or an oblique gaze is seductive, that signals of this kind will be prescribed or sanctioned in a certain culture, depending on how much it prescribes or sanctions those types of social attitudes.

Therefore, my hypothesis is that, in a communication system such as gaze, the norms of use are cultural, but the semantic rules are largely universal. Yes, there will be some specific looks that have a culturally determined meaning (such as the *wink* that in some cultures, but not everywhere, means complicity); but for the most part it is plausible that the communicative system of gaze is universal. Once, in a video of a conversation among Papuans, I was watching the face and eyes of an elderly indigenous woman speaking, and a strange impression of familiarity made me think: but look, I do know that language . . .

The substantive universality of the lexicon of gaze is therefore, for now, only a hypothesis. But there is only one way to verify or falsify it: investigating these lexicons first in a single culture, then in other cultures, and finally comparing the respective lexicons.

### 7.5 Eyes that talk: an empirical study

In Chapter 4, our first steps to write down a lexicon of gaze exploited an ethno-semantic method: scrutinising the words of a natural language to gain insight into the meanings of this lexicon, as well as to shed light on how a gaze is physically produced and perceived.

In Chapter 6, through a method of deductive analysis, starting from a taxonomy of meanings, we singled out a number of gaze items, and then, after observational research, we described various lexical entries in terms of their optology and their corresponding meanings. In all cases we exploited the speaker's judgements, i.e. our intuitions about the communicative value of each gaze; this enabled us to write down a lexicon, i.e. a set of gaze–meaning correspondences. But the theoretical hypotheses that we formulated in this way can also be empirically tested.

The coherence and systematicity of a lexicon of gaze was investigated in an empirical study (Poggi & Roberto, 2007). The hypothesis was that the gaze actually forms a lexicon, i.e. a set of correspondences between signals and meanings that is systematic and shared by people, where the signal is a specific set of traits and movements in the eye region, and the meaning is a set of beliefs that the signal communicates.

The study employed a simulative technique, using the Greta Face Library (Poggi & Pelachaud, 2000; Bevacqua et al., 2007; see Chapter 5), an interactive artificial agent whose facial action library enables the production of all the muscular actions that give rise to facial expressions allowing, among other things, to move not only the muscles of the mouth, forehead and other parts of the face but also the eyebrows, eyelids, and the position of the iris, thus making the values of all the parameters of gaze vary at will.

The following parameters were taken into account, and their values varied correspondingly:

1. Eyelids' aperture:

   *half-closed* (lowered upper eyelids and raised lower eyelids)
   *half-open* (lowered upper eyelids)
   *wide open up* (upper eyelids showing the sclera over the iris)
   *wide open down* (upper eyelids showing the sclera over the iris and lower eyelids showing the sclera under the iris)

2. Eyes' direction:

   *forward, upward, downward, rightward, leftward downward*

3. Eyelids' position:

   *default position, totally raised, inner eyelids raised, inner eyelids lowered and outer eyelids raised*

By combining the values in these parameters, a multiple-choice questionnaire of ten items was constructed, each item featuring the face of Greta with a distinct gaze. A hypothesis regarding the meaning of each item was formulated based on the speaker's judgements. Each meaning was paraphrased by a complete sentence (since a gaze is typically a holophrastic signal), with a performative of information and a propositional content mentioning a physical state (e.g. *I am tired*), a cognitive state (*I am absorbed, I am attentive*), or an emotional state (*I am exasperated, I hate you*). In the multiple-choice questionnaire, for each item four alternative answers were proposed (the meaning hypothesised and three distractors) and a possible open answer (*other*) was added. The questionnaire was submitted to 100 students in a high school, 86 females and 14 males, ages 18–20.

The results generally confirm the hypothesised meanings. Six items were attributed the expected meaning by more than 75% subjects: (*I'm bored* 88%, *I'm tired* 86%, *I'm amazed* 85%, *I hate* 81%, *I repent* 79%, *I'm exasperated* 76%); three items were confirmed by more than a half subjects (*I'm absorbed* 58%, *I scrutinise* 54%, *I'm terrified* 43%), while the meaning of *caution* was confirmed only by 28% participants. But the hypothesis is also confirmed by the meanings with which each item is confused. For example, the gaze *terrified*, correctly recognised by 43% participants, is confused with *alarmed* by 47% of participants; actually, the two meanings share at least one semantic element, the likeliness of occurrence of a dangerous event. And this "confusion" with really close meanings also recurs in the open questions, "other": *terrified* is also interpreted as *astonished, impressed, dismayed, stupefied, amazed*, while *amazed* is interpreted as *alarmed, terrified, surprised, astonished*. In fact, the two items are very similar as to the signal, hence easily confusable: the only difference is that in *terrified*, the eyelids are so open that you can see the sclera both over and under the iris (Figure 7.1a), while in *amazed* you see it only over the iris (Figure 7.1b).

Yet, also on the semantic side, the two gazes share a great part of their meaning: *opening eyes wide* originally has the function of amplifying the visual field as much as possible (Ekman, 1979) to store as much information as possible (Poggi & Pelachaud, 1998) in case of unexpected events. And an unexpected event may elicit surprise (see the meaning "amazed") but, if it is also dangerous, it may even elicit terror ("terrified"). In this case, then, a similarity in the signals corresponds to a similarity in the meanings; which may account for why they get confused. Here, in particular, the similarity is determined by the presence of one and the same

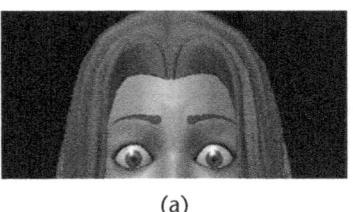 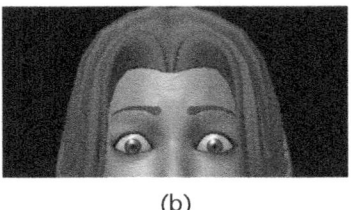

(a)                                         (b)

**FIGURE 7.1**   (a) I'm terrified; (b) I'm amazed

semantic element (UNEXPECTED EVENT) in both meanings: this is the "componential link" seen previously, in which two meanings are connected because they share a same component. In other cases of confusion, instead, the semantic connection is determined by an inferential link: from meaning *a*, you can infer a meaning *b*. To give an example of an inference based on a cause–effect link: 58% participants correctly recognised the item *absorbed*, while 31% interpreted it as *inattentive*, which is seemingly the opposite. But one who is absorbed in one's thoughts is actually disattentive about the surrounding context: one thing causes the other and thus allows one to infer it.

So, on the one side, the answers to the questionnaire, however different from the expected ones, still are semantically congruent with the hypothesised meanings. But more than that, a further confirmation is that the distractors with meanings opposite to those hypothesised were almost never or very rarely chosen: for example, no one chose *attentive* or *sad* for the item *annoyed*, nor was *sad* chosen for the item *terrified*.

The results of this study lead us to conclude that the items of gaze have specific meanings and that hence the lexicon they form is systematic and shared by speakers.

# 8

# EYEBROW WORDS

After our general overview on the lexicon of gaze and its optology and morphology, we will now take a closer look at some specific parts and actions of the eye region that are responsible for specific items of gaze. In this chapter, we deal with the movements of the eyebrows; in the next two we will deal with *closing eyes* and *rolling eyes*.

## 8.1 The eyebrows

In a famous article on the similarities and differences of expressive movements in different cultures, Eibl-Eibesfeldt (1972) distinguished several signals produced by *raising eyebrows*. On the one hand, the *eyebrow flash* (Grammer et al., 1987), in which the eyebrows are raised quickly and repeatedly, communicates acceptance of social contact, readiness for interaction: approval, thanks, greeting, seduction, seeking confirmation. On the other hand, however, *raising the eyebrows* also conveys rejection, disapproval, indignation or arrogance: a look of warning reminiscent of the threatening gaze of some non-human primates. According to Eibl-Eibesfeldt, the raising of eyebrows is originally a simple side effect of the eye-opening that accompanies attention behaviour. This is why eyebrows are raised to signal surprise, and while a pleasant surprise gives rise to a readiness for contact, an unpleasant one can lead to disapproval or threat. Thus Eibl-Eibesfeldt traces all meanings of the raising of eyebrows back to the attention that surprise elicits.

In another important article on the eyebrows, Ekman (1979) attributes all eyebrow signals to the individual or combined movements of three AUs (facial action units), namely AU1, AU2 and AU4, and on this basis he distinguishes the apparently very different cases highlighted by Eibl-Eibesfeldt:

DOI: 10.4324/9781032678344-8

surprise, which can be expressed even when one is alone, even in the absence of communicative interaction; emphasis and the adversative relation, typically used in conversation; and the mental state of doubt or perplexity, generally expressed by one who is the interlocutor in conversation. Finally, he names the *asymmetrical raising of a single eyebrow* the *sceptical eyebrow*.

Ekman also argues that upward and downward eyebrow movements (*raisings* and *frownings*, respectively) are used both in emotional signals, such as expressions of surprise, fear and anger, and conversational signals, such as interrogative expressions, emphasis of words or phrases and signals of approval.

## 8.2 The *eyebrow raising*

*Raising the eyebrows* is, then, a highly polysemic signal, that is, one with various different meanings; yet, for many of them, as already pointed by Eibl-Eibesfeldt and Ekman, a shared semantic element can be found.

### 8.2.1 Question

First, we *raise our eyebrows* when we ask a question. Both in the hearing people's everyday conversation and in Sign Languages of the Deaf, as found for the American Sign Language (Wilbur, 1994; Weast, 2008) and the Italian Sign Language (Volterra, 1987; Volterra et al., 2019), when putting a question we *look at the interlocutor raising our eyebrows*. We do so in order to *open our eyes wide*, to enlarge our visual field and to see more things around us: to acquire more information. In this case, therefore, the *eyebrow raising* communicates our lack of a certain belief and our goal to obtain it.

### 8.2.2 Surprise

Surprise is one of the primary emotions, i.e. those emotions that are of vital importance for human adaptation and that are expressed by an innate and universal expressive pattern. Specifically, it is a "cognitive" emotion (Poggi, 2008; D'Errico & Poggi, 2016), one whose function is to monitor the state of acquisition and processing of the subject's beliefs, a primary device for human survival. In particular, surprise is triggered by the violation of a cognitive expectation, that is, by the sudden acquisition of a belief that is completely unexpected because it contrasts with the subject's previous beliefs, i.e. it cannot be inferred from them (Poggi, 1981; Lorini & Castelfranchi, 2007; Miceli & Castelfranchi, 2014). But why is the violation of an expectation so serious that it triggers an emotion, and why is it so important to express it?

Humans have not only pragmatic or social goals, such as acquiring material resources or being loved and valued by others, but also cognitive goals:

the need to acquire and process beliefs and to store them in memory in networks of interconnected beliefs that explain one another. To be able to make
plans and achieve goals, humans, much more than other animals, need to
have beliefs about themselves and the external world but also to generate
expectations, i.e. inferences about the future, to predict what will happen as
a consequence of their own actions or of external events (Castelfranchi &
Poggi, 1998). Furthermore, it is also important to understand immediately
when an expectation is contradicted by events, and when a new belief cannot
be explained (i.e. inferred) on the basis of previous beliefs, it is necessary to
search for new beliefs apt to explain the unexpected; thus surprise triggers
curiosity, the goal of immediately searching for new information. This is
why we experience surprise whenever something happens that we did not
expect and cannot explain and why we express our surprise by *raising our
eyebrows*: we do so to *open our eyes wide* and see/know more. A person in a
state of surprise is biologically ready to take in as much visual information as
possible, but as a result, his or her *raised eyebrows* and *wide-open* eyes also
become an expressive signal of surprise.

### 8.2.3   Admiration and praise

Admiration is an emotion linked to surprise. Etymologically, its root contains
the Latin verb *miror*, which means "I am amazed", "I am surprised". When
you admire something (e.g. a landscape) or someone, you have a strongly
positive appreciation, and a surprisingly positive one of it because it exceeds
any expectation of the value of objects or people (Poggi & Zuccaro, 2008).
Hence, *eyebrows are raised* and *eyes are opened wider* in expressing admiration but also in praising someone: one who praises someone in fact expresses
not only approval but admiring approval. The facial expression of praise, in
fact, includes a *lowering of the head* – as if to say *yes*, to accept/approve of
what the other has done or the way she has done it – and *more open eyes
with raised eyebrows* (Poggi, 2007).

### 8.2.4   Emphasis

To emphasise means to communicate that something is particularly important, possibly even while showing one's emotion about it; as we do, for example, when we add exclamation marks to a written sentence. This is done
when a whole sentence is very important in a discourse. But often we use
emphasis to make clear what is the most important part of a sentence.

In a sentence, the most important part is the comment, that is, the new,
asserted belief, that the speaker wants to make prominent, asking for higher
attention from the interlocutor; therefore, to highlight the informational

structure of the sentence we generally give little prominence to the topic while emphasising the comment.

Actually, the best way to elicit attention is to show surprise: if I show surprise and hence my need to be attentive to acquire new information, this cognitive attitude, thanks to mirror neurons, is reproduced in the interlocutor: seeing my surprise, the other takes an alert attitude, and credits more importance to that part of the sentence, paying it more attention.

Therefore, *raising the eyebrows* means: "Pay more attention than usual to what I'm saying, because this is the most novel, less obvious, most surprising part of my discourse". In fact, there is a link between surprise and novel information because what is new is potentially difficult to infer from our preexisting beliefs. This is why the idea of something that cannot be inferred from previous knowledge is contained, at least potentially, in the case of emphasis too: "To elicit your attention on $x$, I want you to get surprised about $x$; that is, I want you to know that $x$ cannot be inferred from preexisting beliefs".

### 8.2.5   Adversative meanings

We have an "adversative meaning" when, in a sentence or discourse, the second part cannot be inferred from the first one and even contradicts it. Such contradiction is generally displayed, highlighted, by adversative conjunctions or adverbs such as *but, however, on the contrary, instead, while*. For example, if I say "*This pear is bland but fresh*", from the first part of the sentence, that the pear is bland, one might conclude that it is not worth eating, but from the second one can draw the opposite conclusion. The same relationship between two beliefs contradicting each other may be made explicit by concessive conjunctions or adverbs, such as *even if, although, notwithstanding, all the same* where the contradicted sentence is the one preceded by the concessive one: "*Even if it is bland, this pear is fresh*".

In both cases, adversative and concessive, the adverb or conjunction prevents an inference, i.e. it communicates: "from the first part of the sentence could you draw inference $x$, but I urge you not to do so, because the conclusion I want you to draw is just the opposite of $x$".

As a matter of fact, as we say *but* or *even if* or other similar conjunctions or adverbs, we generally *raise our eyebrows*. Such *raising* is a sort of body synonym of those words, alerting: "Now I will say something that contrasts with what I said so far", but this already codified meaning is but an idiomatised inference of the expression of surprise.

"I am surprised. → You have to be surprised. →
What follows is not predictable from what I have just said."

In this case too, then, the link between unpredictability, novelty, and surprise can account for the polysemy of this eyebrow signal.

### 8.2.6 Perplexity and doubt

A final meaning of the *eyebrow raising* is one of doubt or perplexity. Perplexity is a particular mental state caused in our mind by two contrasting beliefs, that cannot be inferred from each other (Poggi, 1981); until we can decide which of the two to believe, we are in a state of suspension of the mind because we feel less certain of either. To have our interlocutor understand that we do not want to give the belief we are communicating as certain – that is, to alert him to our perplexity – we *raise our eyebrows* but *without opening eyes wide*, unlike what we do with surprise.

The *raised eyebrows* of doubt or perplexity are also used as a backchannel: in this case, it is not the speaker who *raises the eyebrows* but the interlocutor, who thus communicates "I am doubtful about what you are saying": a euphemistic way to say "I don't believe you". Actually, showing perplexity or doubt in giving a backchannel to one who tells us something incredible is like showing surprise because an incredible belief too can't be inferred from my preexisting beliefs.

Another very close meaning, both as to the sender's movement and the addressee's perception and as to its meaning, is just one of Ekman's (1979) *sceptical eyebrow*: by *raising a single eyebrow* we somehow show a fragment of surprise – incredulity (Table 8.1).

### 8.2.7 Polysemy of the eyebrow raising

The semantic element shared by all six cases of *eyebrow raising* – question, surprise, admiration and praise, emphasis, adversative, and perplexity – is a NEW BELIEF THAT CANNOT BE INFERRED FROM PREEXISTING BELIEFS. All six cases entail the lack of a belief, not inferable from preexisting beliefs, which in some cases is necessary to explain a new unexpected one. In the **question**, there is simply the need for a new belief; in **surprise**, in **admiration** and in the

**TABLE 8.1** Surprised, Perplexed, Sceptical

| 1 | *Both eyebrows raised* | Surprise |
|---|---|---|
| | *Wide open eyes* | |
| 2 | *Both eyebrows raised* | Perplexity |
| | *Normal aperture of the eyes* | |
| 3 | *A single eyebrow raised* | Scepticism |

**adversative** meanings, a new belief is coming that is contrasting with preceding ones. In **perplexity**, such a contrast causes indecision about whether to believe the new belief or not. In **emphasis**, we simply have a belief that we want to elicit more attention about because it is new, not necessarily contrasting but different from beliefs already acquired by the interlocutor, and that is not automatically inferable from them.

The six meanings differ:

1. *For the person who is to believe or infer the belief at issue*: With question, surprise, admiration, and perplexity, it is the sender of the eyebrow raising, while for adversative and emphasis, it is the addressee.
2. *For the class of contexts in which the eyebrow raising is performed*: As one asks a question or displays surprise, the new and unexpected belief is caused by a natural event or a human action, while emphasis and contrast and both speaker's and interlocutor's perplexity are expressed during verbal interaction: surprise and emphasis, as well as adversative, concern what the sender refers to, while perplexity can be communicated, both by the sender and by the interlocutor, on what the speaker is saying.

The differences and commonalities in these uses are represented in Table 8.2.

As mentioned, the link among the various meanings of a polysemic signal may be interpreted either as a componential one – a shared semantic component – or as an inferential one – a meaning that allows one to infer another. But also the origin of the signal may be explained by a set of inferences: one can trace how a particular communicative movement derives from a mental state. Here is the causal chain that, for each of the six meanings, carries to the eyebrow raising, seen both in the sender – from the triggering event, to the goal, to the meaning to communicate, to the signal production – and in the addressee – from the signal to the meaning.

Let us start from surprise (Figure 8.1).

This chain of causes describes the ritualisation process that likely bears from actions stemming from a mental state to the development of a communicative signal. I get an unexpected belief (1), I feel the emotion of surprise (2), this triggers the goal of understanding the strange event (3), hence the goal of acquiring more beliefs (4): so I open my eyes wide (5) and raise my eyebrows (6).

Initially, this eyebrow raising is a bare practical action aimed at seeing more to understand better: it is the 0 degree of meaning. But soon the action of opening eyes wide and raising the eyebrows becomes ritualised, no longer do I have the goal of seeing more: that movement has become a signal of surprise.

This is the same for other meanings. (See Figures 8.2–8.6.)

TABLE 8.2 Polysemy of the *Eyebrow Raising*

| Meaning 1 | Meaning 2 | Meaning 3 | Meaning 4 | Meaning 5 | Meaning 6 |
|---|---|---|---|---|---|
| **Question** | **Surprise** | **Admiration** | **Emphasis** | **Contrast** | **Perplexity** |
| New belief | New belief | New belief | New belief | New belief | New belief |
| Belief uninferable from previous ones | Belief uninferable from previous ones | Belief uninferable from previous ones | | Belief uninferable from previous ones | Belief not totally inferable |
| Lacking belief | Unexpected belief | Unexpected belief | Unexpected belief | Unexpected belief | Unexpected belief |
| Belief coming from natural event, human action or communicative interaction | Belief coming from natural event, human action or communicative interaction | Belief coming from natural event, human action or feature | Belief coming from communicative interaction | Belief coming from communicative interaction | Belief coming from communicative interaction |
| | | About object or person | About sender's statement | About sender's statement | About sender's or interlocutor's statement |
| | | Strongly positive evaluation | Request for attention | Warning not to draw the most plausible inference from the previous statement | Doubt or perplexity |

Inferential chain in the sender:

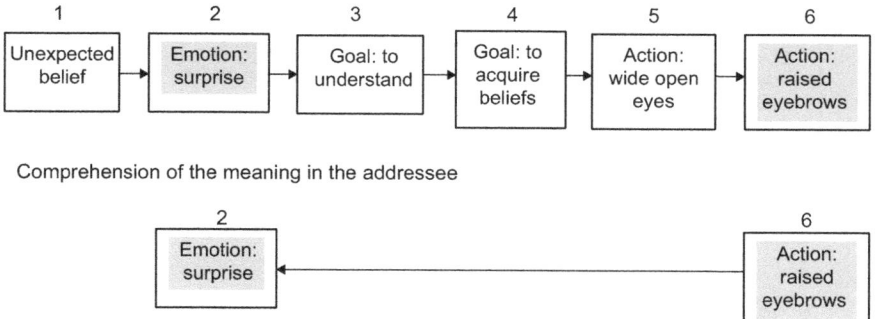

**FIGURE 8.1**  Causal chain for the eyebrows of surprise.

Inferential chain in the sender:

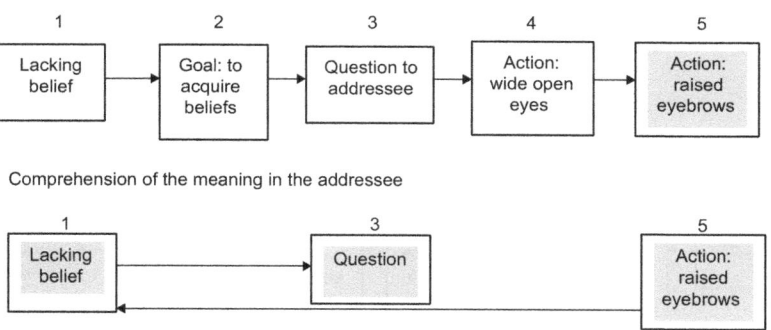

**FIGURE 8.2**  Causal chain for the eyebrows of question.

To sum up, in the rich polysemy of this signal, a semantic element is shared by all its meanings. The *raising of the eyebrows* always signals a lack of beliefs, which we are simply concerned to obtain, in the question (meaning of par. 8.2.1), but in surprise (meaning of par. 8.2.2), it is necessary to integrate an unexpected belief, i.e. to explain it better. The sender may express the surprise felt to display admiration (meaning 3) and may want to trigger it in the interlocutor either to ask for more attention (emphasis, meaning 4), or to warn not to draw plausible but incorrect inferences (adversative, meaning 5), or finally to communicate one's own perplexity (Meaning 6).

Inferential chain in the sender:
1
Emotion: surprise for highly positive evaluation
2
Goal: to praise addressee
3
Goal: to express admiration
4
Action: wide open eyes
5
Action: raised eyebrows
Comprehension of the meaning in the addressee
1
Emotion: surprise for highly positive evaluation
3
Praise to addressee
5
Action: raised eyebrows

**FIGURE 8.3** Causal chain for the eyebrows of admiration and praise.

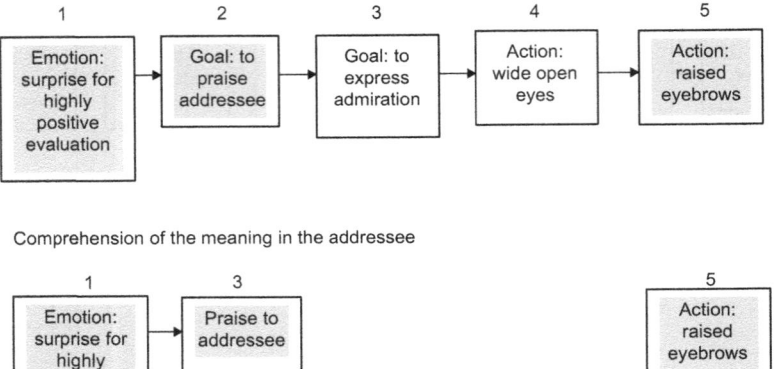

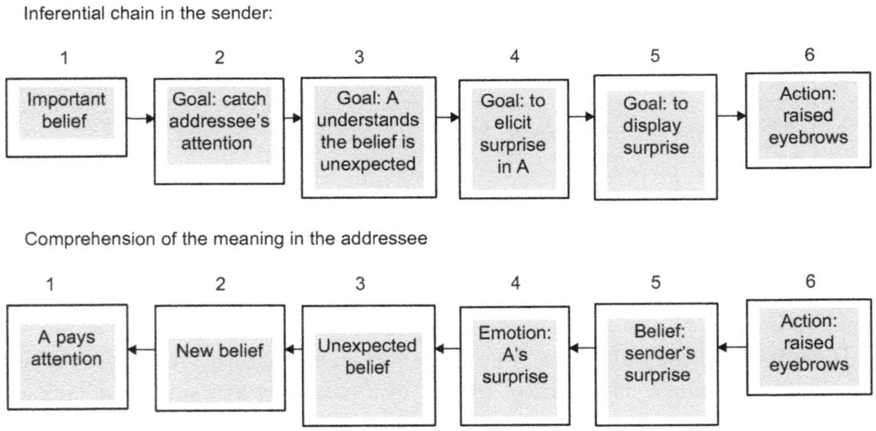

Inferential chain in the sender:
1
Important belief
2
Goal: catch addressee's attention
3
Goal: A understands the belief is unexpected
4
Goal: to elicit surprise in A
5
Goal: to display surprise
6
Action: raised eyebrows
Comprehension of the meaning in the addressee
1
A pays attention
2
New belief
3
Unexpected belief
4
Emotion: A's surprise
5
Belief: sender's surprise
6
Action: raised eyebrows

**FIGURE 8.4** Causal chain for the eyebrows of emphasis.

Inferential chain in the sender:

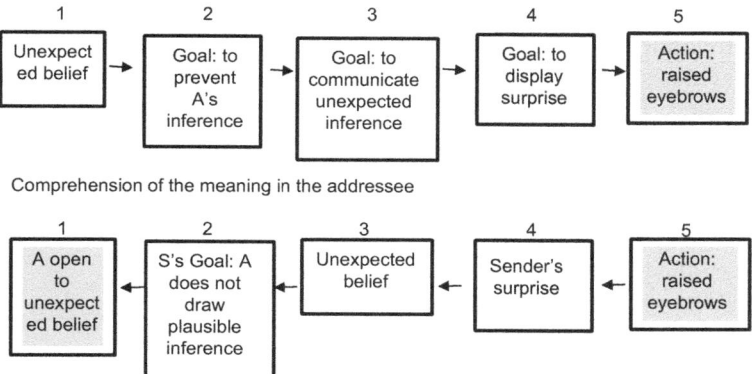

**FIGURE 8.5**  Causal chain for the eyebrows of adversative.

Inferential chain in the sender:

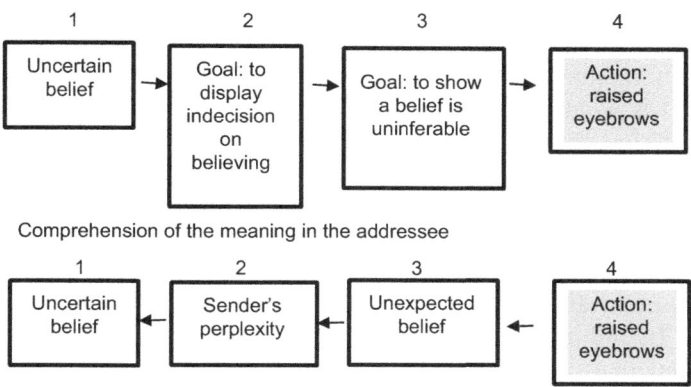

**FIGURE 8.6**  Causal chain for eyebrows of perplexity.

## 8.3 The *eyebrow frowning*

The other eyebrow signal, which is also polysemic, is the *frown*: the eyebrows are pulled together, creating vertical wrinkles on the forehead.

In previous studies (Poggi, 2006, 2007), various uses were singled out of the *frowning*. This signal is produced when:

1. You ask a question;
2. You cannot understand something;
3. You want to convey to your interlocutor that you do not understand what s/he is saying;
4. You want to indirectly communicate you don't agree;
5. You look at something very attentively;
6. You try to remember something;
7. You are doing, telling, or describing something, but you want to do so in a continuous way, without stopping, without distracting yourself;
8. You assert something with certainty and confidence, while conveying you are not kidding;
9. You are worried;
10. You are angry;
11. You are giving a peremptory order.

The meanings 1, 2 and 3 share the lack of a belief: you *frown* when there is something you don't understand (meaning 2), so you look for some belief to explain something by asking a question (meaning 1). If what you do not understand is what your interlocutor is saying (meaning 3), the *frowning* asks the interlocutor to be clearer, but sometimes this is but an indirect way, a rhetorical device or a polite strategy to say: "It is not that I don't understand; indeed, I don't agree" (meaning 4). Meanings 5–8 share an element of attention: you *frown* when you are looking at something attentively (5), but you are also attentive when you are trying to remember something (6), or when you are concentrated doing something continuously without stops or distractions (7); and if you are being serious, to show you are not kidding, you must display that you are attentive to what you are saying (8). The last three meanings have to do with emotions: you *frown* as you are worried (9), but also as you are angry (10); consequently the *frowning* also makes an order peremptory and threatening (11).

So far we have found three components shared by all these meanings: LACK OF BELIEFS, ATTENTION, EMOTION. But we can go further and trace them back to a single element of CONCENTRATION. You concentrate to find the beliefs that you need to understand (meanings 2, 3, 4), and that you can search in the environment (5) or in your memory (6) or by asking other people (1). In addition, concentration also makes you more credible, since you show more responsibility for what you do; for example, when you say something seriously (8) or fervently, without stopping (7); when you show anger (10) or you give an order (11); and finally, when you are worried (9), you are concentrating on what worries you.

But what is the link between *frowning eyebrows* and the meaning of CON-CENTRATION? We may see *eyebrow frowning* and *eyebrow raising* as two symmetrical signals, with symmetrical meanings. If you *open eyes wide* when you want to see more things, on the contrary you *sharpen your eyes* when you want to see better, and, to better focus, you *bring your eyebrows closer together*, that is, you *frown*. Thus *raising* increases the quantity, *frowning* improves the quality of vision. These are, respectively, the original meanings of the two signals, the noncommunicative actions that favour – and hence mean – a search for new beliefs and concentration. Yet since vision is a metaphor of comprehension – seeing with the mind's eyes – then the frowning means not only that we want to see better (meaning 5) but also that we want to understand better (meanings 1–3). And such desire for better comprehension may be displayed not only sincerely but also, rhetorically, to indirectly express disagreement (4). More generally, however, we need concentration, that is, we need to pay particular attention to our own cognitive processing, every time we want to solve a problem that is worrying for us (9), be it the retrieval of beliefs from our memory (6), saying something in a convinced and convincing way (7 and 8), or having someone do something (10 and 11).

## 8.4   Polysemy and synonymy in the eyebrows

Looking at the meanings of the *eyebrow raising* and *eyebrow frowning*, one might have observed that among their different meanings, for at least some of them the two signals are synonyms of each other: for example, the meaning 6 of the *raising*, a backchannel of doubt or perplexity, with its possible indirect meanings of disagreement, is more or less the same as the meaning 4 of the *frowning*, which can be a signal of incomprehension, doubt, or disagreement. (See Figure 8.6.)

So far, to account for the signals' polysemy, we have shown that the different meanings of a same signal share a same semantic component or generate the same inferences.

Now, to account for synonymy, we should wonder: how can two different signals have the same meaning? In this case too, the answer may be in their inferences: in two different signals, their original meanings are different, but both may allow the same semantic elements, although passing through different inferential chains.

Let us see what inferences the addressee may go through which may lead both the *raising* and the *frowning of the eyebrows* to come to be synonymic signals, both working as a backchannel of perplexity, incredulity, or disagreement (Figures 8.7 and 8.8).

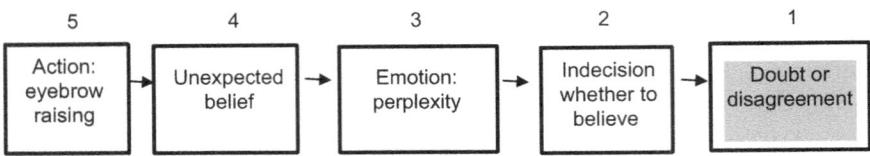

**FIGURE 8.7** Inferential chain in the addressee: from eyebrow raising to doubt or disagreement.

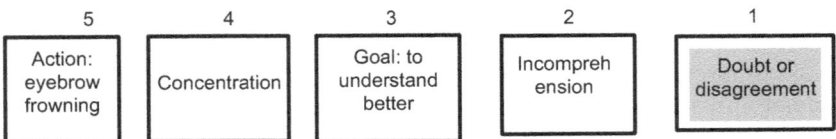

**FIGURE 8.8** Inferential chain in the addressee: from eyebrow frowning to doubt or disagreement.

If your interlocutor *raises his eyebrows* (Figure 8.7, n. 5) you understand that she is thinking of an unexpected belief (4), so she is perplexed (3), and you can interpret such indecision whether to believe or not (2) either as a signal of her being doubtful – if it is she who is communicating that belief – or as disagreement with you – if you or other people are communicating it (1). The final outcome (Figure 8.8) is the same for the *eyebrow frowning* (n. 5): in this case, the inference is that she is concentrating (4) because she wants to understand better (3), but from this you can deduce there is something she does not understand completely (2), so perhaps she wants to indirectly communicate (1) that either she does not believe you (doubt) or does not agree (disagreement).

So two different signals, sometimes even with opposite literal meanings, may be synonyms: if used in different contexts or processed by different inference rules, they may refer to the very same inference and hence to the same meaning included in their respective areas of polysemy.

Therefore, the existence of polysemy and synonymy in gaze signals does not entails any asystematicity in the structure of this lexicon: in various meanings of a polysemic gaze we can single out a shared semantic element accounting for their meanings, while in synonymic signals the same induced inferences may account for their semantic similarity.

# 9

# EYES SHUT AND EYES HEAVENWARD

While in the gaze items seen so far, the main function is fulfilled by the eyebrows, let us now see two gaze families where the eyelid's movements and the direction of the eyes are crucial: *eyes shut* and *eyes heavenward*.

## 9.1   *Eyes shut*

Among the eyelids' movements that can have a communicative function, one is the movement of closing both: i.e. *closing our eyes*.

This was investigated in an observational study (Vincze & Poggi, 2011) on a corpus of seven communicative interactions: six political debates on Canal 9, a TV Channel in Canton Valais, Switzerland, and an interview with Ségolène Royal, a candidate in the 2007 French presidential campaign. Three behaviours of eye closure were singled out, all with communicative and non-communicative uses: *blink*, *eye-closure* and *wink*.

By *blink* we mean a very fast closure and immediate reopening of the eyes; by *eye closure*, closing the eyelids with more eyelids' tension and longer than in a blink; the *wink* is a one-side-only lowering of a single upper eyelid.

The parameters and values relevant for these signals are thus: muscular tension of the eyelids (which may assume the values *tense, normal, relaxed*); speed of the closure movement (*speedy, normal, slow*); duration (*long, normal, brief*); repetition (each closure may be performed only *once*, with value 0, or repeated *twice*, value 2, or *n times*, value n); unilateral or bilateral closure (*only right, only left, or both eyelids* may be closed).

For each of the three gaze signals, before stating their meanings, the non-communicative uses were distinguished from the communicative ones.

DOI: 10.4324/9781032678344-9

### 9.1.1   Noncommunicative uses

The *blink* has three noncommunicative uses:

1. The physiological *blink*, which is very frequent, because it is necessary in humans to constantly moisten the eye. However, too frequent blinks denote agitation, whereas, on the contrary, if they stop, they are a sign of deception (Fukuda, 2001; Leal & Vrij, 2008). Therefore they provide information to those who see them, but by definition are not a communicative signal (to deceive, one must not make it clear that one is deceiving, Castelfranchi & Poggi, 1998);
2. The *blink* of a stuttering person who, while trying to utter a word, repeats the first syllable twice and at the same time *beats her eyelids twice*. This is a case in which the body "cooperates", so to speak, with the effort of the mind by moving on a parallel route (Chiera et al., 2022);
3. The *blink* of the startle reflex (Ekman, Friesen & Simons, 1985). If someone comes up behind you and goes "boo!", you have an immediate startle reflex, which includes a *flinch* and a momentary instinctive *closing of the eyes*.

These are, instead, the noncommunicative uses of the *eye closure:*

1. When you sleep.
2. When you laugh: the laughter often implies eyelids' closures longer than a *blink*.
3. While you are thinking. As we are concentrating, possibly even while talking, we may close our eyes for a few seconds, to isolate ourselves from the context: it is a *cutoff* (Morris, 1977), a noncommunicative signal that is, though, informative concerning the cognitive processes of the one who produces it.

The *wink*, instead, is always a communicative signal.

### 9.1.2   Close your eyes to communicate

Here are the meanings of the three signals of eyelids closure.

An *eye closure with muscular tension* can be used to give information about the Sender's Identity.

1) In a debate at Canal 9 on the Insurance for Disabled people, Richoz, a representative of a disability association, speaking about the efforts of the disabled to obtain a professional qualification, *frowns* and *closes his eyes*, as

if to mimic that effort. But since he himself is visually impaired, this signal shows his own determination, thus giving information about his personality.

Within information about the sender's beliefs, *fast and repeated blinks* confirm the high degree of certainty of the beliefs conveyed, while the *eye closure*, especially if combined with a *head nodding* or even more a *head shaking*, adds an element of categoricity, i.e. of an even higher certainty, to what one is saying or to one's approval of what the other says.

A particularly *prolonged eye closure* and with *pressed eyelids* tells: "I am absolutely certain about this" (Vincze & Poggi, 2022).

*Blinks repeated more than twice* with a flaunted *speed* instead communicate an emotion of surprise, but if this is clearly metacommunicative, i.e. flaunted or ostentatious, the signal may have the supergoal of displaying incredulity.

Coming to Information about the Sender's goals, the *eye closure* with a *high muscular tension* is used in case of self-repair – as one realises one has mistaken a word – to convey one is starting the sentence again; hence, with the function of a metasentence syntactic marker. Within metadiscursive signals, fast and repeated *blinks*, at times accompanied by an *eyebrow raising*, are used as a punctuation of speech: producing *many of these blinks fast one after the other* signals one is stating an important concept to which one draws attention; conversely, an *eye closure* conveys the goal to gloss over a topic or concept, not considering it important to the discourse. It is precisely this signal that is produced, in a Canal 9 fragment, in conjunction with the words "This is not so important".

The *wink*, finally, is a sort of performative that communicates "I am alluding to something". The sender who *winks* is addressing a very specific addressee, with whom the sender himself feels in tune because he shares the same beliefs and goals: he therefore wants to produce a signal that is hidden or incomprehensible to others, to those in the "opposite camp". Hence the furtive and allusive nature of *winking*, which communicates "I want to communicate on this subject, but only to you, so I do it in an allusive, furtive, hidden way". That is why the *winking* is always a sign of complicity, recalling the sender's affiliation to a group, sometimes a very restricted one, which for some reason has to hide its aims from others, and to which both the sender and the addressee belong, while the people against whom the sender's communication is directed are excluded. All this explains the ambivalent nature of the *wink*: a signal at once explicit and hidden, of inclusion and exclusion, of affinity between sender and addressee, of difference from all others.

One more performative signal that means confirmation is a *slow blink*, often accompanying a *nod*, which can be used as a backchannel or a signal of agreement: just like saying *yes*.

## 9.2 *Eyes heavenward* and *rolling eyes*

We now come to another quite widespread gaze item, characterised by a particular position and direction of the irises: *both irises* are *high in the sclera,* and generally they *do not touch the lower eyelids,* thus leaving a *white space* underneath, and they *look upward.* This gaze item has a clear idiomatic name in Italian: *occhi al cielo,* that literally means "eyes to the sky". A corresponding idiom in English is *eyes heavenward,* which is, though, a literary and somewhat obsolete term[1]; the gaze item called in English *rolling eyes* seems to be but a subtype of it, with a more specific meaning, perhaps corresponding to Italian *roteare gli occhi.*

In any case, in both cultures this gaze item is produced quite frequently. In everyday interaction but also in talk shows, often a conversationalist *raises his eyes heavenward,* and while doing so, he may also make a *sigh* or a *puff, tilt his head back*, *open his arms* or *draw his eyebrows closer.* Therefore, *eyes heavenward* is certainly a communicative signal and generally one highly polysemic, but what are its meanings?

In trying to understand it, two empirical studies have been carried out on the occurrences of *eyes heavenward*: a study on corpora of literary texts (Poggi & Ansani, 2018a) and an observational study.

### 9.2.1 Eyes heavenward *in written texts*

With the first study (Poggi & Ansani, 2018a), in a corpus of narrative texts, mentions of *occhi al cielo* were found in 40 texts, 25 Italian novels and 15 translations of non-Italian ones. Here is an example drawn from *The Rampant Baron* by Italo Calvino:

1) "Ma il vecchio prete fuor che un po' di grammatica e un po' di teologia annegava in un mare di dubbi e di lacune, e alle domande dell'allievo allargava le braccia e alzava gli occhi al cielo".

   (But the old priest, except for some grammar and some theology, was drowned in a sea of doubts and gaps, and hearing the pupil's questions used to open his arms and **rolled his eyes**.)

The 40 fragments were submitted to 10 participants, asking them to briefly explain the meaning of this gaze signal in that context but also to provide a verbal paraphrase of it. Here are some answers:

2) Ignorance: I don't know a sense of helplessness and surrender.
3) I can't help it!
4) Acceptance and ok, let's go along with it
5) Resignation to do something

6) Doubt/search for an answer you don't have

7) In a situation in which one does not know something you rise [sic] your eyes to the sky to try to find like in the surrounding space an answer you don't have.

8) Oh my with this, how many questions, my God, help me!

9) The abbot rises [sic] his eyes up to the sky in a sort of prayer, wanting the end of a case he does not find pleasant.

The participants' words or sentences proposed as paraphrases or their descriptions of the events revolve around seemingly disparate concepts such as "help, ask, optative, prayer, hope, thought, remembering, contemplating, worrying, annoyance, helplessness, discouragement, resignation, exasperation, despair, boredom".

When analysing their occurrences and frequencies with the lexicometric software T-Lab plus 2018, four families of meanings emerge:

1. Imploration, grouping words such as *prayer, help, God, lord, entity, supernatural*
2. Helplessness, comprising *resignation, discouragement, surrender*
3. Annoyance: *boredom, annoyance, exasperation, despair, impatience, intolerance*
4. Reflection: *thought, contemplation, memory, thinking*

Actually, these groups of meanings can be traced back to a shared mental state, from which the other mental states or actions can be inferred: a state of IMPOTENCE (semantic family 2), caused by some negative event (3), may give rise to the need to seek help from a supernatural entity and thus becomes a PRAYER, an imploration (1). Or else, a VERY NEGATIVE EMOTIONAL STATE (3) can give rise either to a passive reaction of RESIGNATION and SURRENDER (2) or to a positive reaction, a CALL FOR HELP (1) to an almighty entity that can solve even the problem for which one feels powerless.

From this chain of causes and effects, a type of *occhi al cielo* seems to be excluded that we call COGNITIVE (semantic group 4): a gaze of reflection, a "look of thought" – a type of gaze revealing our attempt to reason or remember.

### 9.2.2   Eyes heavenward *in videos*

To single out real cases of *eyes heavenward* and discover whether the fourth type of meaning (the cognitive *occhi al cielo*) also corresponds to a different type of signal, an observational study has been conducted on a corpus of audiovisual recordings (Poggi et al., 2018). 49 fragments of videos have been collected from political talk shows, parliamentary questions, interviews to famous people, university oral examinations, whether Italian, English, or American.

The types of *eyes heavenward* represented in this corpus are partly different from those singled out in the previous study, based on a corpus of written texts. Moreover, given the particular type of interactions represented, the corpus does not contain some types of *eyes heavenward*, which can be easily found instead by taking a speaker's judgements approach and could be found in different corpora.

*Looking up.* First of all, some cases of *looking up* are not communicative: for example, when someone looks at a person taller or higher than her. In the fiction *L'amica geniale* (The Ingenious Friend), the young girl sitting in the school desk raises her eyes to look up at the teacher who is talking to her.

*Pantomimic looking up.* A communicative case, but not yet a case of *eyes heavenward* proper, is "to look at some tall person" or pretend to. As in a video where Giulio Andreotti, a famous clever and ironic Italian politician, in recalling his encounter with a tall, robust amputee who stepped on his foot on the bus, mimes *looking up* to give an idea of his height.

### 9.2.2.1 Eyes heavenward *of prayer*

Coming back to *eyes heavenward* proper, one case is not represented in the video corpus, the gaze of prayer (meaning 1); we do not find it in today's talk shows, which are so secularised, but it is very frequent in much Catholic iconography: saints and Madonnas gazing in ecstasy or with imploring devotion at heaven, the dwelling place of God, to whom they turn and ask for help (Figure 9.1).

### 9.2.2.2 Eyes heavenward *of impotence*

For the same reason, our corpus does not contain *eyes heavenward* of impotence or despair. This can be explained by the characteristics of the corpus, which is all about public figures, politicians or showbusiness people who cannot leak weakness or incapacity.

On the other hand, two cases of *eyes heavenward* are represented in many of the collected videos: those of thought (type 4 in the previous study) and those of annoyance (type 3).

### 9.2.2.3 Cognitive eyes heavenward

Within *eyes heavenward* that signal cognitive processes taking place, some are produced when trying to remember, others while trying to elaborate a thought.

**FIGURE 9.1**   Imploring Madonna.

### 3.a.   *Eyes heavenward* of memory recall

Luigi Di Maio's gaze during a talk show signals a process of memory recall[2] (Figure 9.2).

10) The journalist Massimo Franco insinuates that the Italian party 5-Stars Movement continues to do well in the polls only because its opponents give it "gifts". Di Maio replies:

"Guardi, io disconosco sempre questa teoria, per cui sono i nostri avversari il nostro merito. Semplicemente per una cosa. Io . . . nel . . . duemilasette ho iniziato questo percorso . . .".

(Look, I always disown this theory that it is our opponents who are our merit. Simply for one thing. I . . . in . . . two thousand and seven started this path . . .)

FIGURE 9.2   Eyes heavenward of memory recall.

After the hesitation following "I", while saying "*nel duemilasette*" (in 2007), Di Maio *looks upward rightward with his eyes high in the sclera*, to recall the exact year in memory, but with his *eyebrows slightly frowning*, as if showing his effort and commitment to remember.

A similar gaze is contained in our corpus of oral examinations, where a student, while answering a question on imprinting, tries to recall details to add to her answer.

11) "Da vari studi, sia suuu . . . i . . . sui macachi, su, su . . . tipi di animali, anche oche".

(From various studies, both on . . . the macaques, on, on . . . types of animals, geese too.)

At first the student keeps her *hands intertwined* on her *crossed legs*, then, during the hesitation "*suuu . . .*", she *opens both hands* in a *fluid gesture of vagueness*, as if communicating "it's not so important who the studies are about"; then she remembers and begins to enumerate, *taking with her right hand the thumb of her left*, "about macaques"; trying to recall further animals subject to these studies, she hesitates again on the preposition "*su, su* . . .", she *casts her eyes heavenward* in trying to immediately recall any other specific ones, but then she settles for the generalisation "*types of animals*" and finally recalls "*geese too*".

Here "*eyes heavenward*" just signal an effort to recall the topics studied in detail.

### 3b.  Reflexion eyes

In other cases, *looking up* instead communicates "I am thinking", i.e. it signals that the speaker is mentally processing what he intends to say: as if he were asking a question of himself and should take time before answering. This is the gaze we find in an interview with the comedian and director Carlo Verdone, who looks up before answering a question in an interview.[3]

12) In an interview to Carlo Verdone after the release of his latest film, Gianni Minoli asks him:

"Ma è un effetto che cambia nel tempo quello del successo, un po' cambia nel tempo?"

(But is success an effect that changes over time, does it change a little?)

Verdone *cants his head to the right, smiling* and *half-closing his eyes* and says, "Un po' cambia, un po' cambia, sì". (It does change a little, it does change, yes.)

Minoli: "In che senso" (Can you explain how?)

Verdone *looks up to the left*. Then, while *lowering his eyes* and *looking at Minoli* again, he says: "che prima avevi più adrenalina, avevi più . . . adesso diventi più saggio, quindi accogli le cose con il giusto equilibrio".

(that before you had more adrenaline, you had more . . . now you become wiser, so you take things in with the right balance" (Figure 9.3).

In this case, Verdone is not trying to remember something; he is trying to process his previous beliefs so as to actively generate one that answers the question: thought, reasoning, inference, not only memory retrieval.

### *9.2.2.4*  Eyes heavenward *of annoyance*

As a matter of fact, the *eyes heavenward* we most frequently find in talk shows are not the eyes of the thinker but those of one who is fed up, bored, impatient, and indirectly conveys this by flaunting a prayer such as "God, make him stop!"

**FIGURE 9.3** Reflection eyes.

Let us see some examples.

13) In Bologna, Matteo Salvini, a member of the right-wing party Lega Nord (North League), during a provocative raid on a Gipsy camp, clashed with a demonstration of students. One of these, interviewed after the demonstration, accuses him of running over them with his car, saying: "Sono le stesse persone neofasciste che loro portano nei loro cortei a Milano". (These are the same neofascist people they bring to their rallies in Milan.) As soon as the student says *neo-fasciste* (neo-fascist), Salvini *raises his eyes up, throwing back his head* (Figure 9.4). Then he *lowers his head* again

**FIGURE 9.4** Matteo Salvini. *Eyes heavenward* of annoyance.

and, *looking into the camera*, he gives the student an only mildly euphemistic curse: "Ma vai a spalare il fango" ("Go shovel mud") Figure 9.4[4]

Here *eyes heavenward* are a display of annoyance, impatience, intolerance, boredom for something the present speaker is doing or saying.

A quite similar nonverbal behaviour is one of Massimo Cacciari (a left-wing philosopher and former politician) during a speech by Alessandra Moretti, also an exponent of a left-wing party, a supporter of the "yes" vote on the Referendum to revise the Italian Constitution, proposed by Matteo Renzi.

14) Alessandra Moretti says: "In settant'anni, lo sappiamo tutti, abbiamo avuto sessantatré governi. Quindi una forte instabilità e un'incapacità a governare".

(In seventy years, we all know, we have had sixty-three governments. So a strong instability and an inability to govern.)

While she says "*a strong* (instability)", Cacciari, until now with his *head slightly tilted to the right*, suddenly, as if he could take it no more, *lifts his head back* and *looks up*, while *opening his arms*: a sign of helplessness (the *open arms*) but helplessness to be able to bear any more and a plea for help, a prayer to God to help him bear.[5]

### 4a. From annoyance to discredit

The last two types of this gaze, Salvini's and Cacciari's, are cases of "facial comments". We define as comment (Poggi, D'Errico & Vincze, 2013; Poggi, 2022) a communicative act of information in which the new belief provided can have an interpretive function – to help the other understand something better, as in the critical comment of a literary text – or else an evaluative function – to express a positive or negative evaluation on some event occurring in the context. When used in a conversation, the comment is a thematically relevant intervention vis-à-vis a previous communicative act, which provides additional but not required information with respect to that turn.

In these two examples, *eyes heavenward* is an evaluative negative comment, more specifically a discrediting act about what the current conversationalist is saying – or the conversationalist him/herself (Poggi & D'Errico, 2020). The set of meanings borne by *eyes heavenward* in these cases is the following:

1) "I ask heaven for help" (literal meaning: the same as in the Madonna of Figure 9.1): From this we infer a helplessness of the sender, in particular.

2) "I cannot cope, I cannot bear this". But what the sender cannot cope with is, in these two cases and in all similar ones, the stupidity or repetitiveness of the previous utterance, especially of the one who uttered it. So the meaning "Oh God, I can't stand the boredom or impatience my interlocutor causes me" lets you infer that . . . .

3) My interlocutor is stupid or boring. In everyday life, these *eyes heavenward* could be the typical comment of the teenage daughter to the umpteenth prohibition of her mother. In a talk show, they are practically always an act of discrediting: attacking the other person's speech is actually attacking the speaker, trying to make him lose face, i.e. to make the audience form an overall negative judgement of him. This, in turn, is done according to persuasive goals: by making the opponent less attractive (if he is boring) or less credible (if he is stupid), the one who makes *eyes heavenward* tries to make himself argumentatively successful.

Such an expression of annoyance and impatience with an intention to discredit the opponent can also be used with defensive aims, to downplay the accusations someone is making against us by making it seem unrealistic or exaggerated. As in Theresa May's *eyes heavenward* when, in 2018, Jeremy Corbin, supported by Donald Trump, accused her of endorsing the attack in Syria.

15) Jeremy Corbin, to the English Parliament:

"Duma was a horrific attack on civilians using chemical weapons part of a civil war that killed hundreds of thousands of people. Mister Speaker this statement serves as a reminder the Prime Minister is accountable to this Parliament, not to the whims of the US president: we clearly need a War Powers Act in this country to transform our now broken convention into a legal obligation".

While Corbyn says "not to the whims of the US president", Theresa May makes a *sigh, raises her eyes heavenward*, then she shakes her *head*, as if saying: "Oh how boring".[6]

### 4b. Rolling eyes

Actually, Theresa May produces a variant of the *eyes heavenward* of annoyance: the *rolling eyes*. In some cases, the sender not only *raises his eyes in the sclera* but also *rolls them*, i.e. repeatedly *moves them from left to right, always upwards*. This sometimes gives an even more aggressive sense to this type of gaze, making it resemble the threatening eye-rolling of the psychopath close to homicidal rapture. And this may be precisely the intention of the person who *raises his eyes to the sky* and *rolls them*: to mimic in a somewhat parodistic manner the stereotype of the psychopath in the throes of a rapture, with the aim of making himself appear closer to an agitated aggressiveness, which he may be ostensibly inhibiting, than to the (apparently) mild mockery evoked by the simple *eyes heavenward*.

### 9.2.3 *Semantics of* eyes heavenward

Recall, reflection, prayer, impotence, resignation, annoyance – exasperation, impatience – discredit, restrained aggression. These are the meanings that the *eyes heavenward* can express. Is it possible to trace a logic of this polysemy, i.e. to identify shared semantic elements among its various readings?

It is not easy to find an element that is shared by all of them, but two big groups of meanings can be distinguished: on one side, "cognitive" *eyes heavenward*, on the other all the remaining readings.

For the first two, recall and reflection, it is not difficult to find a link: the former signals the search for beliefs in long-term memory, the latter the manipulation of beliefs aimed at generating inferences. But also among the other meanings we can find a chain in which one event generates another.

First there is a NEGATIVE EVENT, either caused or not by an animated agent. It can be a weather event – I look out the window and see it's still raining, when I wanted to go out and play football – or else a communicative or non-communicative action of ours or someone else's: while going out I realise I forgot my mobile, or in uttering a long word I make a mistake in concatenating the syllables, or my kids have once again scattered all their toys across the living room, or mummy forbids me to go out. There is, however, a further element of REPETITIVENESS: it's been raining for a long time, or it's not the first time I forget my phone, or I am bungling, or the kids make a mess, or mummy is strict.

Furthermore, there is a subjective feeling of IMPOTENCE to find a solution to change the negative event. This causes ANNOYANCE or EXASPERATION and, if the negative event, possibly a communicative act, is caused by other people, IMPATIENCE; hence the need for seeking HELP from a higher entity – God, Heaven – to help us solve the problem or at least bear it: PRAYER. Yet if we think that nothing can help us, a sense of RESIGNATION can even be triggered.

This set or sequence of mental and emotional states can either be expressed sincerely or "acted out", "recited" (Castelfranchi & Poggi, 1998); that is, they can be mimicked while letting people understand that they are not true, with the aim of discrediting others: thus we deliberately flaunt an expression of impotent annoyance to make it clear that it is the other who is the cause of our annoyance, and this is so because what he says or does is stupid, boring or useless. In this case we want to induce, about the other, an evaluation not of power, malice or harmfulness but of impotence, insipience (Castelfranchi, 1988).

Sometimes, on the other hand, we at least want to make it clear that what has happened provokes in us a desire to indulge in aggressive acts – a desire, however, that is also only ostentatious and thus a RESTRAINED AGGRESSION.

This polysemy of *eyes heavenward* is thus held together by a common thread, and a set of semantic components (or mental ingredients) more or less salient in one or the other meaning. And yet the different meanings, although connected to one another, are often distinguished by particular aspects of the signal, i.e. other bodily signals in addition to the pure *raising of the eyes in the sclera*.

For example:

1. In the meaning of PRAYER, the head movement of *raising one's face* is almost necessary.
2. In the meanings of ANNOYANCE, EXASPERATION, IMPATIENCE – and hence in using *eyes heavenward* as a discrediting move, the raising of the eyes can still be accompanied by the movement of *pulling back the neck* but also by two mouth signals: one visual, the *lower lips slightly protruded and pressed against the upper ones*; the other possibly also acoustic: a slight *puffing*.
3. In RESIGNATION (whether true or flaunted), while *the eyes are raised, the eyelids are lowered*, thus expressing the relaxation of one who thinks that nothing can be done (see Chapter 5), but the *raised eyes* are also often accompanied by a *sigh* and the *shaking of the head* of helplessness.
4. In RESTRAINED AGGRESSION, finally, the eyes not only *roll up* in the sclera but also *roll up to the left and right*, and sometimes the *head also rolls*.

### Notes

1 I am indebted to Salvatore Attardo for his scholarly disquisition about this idiom.
2 https://www.youtube.com/watch?v=DpQh9j-Y8–0, minute 2.04, accessed 2023-8-22
3 https://www.youtube.com/watch?v=Dc3tBtWKKqE&t=161s, accessed 2024–8-19
4 https://www.youtube.com/watch?v=gqDl5N_5_iM, minute 1.25, accessed 2024-8-19
5 https://www.youtube.com/watch?v=4lNbiI7SUaY, minute 0.12, accessed 2024-8-19
6 https://www.youtube.com/watch?v=xPP5cbGAI64, minute 0.52, accessed 2024-8-19

# 10

# THE POWER OF YOUR EYES

The hypnotist influences people by his eyes. But we all do: our gaze is a strong means for influence. Because if you look at me – and I look at you – I can make you do what I want, subjugate you.

But does people's gaze really have such a power? Other people's eyes influence us and do so in many ways. First of all, vision is the first form of power acquisition, being acquisition of knowledge. But if to know is to have power, to know about another is to have power over him, to exercise control. In fact, what is control? To continue to have information about something in order to make sure it continues to be, or to work, the way we want. But in addition to knowing about him, to look at the other is to make a request of him.

## 10.1   Power and impotence in gaze

The signals of gaze we use in everyday life very often in their meanings contain a semantic ingredient of power: specific gaze items, along with other contents, communicate an important belief like "I have more power than you" or "I have less power than you", which transpires both in the expression of our emotions and in our communicative intentions.

## 10.2   Emotions of power

As was early acknowledged in '900 emotion research by Osgood, Suci and Tannenbaum's (1957) "The measurement of meaning", while studying the words of emotional lexicon, each emotion is characterised by a certain level of *arousal* (physiological activation: fear is less activating than terror) and a certain *valence* (happiness is positive, sadness is negative), but also by an

DOI: 10.4324/9781032678344-10

ingredient of *potency*. Anger contains an idea of power, i.e., the belief "I have the power to confront the one who did me this wrong"; fear, an idea of impotence, "I do not have the power to confront this danger". Such belief about power consequently activates a congruent goal: anger leads you to aggress the one who hurt you, fear leads you to escape from what can hurt. This is why in the gaze signals that express emotions, we can read information about the power of the one who is looking and the one who is looked at.

Let us see some "emotions of power" and the gaze signals that express them.

Some primary emotions, such as anger, fear and sadness already contain in their meanings beliefs about having or not having power over others or the situation.

### 10.2.1   Anger

Anger is the emotion I feel when I think that someone has harmed me unjustly, that is, has thwarted a goal of mine without my having done anything to deserve it; I am then activated to attack him – as retaliation, revenge or punishment – also because I think that I have the power to do so without the other person getting the better of me: I am stronger. This aggressive intention is communicated by a *strong frowning of the eyebrows*, which are close together but also lowered, and by a direction of the *eyes that points insistently and prolongedly towards the offender*: I therefore look at the other person carefully, as if planning aggression, and my *frowning eyebrows* (an expression opposite to the *open gaze* of joy), lets him know that I am not at all happy (Figure 10.1).

**FIGURE 10.1**   Anger.

### 10.2.2  Fear

Let us now see instead the cognitive structure of fear. Nothing has happened yet – fear is an emotion of future, of expectancy (Miceli & Castelfranchi, 2014) – but I believe an event might or is going to happen, or someone is going to do some action, which very likely might thwart a very important goal of mine, perhaps even my survival. Yet I believe I am not able to actively contrast this event or action, so my goal of flight is triggered: the intention to escape that situation as soon as possible. In fear, *eyes* are *wide open*, with *highly raised eyebrows, raised upper eyelids* that leave the whole eye visible, and *tense lower eyelids*. *Wide open eyes* actually also characterise another emotion, surprise, in which their function is to widen the visual field as much as possible to look for an explanation of an unexpected event. Actually, in fear too we can find an urgent need to acquire any useful information to evade danger; so the expression of the eyes in fear does not seem so much linked to the sense of impotence as to the need to acquire beliefs (Figure 10.2).

### 10.2.3  Sadness

In the case of sadness, an event has happened, possibly even one not dependent on others' action, that has irreversibly thwarted a very important goal of mine, for example, the life or affection of a beloved person. I therefore think that I have no power to remedy, and this results in a withdrawal from action – the abulia of sadness, mourning or depression – then also in a physiological relaxation, which is usually expressed by the *half-open eyelids*, but

**FIGURE 10.2**    Fear.

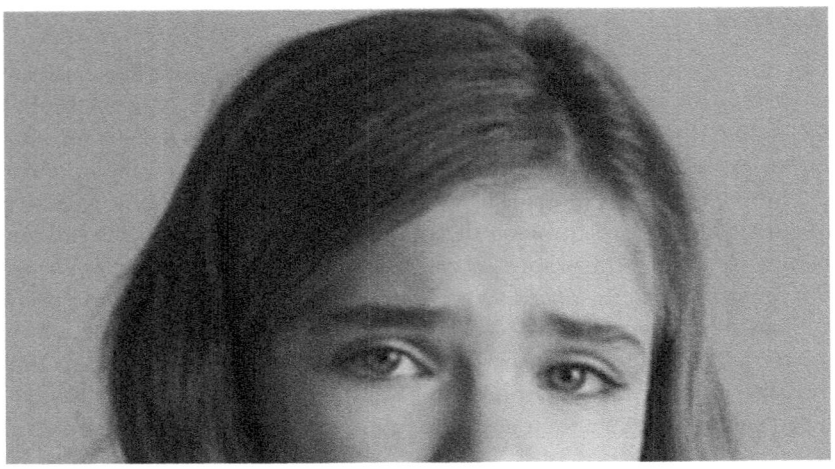

**FIGURE 10.3** Sadness.

often also by the "roof", or *A-shaped eyebrows* (Tipples, Atkinson & Young, 2002), i.e. inner eyebrows raised (Figure 10.3).

### 10.2.4 Shame

If an ingredient of power or lack of power is present in the cognitive structure of primary emotions, it dwells by definition in the emotions of image (the self-conscious emotions, Lewis, 1995, 2008): those that monitor our goals of being evaluated positively by others or ourselves, such as pride, shame, embarrassment.

When you feel the negative emotion of shame, the typical behaviour of your eyes is *eyes down*.

Shame is the displeasure or fear of losing face, of making a bad impression, of attracting a negative evaluation from others or from yourself (Castelfranchi, 1988; Castelfranchi & Poggi, 1990). And since every evaluation is a belief about the power – or lack of power – of a person with respect to certain goals, you regret or fear a negative evaluation whenever you think you did not or do not have the power necessary to be a certain way or do a certain action. And when that certain or feared negative evaluation comes to you from others because you have not lived up to a standard or value that is important to yourself, then you feel the need to apologise to the group, acknowledging your ineptitude but trying to make it clear that you share that standard – even if you have occasionally not honoured it. So you make an act of submission to others, apologising to prevent their aggression towards you. And since, as mentioned previously, looking is already a way of acquiring power, you *lower your eyes*, thus accepting that you have less power and acknowledging the other's power over you.

Connected to shame is shyness, a temperament type characterised by fear of social relationships and related evaluations, which is accompanied by a tendency to observation and reflection. The typical behaviour of the shy person is to *avoid eye contact*, to *look away*, to *avert gaze* from the other person's face, which may arise partly from intense sensitivity to shame, partly from the need to withdraw in order to reflect.

### 10.2.5   Pride

But let us look at the eye signals in the opposite emotion to shame, namely pride: the positive emotion that signals the achievement of a good image or self-image. You experience it when an action or quality of yours, or simply an event, related to your identity causes you to be positively evaluated by yourself or others. Poggi and D'Errico (2012) distinguish four types of this emotion:

1. A *self-image pride*, when you are satisfied with yourself because of how you are or what you do, without caring about the evaluation of others. Further, three types of image pride are related to how you want to be judged by others:
2. *Superiority pride*, when you attribute to yourself – and think you deserve – a more positive evaluation than others, i.e. you believe you have more power than them, thus considering the others inferior.
3. *Dignity pride*, when you want to be considered, not superior, but at least not inferior to others, and you want to be recognised as an equal.
4. *Arrogance pride*: in which you currently do not have more power than the other, but you are certain that you will soon be able to overpower the one who currently has more power than you. You place yourself towards him in an attitude of defiance, assuring him that you will soon become superior to him.

While self-image pride can be felt even in solitude – it means to be satisfied with oneself – with no need of an audience and therefore no need to display it, some differences have been found (Poggi & D'Errico, 2012; D'Errico & Poggi, 2013) in the body display – and in the gaze – of the three types of image pride, the ones that are communicated to others.

In superiority pride, a typical expression is one of haughtiness, *looking down on others*, where looking down is made necessary by the *erect head*, with *chin up* and *neck back*, and the gaze is characterised by *raised eyebrows* but *half-closed and relaxed eyelids*, as if to say "I look down on you from the height of my superiority, but I can relax, I don't even have to check you too much, because you have less power than I do" (Figure 10.4).

**FIGURE 10.4** Superiority pride.

**FIGURE 10.5** Contempt.

As one's own superiority is displayed by stigmatising the other's inferiority, pride comes close to contempt (Figure 10.5), but often this is expressed by the "sceptical eyebrow" (Ekman, 1979; Chapter 8 in this volume): the *asymmetrical eyebrows*, one up and one down, denouncing a judgement of the other's unreliability: "I don't trust you" (Figure 10.6).

Dignity pride, on the other hand, is expressed by *looking the other person straight in the eye* – as if to present oneself at her level – with the *eyelids open* and with a *frown less intense* than in anger but more like the expression of seriousness of someone who feels sure of what he or she is saying and who makes it clear that he or she is not joking.

**FIGURE 10.6**   I don't trust you.

In arrogance pride, finally, as in superiority pride, the most salient signal is the *head erect* with *chin up*, but there is *no frowning*, and often the *eyelids are open*.

The *opening of the eyelids* in these three cases of image pride might possibly depend on the just mentioned mechanism for which gaze is a means of control: the more superior I feel, the less I feel the need to look – just as in animal groups in which the dominant does not look at others but is the most watched by them. But if I am not yet superior to the other – as in arrogance, in which my superiority is not yet established – I look at the other in order to continue to maintain control over his present and future actions.

### 10.2.6   Admiration

I call "emotions of the other's image" those that monitor our goal to evaluate others so as to decide which types of social interaction to have with them, ones that are functional for an effective cooperation, not marred by conflictual relationships. In their cognitive structure, some positive emotions (such as admiration) contain the idea that the other has more power and capabilities than us, some negative ones (such as pity), an ingredient of a lack of power of the other.

Admiration is a positive emotion you feel towards something (e.g. a sublime landscape) or someone (a person with great gifts) who is endowed with a positive quality at a surprising extent – as shown by the Latin origin *miror* = I am surprised (Poggi & Zuccaro, 2008). Sometimes I would also like to be endowed with such a quality myself, and in these cases I generally wish to have a close relationship with that person, not only to admire her and her qualities but also to absorb them by imitating her.

The sense of happy amazement at something greater or more beautiful than I expected is displayed, in admiration, by the *wide-open eyes* typical of surprise (Figure 10.7).

**FIGURE 10.7** Admiration.

### 10.2.7 Contempt

Contempt is a negative emotion "of the other's image": by displaying it, I show my negative evaluation of the other, which makes me consider him morally inferior to me, and my intention to avoid any interaction with him (Figure 10.5). The expression of this emotion is mainly characterised by a grimace, an *asymmetry of the mouth*. But since contempt is partly a metaphorical extension to a person of the primary emotion of disgust, the instinctive shunning of a noxious substance, it can also be expressed by *narrowed eyes*, with *raised lower eyelids* and *lowered, curled upper eyelids*. Two other, slightly less direct ways of expressing contempt are the *asymmetrical eyebrows* of scepticism seen in Figure 10.6 and the *eyes heavenward* or *rolling eyes* seen in Chapter 9.

### 10.2.8 Pity

Pity is one more emotion "of the other's image". Here the other's lack of power is a source of suffering for him alone (Castelfranchi, 1988), but through identification and empathy I suffer for the other, and I show this with the *A-shaped eyebrows* typical of sadness: I am sad for his lack of power that causes him suffering (Figure 10.8).

### 10.3 Power in performatives

Communication is an act of influence: with each sentence you utter, you make a request to the other, to do something, to let you know something, or to pay attention, understand and believe what you say. Thus in the sentence,

**FIGURE 10.8**  Pity.

the propositional content specifies the content of the request – what you are asking to do, to let you know, or to believe. But the performative (according to Poggi, 2007, 2022a) contains various meanings: the type of action performed (request, question, information); the degree of certainty of the information provided (*asserting* is different from *hypothesising*); in whose interest is the action requested (an action I *beg* you to do is in my interest, one I *recommend*, in yours). Many performatives also contain information about power relations between sender (S) and addressee (A): in an *injunction*, S has more power, in a *prayer*, less power than A; in a *proposal*, S and A have equal power. Again, the performative may contain information on the actual or potential affective state of the sender, as well as a positive or negative evaluation of the sender or the addressee.

Some communicative behaviours of the eyes just express the relation of power, the evaluation, and the affective state embedded in some performatives.

### 10.3.1  Order

In the performative of the peremptory order, the speaker communicates: "I request you to do this action, but since I have more power than you, you must do it, and if you don't do it, I'll get angry". The *frowning of the eyebrows* in the face of the performative of order – a strict face – expresses anger and the potential desire of aggression towards the addressee, should she not comply with his request (Figure 10.9).

**FIGURE 10.9** Strict face of the order.

### 10.3.2 Imploration

The performative of imploring, on the contrary, communicates: "I acknowl-edge that you have more power than me – or power over me – and I ask you to do this action (which I do not have the power to do and which is very important to me), but if you do not do it, I will be very sad". The *A-eyebrows* express precisely the potential sadness prefigured by the implora-tion (Figure 10.10).

### 10.3.3 Threat

Threat is a communicative act of influence in which the sender S wants to make it clear to the addressee A that if A does not do what S asks, S will thwart a very important goal of A. It is therefore a case of influence based on an unbalanced power relationship between S and A: S can afford it because he has more power than A. In the performative of threat, the request is presupposed, while the anger and the intention to attack prospec-tively, in case the addressee does not comply, are a much more real poten-tiality than in the simple order. A face with *frowns* of anger is considered threatening, especially if the *direction of the gaze* is *towards the addressee* (Figure 10.11).

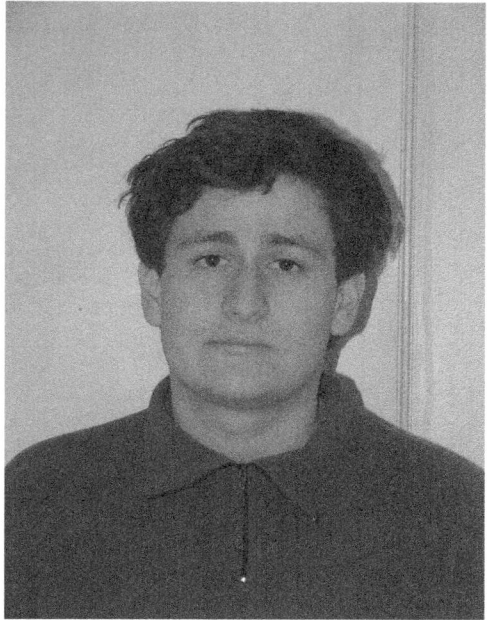

**FIGURE 10.10**    Imploration.

**FIGURA 10.11**    Threat.

**FIGURE 10.12** Reproach.

### 10.3.4 Reproach

While the threat is intended to prevent the addressee's unwanted action, the reproach comes after it has already been carried out. The one who scolds or reproaches has more power and, more precisely, has or arrogates to himself a pedagogical role towards the addressee and can thus afford to express an explicit negative evaluation of his actions by expressing one's anger. Reproach is a form of blaming (Miceli, 1992); therefore, unlike the threat that induces fear, it instils in the other an uneasiness, a dissatisfaction with herself.

In this case, the anger of one who is reproaching is expressed by the *wide-open eyes* that *stare fixedly at the culprit* of the execrated action. Here is a choral conductor's reproach for an error during a performance considered particularly serious (Figure 10.12).

### 10.4 Persuasive gaze

An important form of power is the skill to persuade, and in persuasive speech we make use of all the resources of multimodality, including gaze. But are there such things as persuasive gazes? For example, in the speech of a candidate in an election, are there looks that persuade me to vote for him more than others? In a parson's sermon, do his eyes play a role in persuading me to behave differently?

In fact, we might sometimes say: "His look was tremendously persuasive. I immediately did what he wanted", and we may perhaps refer to a very angry or threatening look. However, this is a somewhat ironic use of the adjective "persuasive". When we say "he was very persuasive" in this sense, we mean that, to get me to do something, the other used or showed she wanted to use a weapon that was certainly successful: violence. But here I mean persuasion in a nobler and higher sense.

### 10.4.1 Persuasion

In my definition (Poggi, 2005, 2022a; Poggi & D'Errico, 2020, 2022), persuasion is a case in which the sender S tries to influence the addressee A to decide to perform or not to perform an action (i.e. to pursue a goal), yet not by means of coercion (the use of force) or induction (threats or promises) but rather by means of persuasion: A ultimately strongly believes (is convinced) that what S proposes to A is not only in the interest of S but also in the interest of A; so much so that if S had not proposed it, A would have considered it appropriate to do so anyway.

Persuading A means, for S, proposing a goal SG (sender's goal) to A and trying to convince him to pursue it by linking it to AG (addressee's goal), a goal of A, i.e. by showing him that pursuing SG is a means to realise AG, so that SG becomes an important goal for A. If I know you are a vegan and I want you to buy a certain food, I tell you that it is without animal protein, so eating the food I sell (SG) serves to maintain a vegan diet (AG).

To persuade, the sender uses three strategies already identified by Aristotle: logos (the logical argument), pathos (the emotions of the audience) and ethos (the character of the speaker). What ultimately persuades me to do something is not only what they tell me but the emotions that the thought of doing that thing arouses in me and who it is that is asking me to do it – someone I trust and rely on. Moreover, this trust implies that I evaluate the other person positively on the basis of criteria of benevolence – he looks after my interests, he does not want to harm me, he does not deceive me – and of competence – he knows things, he has the ability to acquire information, to reason, to make plans; furthermore, as regards the people to whom I have to delegate public responsibilities, such as politicians, I also judge them on the basis of a criterion of dominance: the ability to influence others, to stick to the point, not to be misled or subordinated.

Every act of persuasion thus contains a series of "ingredients", beliefs that define it and constitute its cognitive structure. When S wants to persuade A, in order to convince him to pursue the SG proposed by S, he must:

1. Communicate SG, the goal of S.
2. Communicate that SG is a goal of high value, and possibly of higher value than alternative goals of A, B, C, etc. (an ingredient of EVALUATION: IMPORTANCE of SG).

3. Remember/emphasise that A has AG, the goal of A.
4. Show that SG is connected to AG, the goal of A, by a means–goal relationship.
5. Induce emotions in A that generate or activate in A the goal AG (PATHOS).
6. Convince A that what S says about the desirability of SG and its means–goal relationship to AG is true, through logical argumentation (LOGOS).
7. Give the impression that S is reliable (ETHOS) by showing that:

   a. S is certain of what he says, to induce confidence in A (CERTAINTY).
   b. In proposing to A to pursue SG, S does not do this in its own interest, but in the interest of A's goals (BENEVOLENCE).
   c. S has good understanding, planning and action skills (COMPETENCE).

### 10.4.2  In search of the persuasive gaze

An observational study (Poggi & Vincze, 2009a, 2009b; Poggi & D'Errico, 2020, 2022) has posed the following questions: do some gestures and gaze items exist that may be defined as persuasive? how could they be characterised? Is it possible to single out a repertoire of them? and how frequent are they? The working hypothesis was that these signals are endowed with a higher or lower degree of persuasiveness to the extent to which their meaning contains these ingredients of persuasion: CERTAINTY, EVALUATION, IMPORTANCE, LOGOS, PATHOS, ETHOS/BENEVOLENCE, ETHOS/COMPETENCE.

To test this hypothesis, the persuasive use of gaze has been investigated in two pre-election TV talk shows: a debate between Romano Prodi and Silvio Berlusconi before the 2006 elections in Italy, and the interview on France 2 Channel of the journalist Arlette Chabot to Ségolène Royal, during the French presidential campaign in 2007.

Table 10.1 presents two examples of analysis.

In example 1, Ségolène Royal stigmatises the case of a manager who has bankrupted his company and does not suffer sufficient sanctions. While saying (Col. 2): "And to the high managers who make companies fail, like Monsieur Forgeat" (*Et aux hauts dirigeants qui abîment l'entreprise en faillite comme Monsieur Forgeat*), she *looks at the interviewer*, Arlette Chabot, with a *fixed stare* (col. 3), which means "I'm strict, I won't let you look away": information about her own personality, the fact that Ségolène Royal is a serious and determined person, thus an ingredient of ETHOS, in particular of COMPETENCE (col. 6); furthermore, this gaze suggests (indirect meaning, col. 7) that she is a person who fights against injustice: again information about her personality (col. 8), this time in its moral aspects and thus about her BENEVOLENCE (9).

In example 13, Royal refers to a proposal by Sarkozy to force the unemployed to choose a job by giving them an alternative between a maximum

TABLE 10.1 Ségolène Royal's Persuasive Gaze

| 1. Time | 2. Speech | 3. Gaze description | 4. Literal meaning | 5. Type of meaning | 6. Persuasive ingredients | 7. Indirect meaning | 8. Type of meaning | 9. Persuasive Ingredients |
|---|---|---|---|---|---|---|---|---|
| 1 48.10 | *Et aux hauts dirigeants qui abîment l'entreprise en faillite comme Monsieur Forgeat* And to the high managers who make companies fail, like Monsieur Forgeat | *Stares the interviewer in the eye, half-closed eyelids, leftward head canting* | I am strict, I won't let you look away + I feel anger and indignation. | Personality Emotion | ETHOS COMPETENCE PATHOS | I struggle against injustice I ask you to feel indignation too. | Personality Performative | ETHOS BENEVOLENCE PATHOS |
| 13 49.10 | *Non, là, il faut . . . il faut accepter cet emploi,* No, come on, you have . . . you have to accept this employment | *Looks downward, first right then left, as if to choose between two alternatives Raised eyebrows, Eyelids in default position* | Choice, to choose a job I command you (to choose one) | Action Performative | | I am mocking Sarkozy's proposal. ↑ His proposal is too punitive. | Emotion Amusement Negative evaluation of the opponent | PATHOS LOGOS |

Legend: CAPITALS = persuasive ingredients.

of two jobs, on pain of withdrawal of unemployment benefits. Royal argues that this choice is only acceptable if the conditions of the two jobs are not too punitive. So, in saying "No, come on, you have to . . . you have to take this job", she *looks down, first to the right then to the left*, as if looking at two things to choose from: an iconic gaze that mimics the action of choosing between two jobs. She then *raises her eyebrows with her eyelids in the default position*, another iconic gaze that mimics the performative of ordering the unemployed person to choose. With these two glances Royal impersonates two roles, the unemployed person who must choose and the person who proposes the two jobs and orders him to choose one of them: that is, she enacts, with a sort of serious parody, Sarkozy's proposal, and in this way indirectly communicates an ingredient of negative evaluation of the opponent, using a strategy of pathos.

The analysis of Prodi's and Royal's communication made it possible to identify the different frequencies of the four persuasive ingredients of LOGOS, PATHOS, ETHOS COMPETENCE, and ETHOS BENEVOLENCE in 20 items of gaze. Prodi mainly exploits ingredients of COMPETENCE (62%), then LOGOS (25%) and PATHOS (13%), but not of BENEVOLENCE; in Royal, the most frequent strategy is LOGOS (54%), followed by COMPETENCE (27%), and a low frequency of BENEVOLENCE (5%), while PATHOS stands at very similar values to Prodi's (14%). The differences in the respective patterns of persuasive gaze seem to be determined by differences in political strategy. Prodi does not emphasise his BENEVOLENCE aspects because he does not need to corroborate his image as an honest person, especially in the comparison with Berlusconi who is attributed a political action often bent to his own interests. On the other hand, Royal's frequent use of a LOGOS strategy could depend either on her desire to counter the stereotype of the woman more prone to emotion or irrationality (Fiske, 2012) or on a cultural difference between Italian and French speakers, a greater disposition of the French to rational argumentation, a prevalence of their *esprit de géométrie*.

## 10.5 Magnetic gaze

When Adolf Hitler was reviewing troops of young soldiers, many were impressed and awestruck by his gaze that incited action. His eyes "were startling and unforgettable – they seemed pale blue in color – and were intense, unwavering, hypnotic" (Dodd, 1939). As witnessed by Shirer (1941), Hitler's eyes "stared through you. They seemed to immobilise the person on whom they were directed, frightening some, fascinating others, but dominating them in any case. I would observe hardened old Nazi party leaders freeze as he paused to talk to one or the other of them, hypnotised by his penetrating glare". This is an impressive description of how a person's eye may have an influence on others. But already according to Suetonius (335), Augustus

**FIGURE 10.13**   Luigi Nono.

believed his eyes were endowed with divine power, so that when someone was *fixedly stared at* by him, he would *lower his eyes* as if dazzled by sunlight.

Nuria Schönberg, the daughter of the founder of dodecaphony, fell in love at first sight with her father's pupil, Luigi Nono, because of his magnetic gaze (Figure 10.13).

Charles Manson, perpetrator with his followers of the Cielo Drive massacre, where Sharon Tate died among others, and charismatic leader of a kind of sect called "The family", scholar of mesmerism and hypnosis who passed himself off as the reincarnation of Christ and Satan, was forbidden to look the judges in the face during the massacre trial, to prevent him from subjugating and manipulating them with his gaze.

But does the magnetic gaze really exist? Makeup artists and cosmetics experts lavish women with advice on how to make their eyes look like that, giving an identikit of them: narrow, outwardly elongated eyes, "deepened" by mascara or long false eyelashes, eyebrows defined and protruding. Cosmetic surgeons retouch men's "prey" eyes, which are too round, to make them "hunter's eyes", more elongated, with protruding eyebrows covering the upper eyelid, making the gaze more intense, virile, dominant.

In part, the magnetic gaze is close to the "hypnotic" gaze: the hypnotist stares at you for longer than those 2 seconds allowed by the laws of eye-to-eye (Chapter 1); and the direct gaze in itself communicates firstly a request for attention, then a request for action that tenses you up by demanding a response. But immediately afterwards he looks a few metres beyond, as if looking through you: this is perhaps precisely what is verbalised as a "penetrating" gaze.

Yet if according to these descriptions the notion of magnetic gaze comes close to 18th-century theories on mesmerism and animal magnetism, is it possible to take it away from such a somewhat magical and naïve idea and restore scientific rigour to it?

My hypothesis is that magnetic gaze is one of the visual manifestations of a person's charisma.

The notion of charisma, defined by Max Weber (1920) as an outstanding quality of a leader, in the definition of our model (Poggi & D'Errico, 2020, 2022; Poggi, 2022a, 2022b) is a set of internal features of a person, manifested by a set of communicative and noncommunicative traits and behaviours that, eliciting in other people trust, faith, admiration, have the effect of inducing them to pursue the goals proposed by the charismatic person in a convinced way, with passion and enthusiasm.

A political leader, a teacher, a singer, a musician, a doctor can be charismatic, but so can the old grandmother in the village to whom people turn for advice; and charisma can be expressed in their sentences, their voice, their gait, their face, their gaze (charisma of the body) but also in the beauty of the music they compose or the visionary ideas they propose (charisma of the mind).

According to previous works (Signorello et al., 2012, 2013; Poggi, 2022a), the internal features that constitute charisma can be traced back to the persuasive elements of ethos and pathos: the adjectives used by people to describe a charismatic person credit her with gifts of competence (*visionary, intelligent, smart, organised, creative, wise, determined)*, benevolence *(spontaneous, trustworthy, honest, just, sociable, friendly*), dominance (*dynamic, lively, courageous, confident, strong, energetic, leader, authoritarian*), capacity of feeling emotions (*passionate, empathic*) and to induce them in others (*charming, attractive, nice, seducing, bewitching, engaging, exciting*).

A study investigated the voice of Umberto Bossi (D'Errico et al., 2013), a charismatic Italian leader whose language changed dramatically after a stroke. First it identified the acoustic characteristics of his voice and their changes before and after the stroke. Then, based on the adjectives attributed to the speaker in the two cases by non-Italian participants (who did not know Bossi and did not understand his words), it distinguished three types of charisma, proactive-seductive, calm-benevolent and authoritarian-threatening, and it showed in Bossi's voice, from before to after the stroke, a strong decrease in the proactive-seductive and authoritarian-threatening types of charisma and an increase in the calm-benevolent one.

On the basis of these studies, my hypothesis is that the magnetic gaze is a visual analogue of the charismatic voice, that is, a visible feature or behaviour that manifests a person's charisma.

This hypothesis was tested in two empirical studies carried out in collaboration with Alessandro Ansani, Giulia Galdo and Elena Rinallo.

### 10.5.1 *Study one*

The first research questions were:

1. Is the concept of "magnetic gaze" present in common sense? And how is it defined?
2. What are the visual elements that make a gaze magnetic?
3. What are the effects that people attribute to this gaze? What are the goals it induces one to pursue, the emotions it triggers, the personality traits it lets you infer in its sender?

#### 10.5.1.1 *Does the magnetic gaze exist? And what is it?*

A sample of 91 participants, 73% females, mean age 34, was submitted a questionnaire with 3 open and 7 Likert questions. In the open answers about the existence and definition of magnetic gaze, 31 participants say that it triggers attention and 23, attraction. Ten participants answer that you cannot stop looking at it, and six that you feel subjugated and you cannot resist it.

#### 10.5.1.2 *The signal*

As to the open questions about what makes a gaze magnetic, 24 answers mention intensity and 20 depth of the eyes, while 7 mention the colour, 5 the shape, and 1 its sensuality. Many of them only describe it by mentioning the effects of attention (3 participants), attraction (11), and emotion (5). Other answers attribute magneticity to features of the person as intelligent, determined, confident (competence and dominance,7 participants), or interesting, with charm, empathic, tender (pathos, 7).

Concerning the features of the signal, from a multiple choice question asking to describe a magnetic gaze in terms of colour and shape of the eyes, position of the eyelids and of the eyebrows, gaze duration and direction, it results that the most magnetic one is a *directed gaze, concentrated*, and with *dark, shining eyes*, with *elongated shape* and *half-closed eyelids*. But when asked to find an example on the web, the participants more often propose pictures with *elongated shape* and *light eyes* (blue or green). The most quoted are Ian Somerhalder (Figure 10.14) (6 participants) and Angelina Jolie (4 participants) (Figure 10.15), then *dark eyes with elongated shape* (20), like Johnny Depp (3). The only *dark eyes of round shape* proposed are those of Penelope Cruz, while *light and round* were twice noted in the famous picture by Steve McCurry, the "Afghan girl" Sharbat Gula.

**FIGURE 10.14** Ian Somerhalder.

**FIGURE 1015** Angelina Jolie.

*10.5.1.3  Induced goals and emotions*

Concerning emotions, first the participants were proposed Plutchick's wheel, a representation of emotions on the axes of valence and intensity (Plutchik, 1980), and they were asked to indicate the two emotions most often induced by a magnetic gaze; then they were asked to quantify, in terms of a Likert scale, a set of emotions typically induced, respectively, by the three types of charisma found in the study: authoritarian-threatening, proactive-seductive, and calm-benevolent.

In the former question, the emotions clearly cluster around the positive and high activation quadrant, with a clear preference for *interest* (41 participants) and *admiration* (22), sometimes also pointing at *expectation* and *ecstasy*.

From the latter question, the result is that the magnetic gaze mainly elicits emotions or internal states such as *attraction* (mean score 3.75) and *admiration* (3.11), followed by *confidence* (2.98), *amazement* and *enthusiasm* (2.85); on the contrary, the most seldom triggered emotions are *anxiety* (1.83), *worry* (1.66), *disgust* (1.31.), and *contempt* (1.22), as well as *subjection* (1.76). The participant does *not* feel *induced to do anything* (1.99) but *feels like* doing something with the one who has this gaze (3.46): he does not feel this as an *obligation*, it is something he *chooses* to do. He feels *charmed* (3.78) and *attracted* (3.65), *seduced* (3.55) and *engaged* (3.33), and finally he may be possibly keen to *fall in love* (3.27). Very rarely instead do the participants mention negative emotions such as feeling *frightened* (1.66), *terrified* (1.39) or *disgusted* (1.20).

The person with a magnetic gaze is mainly seen as *charismatic* (3.94) and *beautiful* (3.58), often with the positive features of Dominance (*convincing* 3.71, *strong* 3.54), much less so the negative features (*threatening* 1.91, *disturbing* 1.93); among the features of Competence, *intelligent* emerges (3.53).

Given the high frequency of features such as *charming* (4.09), *attractive* (4.06) and *bewitching* (4.02), the magnetic gaze is mainly associated with a proactive-seductive type of charisma, followed by the authoritarian-threatening one (*confident* and *determined*, 3.83, and *leader*, 3.67); much less to the calm-benevolent charisma, given the lower scores of the adjectives *calm* 2.77, *sincere* 2.76 and *fair* 2.71.

### 10.5.2  Study two

The second study further investigated the shape and colour of a magnetic gaze. A total of 6 photos, 3 males and 3 females, each showing the eye region only, were retouched so that each had light or dark eyes with round or elongated shape, in the following combinations:

1. Light eyes, round shape
2. Light eyes, elongated shape
3. Dark eyes, round shape
4. Dark eyes, elongated shape

The 24 stimuli were submitted to 150 participants in an online survey in the form of IAT (Implicit Association Test), to obtain an immediate unreasoned answer. For each gaze, they were asked to decide within 2 seconds whether it was magnetic or not.

The results confirm that participants tend to judge eyes of *light colour* and *elongated shape* as magnetic. This contradicts the result of the closed question in Study one, showing that the perception of magneticity is instinctive and does not depend on reasoned judgement. Moreover, strangely enough, there is a gender difference in the importance attached to eye colour: when judging the faces of women, women are indifferent to the colour of the eyes, whereas when judging the faces of men, the colour plays an important role, and the light colour is preferred. Men, on the other hand, prefer light-coloured eyes for both women and men.

### 10.5.3 Conclusion

The two studies show that people have quite a clear idea of what a magnetic gaze is: they connect it, sometimes explicitly, to the charisma of a person, in many cases an authoritarian-threatening charisma but more often a proactive-seductive one; the emotions it triggers are almost always positive, and the goals it induces are then chosen freely.

As far as the signal is concerned, we can conclude from the second study that light and elongated eyes are more often magnetic. The dimension of movement, on the other hand, has not been explored: some responses in Study one suggest that the way you look at the other person is also important, for example, looking into his eyes for a long time. But to test these hypotheses empirically, a comparison between non-static stimuli would be needed, for example an actor or a virtual agent looking in different ways.

Finally, the distinction between beautiful and magnetic eyes should still be investigated: since one of their main effects is attraction, it is not clear if such attraction is determined only or mainly by beauty, if it is but an erotic attraction, or if there is something else in a magnetic gaze that makes it magnetic.

# 11

# THE TEACHER'S GAZE

An area of human activity in which communication is particularly important – and a very interesting area of communication – is education: a type of social interaction aimed at conveying beliefs, but also goals and emotions. As to the first objective, the teacher's social role is not only to provide beliefs but also to teach pupils how to process them, that is, to develop their learning capacity; so the teacher must induce goals in the student: epistemic goals – the goal of learning – therefore also trying to wake and maintain attention and learning motivation; but she must also care about their goals of image and self-image and the goals of equity, attachment, affiliation. And to sustain these goals, she must also be able to induce emotions: cognitive emotions such as interest, curiosity, the lust for knowledge, the enthusiasm of investigation, but also emotions of image and self-image, such as the pride for succeeding, or emotions of the others' image, such as admiration and emulation for those worth imitating and contempt for unjust and unfair people.

## 11.1   How does the teacher look at you?

Verbal communication between teacher and pupil has been studied in both cognitive and interactional terms. While some works have tackled how the teacher's work may enhance contents' comprehension and the acquisition of a research method (in Italy, Lumbelli, 1981; Ajello, Pontecorvo & Zucchermaglio, 1991; Orletti, 2015), others have stressed the social, interactional, and communicative devices at work in the teacher–pupil(s) interaction: from Flanders (1965), taxonomies of the speech acts used by the teacher, to Amidon and Hunter's (1966), Fele and Paoletti's (2003) and Englehart's

DOI: 10.4324/9781032678344-11

(2009) analysis of classroom verbal interaction, through Babad's (2005) investigation on nonverbal behaviours in education.

Research on gestural communication has shown how the teacher's gestures, besides revealing her personality and type of relationship with students (Merola & Poggi, 2003), foster content comprehension (Ferrara, Nemirowski &Terc, 2005); Alibali & Nathan, 2012; Macedonia, 2019), while the student's beliefs, sometimes more correct than those expressed verbally, often emerge through her gestures (Goldin Meadow, Kim & Singer, 1999).

As regards the teacher's gaze, some works investigate her "professional" use, i.e. how she uses her eyes to study students, in order to acquire information about them (Minarikova et al., 2021); others ask students to judge how the teacher looks at them to assess how dominant or friendly she is, and they discover that such impressions do not vary across cultures (McIntyre, Mulder & Mainhard, 2020). But already the famous study about the Pygmalion effect (Rosenthal & Jakobson, 1968) had shown how the teacher's nonverbal communication determines the students' attention, as well as their sensation of being subject to her positive or negative evaluation and to her confident or resigned expectations.

So what do the teacher's eyes communicate? The following three studies tried to answer this question.

## 11.2   Gaze at school, in true life and fiction

Two studies (Liberati, 2002; Poggi, Merola & Liberati, 2003) tried to assess in general terms the types of meanings carried by the teacher's gaze during classroom interaction, in order to understand, on the basis of their respective frequencies, the predominant functions and the different gaze communicative styles of different teachers.

In order to assess which meanings are carried by the teacher's gaze, an observational study was conducted on two corpora. One contained fictional but realistic material taken from fragments of the fiction *Compagni di scuola* (Schoolmates), produced by the Italian television channel Rai2, and from three Italian films: *La Scuola* (The School), *Auguri professore* (Many Wishes, Professor) and *Io speriamo che me la cavo* (I hope I Can Get away with It), from which 100 gaze items were selected. The other corpus included real cases of school interaction, namely the video recordings of two classes in a third grade of a primary school in Rome, one class of French language and one about Carnival, in which 76 gaze items were singled out.

For each gaze, the signal was analysed in terms of its parameters (see Chapter 5); on the semantic side, the verbal context was transcribed, and the supposed meaning of the gaze was translated into words and classified according to the semantic taxonomy presented in Chapter 4. For example, a gaze is classified as DEICTIC if the *eyes*, to point at the teacher's desk, are *directed towards the place* where the desk is; it is ATTRIBUTIVE when the *eyelids open wide* to mean "big", or when the *upper eyelids lowered* and the *lower eyelids raised and corrugated* means "difficult"; a gaze is of the PERFORMATIVE type when the *eyebrows are lowered and closer* and the *eyelids are corrugated* in asking a question, or when *raised eyebrows and eyelids*, along with a *nodding*, communicate approval; we have an EMOTIONAL gaze if *raised eyelids and eyebrows* express surprise; a CERTAINTY gaze when *raised eyebrows* are accompanied by *upper and lower eyelids raised and tense* and by a *nod*, to convey "I am sure of this"; a METACOGNITIVE gaze when *raised eyebrows along with lowered eyelids* mean something like "I am trying to retrieve a word I don't remember"; it is METADISCURSIVE with a short *closure of the eyelids* following a lexical error that means "I am going to rephrase"; and TOPIC-COMMENT gazes are those occurring during *eyelids in default position* for an *average duration* – which mean "This is the topic of the sentence" – and are followed by a *total aperture of the eyelids* for a *short duration*, which means "This is the comment".

The results tell us how the meanings communicated by the teacher's gaze in his interaction with students are distributed in real and fictional teachers, respectively (Figures 11.1 and 11.2).

In both cases, the most frequent types of gaze are the performative ones, i.e. those that make the teacher's interactional goals explicit. A relevant difference is in the emotional gazes, more frequent in fictitious (16%) than in real teachers (3%); this is even more unexpected, given that the real classes are with primary school children, which might predict a wider affective expression on the part of the teacher.

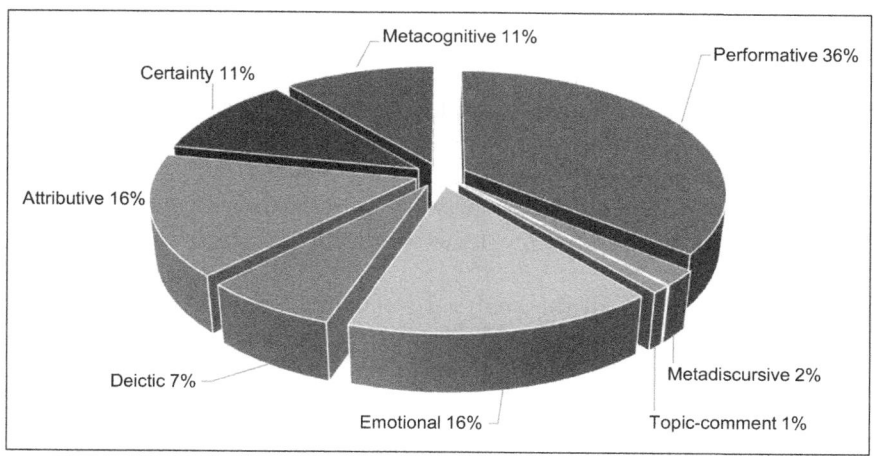

**FIGURE 11.1**   Teacher's gaze in films and fiction.

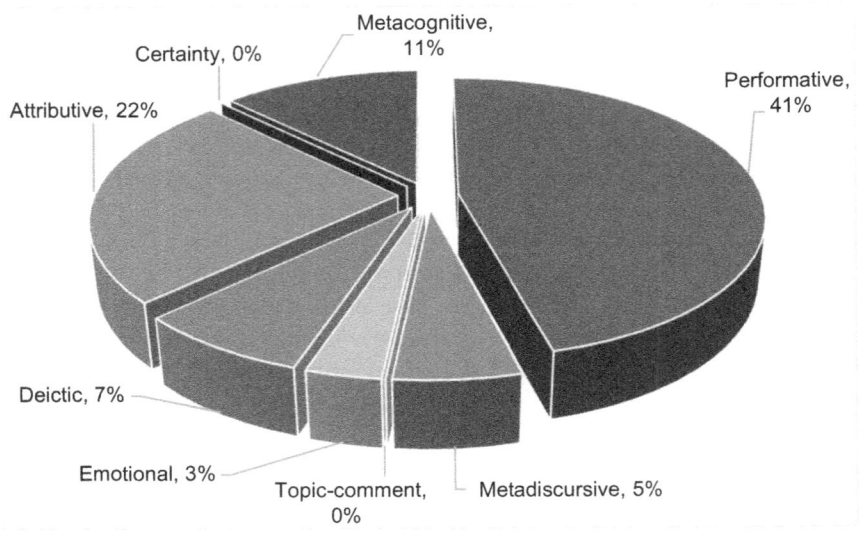

**FIGURE 11.2**  Teacher's gaze in real school.

The use of deictic and attributive gaze, instead, is quite similar between real and fictitious schools: the deictic are 7% in both corpora, while the attributive are slightly less frequent in the fiction (16%) than in the real context (22%), where they are often used by primary school teachers to illustrate their discourse by iconic signals.

An unexpected difference is one in certainty gazes, that are totally absent in the real teacher but fairly represented in fiction (11%), while metacognitive and metadiscursive gazes, interestingly enough, are quite frequent. The metacognitive are 22% in the real teacher, twice as much as the fiction teacher. And the metadiscursive too, although less frequent (5%) than the metacognitive ones, are in the real teacher twice as much as in fiction (2% metadiscursive + 1% TOPIC-COMMENT).

To account for these differences between the behaviour of the real teacher vs. one of the narrative stereotype, let us see these types of gaze more in detail.

*Deictic gaze.* Out of all the analysed fragments, the deictic gazes are 12 (7%): 5 in the fiction *Compagni di scuola*, 2 in the film *Io speriamo che me la cavo*, and 5 in real classes, 4 in that of French and 1 in that on Carnival.

All of the deictic gazes employed in real interactions are used by the teacher to get into the reality lived by her young students and to make her explanation clearer. The teacher DP, in the French class, uses two deictic gazes to facilitate the children's lexical retrieval of the words she is uttering: while saying *sole* (sun) and then *luna* (moon), she *raises her eyebrows and her head* and she *looks upward*, as if saying: "I refer to those two things that are in the sky". In *Compagni di scuola* and in *Io speriamo che me la cavo*, on the other hand, the deictic gazes occur in a conflictive situation, for example, when the teacher exploits his power to command to get out the door or to ask one to come to his desk. To the opposite, in *Auguri professore* and *La scuola*, in which the teacher–students relationships is not marked by a traditional authoritarian style, no deictic gaze occurs.

*Attributive gaze.* As expected, the attributive gaze often bears meanings of quantity, size, intensity: like when the teacher, referring to the Carnival masks, says *"Un dito grosso così"* (A finger as big as this) or *"Sarà enorme"* (It will be huge), while *raising her eyebrows and upper eyelids* to mean big size. The attributive gaze, especially in its meaning of intensity, is more often used with little kids to emphasise and thus to make the class more engaging.

Yet the same type of gaze is produced by the actor Massimo Lopez, acting as a teacher in *Compagni di scuola*, who says: *"Si sentiva investito di un compito altissimo"* (He felt invested with a very high task). And in other examples that gaze reinforces the words *very, many, more*. But other properties too are evoked by eyes. During the class on Carnival, while saying that adult people *"sono proprio tristi"* (are really sad), the teacher *lowers her eyebrows and corrugates her eyelids*. And in *Compagni di scuola* a professor, reciting a Shakespeare sonnet, while saying "treacherous females", *squints his eyes*.

The last two are both iconic gazes, in which eyes predicate a property by mimicking it: in the first example, by imitating the emotional gaze of sadness, the teacher attributes adult people the property of being sad; in the second, what is the link between treachery and squinting eyes? We can say a person is treacherous if when dealing with her one must be cautious, that is, squint one's eyes, not to be cheated – so the one who has to squint his eyes is the one who deals with the treacherous person; or else, it is the treacherous person herself who always has a furtive, not open gaze. In both cases, one attributes a personality trait to a person by imitating, either what the person herself does or what others do with her.

*Performative gaze.* The performative glances (67 cases) are the most frequent in the whole corpus: 16 in the fiction, 20 in the three films, 31 in the real classes. In the French class, when the children recognise a word, the teacher produces gazes of approval and praise, often also while *nodding* or saying *"E' giusto"* (It is right), *"esatto"* (correct). In *Auguri professore*, while a child recites a poem, a primary school teacher conveys approval with a *fixed*, attentive gaze.

Performatives of disapproval or rejection or those connotated by an aggressive attitude, such as orders or reproaches, are generally expressed by *lowered eyebrows* and *squinting* and *corrugated eyelids*.

In the film *La scuola*, the teacher produces a gaze of peremptory order, with *raised eyelids* but *lowered eyebrows*, when saying "*Zitta tu*" (You shut up). In the fiction, the teacher, while saying "*calma, Orietta, non ho ancora cominciato*" (easy, Orietta, I have not started yet), *raises the eyebrows*, but with *lowered upper eyelids*: a gaze akin to haughtiness, which counts here as a benevolent rebuke.

These negative performatives, though, only occur in acted interactions, while in the real ones attention requests prevail, expressed by *eyebrow raising* and *wide eyelids aperture*: like when a new topic, or an important definition or a new word to learn is coming.

*Certainty gaze.*   Contrary to the hypothesis put forward in Chapter 4, the gazes in the corpus that communicate a high degree of certainty are mainly characterised by *raised eyebrows* and *eyelids raised* or in *default position* – what we might perhaps call an "open" or "frank" gaze. Those that express doubt – and in some cases have as an indirect meaning a performative of request for clarification – have *frowning eyebrows* and *squinted eyelids* (the *upper ones lowered*, the *lower ones raised*).

Yet the certainty gaze only occurs in acted interactions. In the two real classes, there is none; perhaps because a primary school teacher, unlike a high school counterpart, does not need to reaffirm his reliability with frequent reminders of his confidence but tends to take it more for granted that the children "hang on" to his or her words.

*Metacognitive gaze.*   The metacognitive type of gaze is more frequent in the real (17) than in the fictitious teacher venue (11). It is precisely in real classes that most often the teacher, while explaining the lesson content, communicates with a gaze that she is thinking, searching for the right term or the most appropriate definition. It is no coincidence that these looks are most frequent in French lessons, where the teacher, who is not a native speaker but who speaks almost only French with the pupils, often *bends her head back* and *raises her eyelids and eyebrows* during a sentence in order to retrieve the foreign word from memory: the *eyes heavenward* of memory recall illustrated in Chapter 9. In other cases, after pronouncing a new French word, e.g. *école* (school), she produces *eyes heavenward* of reflection to help the children find a translation for that word. But also in the lesson on Carnival there are metacognitive gazes, for example, one that signals the beginning: before starting the lesson, as if to collect thoughts, the teacher *squints her eyelids* saying "*vediamo un pochino*" (let's see a little bit).

*Metadiscursive gaze.*   Out of the rare gazes that metacommunicate on one's own discourse (6 in all the corpus), here are, in *Compagni di scuola*, a gaze of self-correction and one of coming back from a digression.

1. Talking about the poet Leopardi's *Operette morali* (Little Moral Works), the teacher has a slip of the tongue and says "The Canticle of the Sylvester Cat"; she immediately *shakes her head bent forward* and *closes her eyes* as if to indicate "I have made a mistake, I correct myself"; then she opens them again and utters the correct sentence: "The Canticle of the Sylvester Rooster".

2. Another teacher, to close a digression and come back to the main topic, while saying "*Adesso andiamo avanti*" (now we go on), *lowers her head and closes her eyelids*, as if to undo what was said and get back on track.

One more case is the adversative relation set during the lesson about Carnival:

3. While saying "*però in genere*" (yet generally), the teacher *rises her eyebrows and eyelids*, as if requesting attention and pre-alerting to something unexpected. This is the equivalent of an adversative that communicates: do not draw the inferences that seemed plausible to you, be aware that just the opposite is the case.

*Topic-comment gaze.* The only instance in which two items of gaze alternate in marking first the topic then the comment is in the fiction *Compagni di scuola.*

4. The chemistry professor, talking about a type of battery, says "*il dispositivo si chiama Pila . . . Daniell*" (the device is called a battery . . . Daniell)". Here the word "battery" is the topic because it is already clear from the context that one is talking about batteries, while the name "Daniell" is the comment, the new information. The two concomitant gaze items, respectively, with *pila* and *Daniell* are similar because in both the *eyebrows* are in the *default position* and the *eyes look towards the class*; but the latter differs from the former because the *eyelids are raised higher* and the *duration* of the gaze is *shorter*: almost a stress on the new word.

*Emotional gaze.* Two emotional types of gaze were found in the real lessons, both of surprise, and sixteen in the acted lessons.

5. In the French lesson, while saying "*l'école . . . non lo sapete!*" (*l'école . . .* you do not know it!), the teacher *opens her eyes wide* (i.e. *eyebrows and upper eyelids raised*) from surprise.

6. In the lesson on Carnival, while saying "*anche i nonnetti talvolta si mascherano*" (grandparents too sometimes disguise themselves), the teacher by *opening her eyes wide* is seemingly expressing her surprise but actually she wants to elicit it in the kids.

7. In the film "*Io speriamo che me la cavo*", the teacher acted by Paolo Villaggio, while reproaching the kids by saying "*seconda regola venire a scuola con le unghie pulite*" (second rule, to come to school with nails

clean), expresses embarrassment by *lowering the eyelids* and *looking downward*.

8. Villaggio again, silently, expresses his anger with *closed and lowered eyebrows*.

## 11.3 The teacher's eyebrows

As seen already, the movements of the eyebrows play a very important role in our talking by eyes. Particularly relevant are the meanings carried by the eyebrows in the teacher's gaze. The signals of the eyebrows produced by teachers were investigated in more detail in an observational study (Remondini, 2000; Poggi, 2001), aimed at assessing whether the teachers use them in their classroom interaction, how frequently, and with which meanings.

Two schoolteachers, MP and PC, both teaching in the same primary school to third grade 8-year-old students, participated in the study. Four lessons of 20 minutes each were videorecorded, two for each teacher, both concerning the same two topics: air, and water. In the videos, the fragments in which the teacher produces a *raising* or a *frowning of the eyebrows* were selected, and each fragment was analysed in terms of the "score or multimodal communication" (Poggi, 2007): for each selected item of gaze the verbal context was annotated, and for each gaze a verbal translation was provided for both the literal meaning, and the indirect meaning assumed in that particular context. Table 11.1 shows the analysis of a fragment.

In this fragment, the teacher is explaining the importance of water to grow the seeds, and she asks the children to recall an experiment they did together some months before. So she *raises her eyebrows* while saying *vasetti diversi* (different pots): the literal meaning is to ask for attention, the meaning in context is to solicit the children to recall the experiment.

By computing the observed movements with their meanings, some differences result between the styles of the two teachers as far as the communicative use of the eyebrows is concerned (Table 11.2).

**TABLE 11.1** Analysis of the Eyebrow's Movements

| | *Verbal* | *Eyebrows* | *Literal meaning* | *Meaning in context* |
|---|---|---|---|---|
| 1 | *Se vi ricordate avevamo seminato i semi di fagioli in due **vasetti diversi*** (if you remember, we had sowed bean seeds in two **different pots**) | *Raises her eyebrows* | It is important, I ask for attention. | You have to recall what we did. |

TABLE 11.2 Signals of the Eyebrows by Two Teachers

| Teacher | Raisings | Frownings | Total |
|---------|----------|-----------|-------|
| MP | 11 | 21 | 32 |
| PC | 9 | | 9 |
| Total | 20 | 21 | 41 |

TABLE 11.3 Meanings of the Eyebrow Raising

| Literal meaning | Type of meaning | Meaning in context | Type of meaning | n. |
|-----------------|-----------------|--------------------|-----------------|-----|
| I ask for attention. | Performative | Emphasis | Topic-comment | 16 |
| I ask for attention. | Performative | But | Metadiscursive | 2 |
| I ask for attention. | Performative | Surprise | Emotional | 2 |
| Total | | | | 20 |

First of all, the two teachers strongly differ as for their eyebrows expressivity: while MP produces 32 signals of the eyebrows, PC performs only 9, and only *raisings*, no *frownings*. In general, her face is much less expressive than MP's.

Coming to the meanings conveyed, Tables 11.3 and 11.4 summarise the number of meanings, literal and "in context", of the *raisings* and *frownings*, and their classification in terms of the typology above.

For all the *eyebrow raisings*, the literal meaning is a request for attention – they are, then, performative gazes – but out of the 20 total occurrences, for 16 of them the meaning assumed in context is one of emphasis – that is, to distinguish the comment from the topic. In some cases, they only signal that the concomitant word or phrase is the new part of the sentence; in others, instead they emphasise a certain belief to recall student beliefs acquired in previous lessons. Therefore the *raising* means either "pay attention to this belief that is new for you" or again "pay attention to this belief that you already know but is stored in your memory".

In two cases, the eyebrow *raising* has an adversative meaning – so it belongs to the metacognitive type; in fact, the concomitant sentence is preceded by *però* (however). In two cases, finally, the *raising* is an emotional signal of surprise. Thus the teacher wants to awaken surprise: more specifically, either to recall the children's attention on an unexpected event or to communicate admiration (i.e. acknowledgement of surprising qualities) and hence praise for a boy who recalled something before the others did. Typically, in fact, in praising someone, one *raises the eyebrows* to show admiration.

Let us now see the meanings of the eyebrow frowning (Table 11.4).

**TABLE 11.4** Meanings of the Eyebrow Frown

| | 1 Literal meaning | 2 Type of meaning | 3 I meaning in context | 4 Type of meaning | 5 II Meaning in context | 6 Type of meaning | 7 n. |
|---|---|---|---|---|---|---|---|
| 1 | I'm attentive. | Metacognitive | I look. | Sender's action | The droplet looks far away. | Character's action | 3 |
| 2 | I'm attentive. | Metacognitive | I am worried. | Sender's emotion | The droplets are worried. | Character's emotion | 3 |
| 3 | I'm attentive. | Metacognitive | I am serious. | Certainty | | | 1 |
| 4 | I'm attentive. | Metacognitive | I am trying to remember. | Metacognitive | | | 4 |
| 5 | I'm attentive. | Metacognitive | I ask you. | Performative | | | 7 |
| 6 | I'm attentive. | Metacognitive | I forbid you. | Performative | | | 2 |
| 7 | I'm attentive. | Metacognitive | I am listing. | Metadiscursive | | | 1 |
| Total | | | | | | | 21 |

Out of 21 *eyebrow frownings* by teacher MP, all convey, as a first meaning, that the sender is paying attention or is even concentrating; so all of them belong to the metacognitive type. But looking at the meanings that this signal acquires in the context of the lesson, the most frequent one (7 cases, line 5 of Table 11.4) is to accompany a question: the teacher shows attentiveness to metacommunication when she is asking some information from the students, and she concentrates to better understand their answer: thus a performative gaze. The second more frequent meaning (4 occurrences, line 4) is "I concentrate because I am trying to remember something" – so a metacognitive gaze also as to the meaning in context. Further occurrences are the *frowning* of the "serious gaze", that the teacher uses twice (line 6) to forbid a boy to speak – a performative gaze – and once (line 3) to show an assertive expression such as "I'm not kidding", thus as a gaze of certainty.

The other *frownings* are produced by the teacher with narrative aims. To explain the cycle of the water, the teacher tells a story of a droplet (*GocciaLina*, a pun with the noun *gocciolina* [droplet], the diminutive of *goccia* [drop] + the name *Lina*) and her droplet friends, by assuming in the narrative sometimes the role of the storyteller, sometimes instead by taking on herself the role of the droplets. Consequently, some of her gaze items are iconic, i.e. they represent actions or emotions of the characters of the story. Viewing all this in terms of the notion of "Observer vs. Character viewpoint" (McNeill, 1992; Merola & Poggi, 2003) for the analysis of iconic gestures, in this case, for some *frownings* the teacher at a first level takes the role of the storyteller and represents her own physical actions such as looking or emotions such as worry (lines 1 and 2, cols. 3 and 4, 3 cases each), but at a second level (lines 1 and 2, col. 5 and 6), these actions and emotions allow her to take on the role of the droplets themselves. So at the first level the teacher takes up the viewpoint of the Observer, at the second level the one of the Character. In the three cases, while saying *"guardava lontano"* (she was looking into the distance), the teacher produces an iconic *frown*, i.e. she mimics the action of someone who looks in the distance to focus on something. Therefore, the literal meaning of the frown (line 1, col. 1 and 2) is, like in all other cases, one of a metacognitive gaze expressing attention; the first meaning in context is "I am looking into the distance" (line 1, col 3), i.e. it refers to an action (col. 4) of the teacher herself in the role of the storyteller (Observer's viewpoint). The second meaning in context is "the droplet looks into the distance" (col. 5), i.e. a description of the droplet's action, which then adopts the Character's viewpoint (col. 6). In three more fragments of the narration (line 2), by the literal meaning of the *frowning* (col. 1) the teacher displays attention, thus again a metacognitive meaning (col. 2), whose first meaning in context is an expression of worry (col. 3), an emotion felt by herself in the role of the Storyteller (col. 4). But, as a second meaning in context, she mimics an emotion of the Character (col. 6), the droplets worried about evaporating under the sun (line 2, col. 5): thus the Storyteller, by expressing one's own emotion, mimics the Character's emotion (Poggi, Merola & Liberati, 2003).

Finally, teacher MP's communication provides one more intriguing example. At the beginning of the story, while describing the droplet personality and assuming the role of the Storyteller, she lists the droplet's qualities: "*era una gocciolina allegra, spensierata, vivace*" (she was a cheerful, carefree, lively little droplet), and meanwhile *frowns* and *shakes her head left and right rhythmically* with each adjective. This frowning can be interpreted (also in the light of other studies, see Chapter 12) as a metadiscursive signal communicating: "I am attentive, concentrating because I want to list these qualities without interruption, without stopping or pausing" – a metadiscursive signal often found in enumerations but also when the sender is caught up in the "flow", the flow of her own speech or action. In fact, we will also see it in the gaze of the conductor when he shakes his head accompanying the flow of music he is conducting but also enjoying the pleasure and feeling of aesthetic abandon that the music gives him.

## 11.4   Does the teacher's gaze affect learning?

We have seen how rich and subtle the teacher's gaze communication is. But . . . does this serve learning? And, if so, how and why? To investigate the effectiveness of eye communication in teaching, a study was conducted on the cognitive effects of body communication in the classroom (Poggi, Merola & Liberati, 2003). The research question was whether the teacher's multimodal communication promotes students' cognitive processes of comprehension and memory.

Three primary school teachers participated in the study, teaching, respectively, to classes of 9, 9, and 7 fifth grade students, respectively, for a total of 25 students.

The students of each class were divided in two groups: the control group read a story, while the experimental group was told the same story by the teacher who made use of all her multimodal communicative resources: verbal, prosodic, gestural, facial, and gaze communication. In this case, the lesson was videorecorded. After reading or listening to the story, all students had to write a summary of the story they had read, or seen and heard.

The textual part of the teachers' narratives was analysed by dividing it into information units, while the videorecorded lessons (10 minutes for each teacher) were analysed in terms of the "score of multimodal communication" (Poggi, 2007); also in this case, the units of information were singled out in both verbal and bodily communication. Finally, in the students' summaries, the units of information retained were singled out, taking them as evidence

**TABLE 11.5** Effects on Memory of Written Text and Multimodal Lesson

| Modality | A | B | C |
|---|---|---|---|
| Prosody | 9 | 10 | 4 |
| Gestures | 7 | 27 | 4 |
| Face | 27 | 12 | 1 |
| Gaze | 4 | 12 | 1 |
| Total | 47 | 61 | 10 |
| Memory score after multimodal lesson | 41.8 | 42.5 | 28.8 |
| Memory score after written text | 39.77 | 45.34 | 37.9 |
| Written–multimodal gap | +2.03 | –2.84 | –9.1 |

that those units of the texts or multimodal narratives had been comprehended and memorised.

Table 11.5 summarises the effects of the written texts and of the multimodal lessons, respectively, on the students' memory of the information units.

Considering the number of information units maintained in the summaries, the students with the lowest scores, for both written text and multimodal lesson, are those of teacher C, who is the least expressive one: she uses very few prosodic (4) and gestural (4) signals, only 1 by facial expression and 1 by gaze. These students show the highest gap (–9.1) vis-à-vis the other groups between performance after the multimodal lesson and after the written text: the multimodal support to the speech of this teacher seems to be very low.

The students with best performance in both conditions are those of teacher B, the most expressive of the three, with 61 body signals, among which 10 prosodic, 27 gestural, 12 facial and 12 gaze items; here, though, the score of the information units retained by the group taking the multimodal lesson (42.5) is slightly lower than the one obtained by the group reading the written text (45.34), with a negative gap of –2.84.

Finally, teacher A has a multimodal communication globally less conspicuous than teacher B but very rich in facial expression: after her multimodal lesson, even more information units are retained (41.8) than with the text reading (39.77), with a positive gap of +2.03.

These results tell us that a wide use of multimodality enriches the verbal message providing beliefs that sometimes repeat or confirm those carried by words and sometimes make them clearer, adding vividness and thus favouring the welding of beliefs into an interconnected, hence more memorable network. A contribution to this is given mainly by gestures in teacher B and mainly by face in teacher A. Yet B's communication, in which face and gaze are used frequently too, is the most rich and balanced and produces more comprehension and memory. Therefore, the summaries retaining the most information units are right those of the students whose teachers produce more facial and gaze signals.

This demonstrates in general the usefulness of multimodality in teacher communication and in particular the importance of gaze and facial expression as tools of educational interaction.

# 12

# THE EYES OF MUSIC

In the first chapters of this book, we have seen that eyes are used to see, to look, to feel, to think, and to communicate. These different functions are at work also in a very peculiar behaviour of humans: making music. When a pianist or a violinist is playing, a soprano singing, a conductor conducting, their eyes can do all of these things. The conductor who *turns his eyes* around over all the orchestra members does so to look, i.e. to check that all are ready to start; but if his *eyes address a single section* of the orchestra, he is conveying an order to keep ready to start. A singer raising her inner parts of eyebrows conveys to the audience the emotion of sadness or yearning she wants to imprint on the song she is singing.

In this chapter, we will overview the functions of gaze in making music, particularly in the behaviours of pianists and of orchestra conductors.[1]

## 12.1   The pianist's eyes

A first observational study (Poggi, 2006b) analysed the multimodal behaviour – specifically, the movements of head and trunk, face and eyes – of a pianist during performance. The fragments of video recordings analysed are taken from performances in rehearsal and concert of the piano and orchestra concert K 488 by Wolfgang Amadeus Mozart, played by the pianist Marcella Crudeli with the amateur orchestra "Res Musica" of Rome, conducted by Fabrizio Santi.

The goal of a performer is to produce music by taking care of all its constitutive parameters: melody (the sequence of notes to play or sing), rhythm (their succession and grouping in time), harmony (the relationships between contemporary or successive sounds), timbre (the quality of sound), tempo

DOI: 10.4324/9781032678344-12

(fast or slow), intensity (loud or soft), expression (the modulation of all parameters that express or induce emotions).

In the performer's mind and body, various processes are at work, finally triggering the motor processes of playing: the cognitive processes of attention, concentration, memory, imagination and the emotional processes, among which four types of emotions can be distinguished (Poggi, 2006b). First, the emotions may be either "felt" or "enacted". The former are the emotions the performer actually feels while playing or singing: first, the "process emotions", those caused by the very process of making music, such as flow, the sense of doing something without stopping, with ease and pleasure (Csikszentmihalyi, 1990) or else tension or fear of making mistakes; then "outcome emotions", like shame if you made an error, pride or pleasure when you hear you are playing well. The "enacted emotions" are those the musician has to pretend, to fake to be feeling himself; the "meaning-oriented" ones are those functioning to convey the emotional meaning of music, to be imprinted into the music performed: feeling sad in playing a sad dirge, buoyant in a march. The "movement-oriented" ones, instead, are those enacted because the mood they induce may facilitate the technical movement: such as, as we shall see in this chapter, the frowning of anger that may help playing "forte".

From the analysis of the pianist's movements in the videorecorded corpus, it was clear that, apart from the movements of the hands, which are deputed to materially produce the music, the other movements of her body during performance – movements of the torso and head, facial expressions, movements in the eye region – can fulfil three functions: communicating, expressing internal states and collaborating in the technical gesture. Let us look in particular at what the eyes of the musician do.

*Communicating.* During the rehearsals, the pianist uses her eyes to communicate to the orchestra. The ensemble that accompanies her is an amateur group of young people, with whom she has a pedagogical, almost maternal relationship. Besides the *looks* of understanding aimed at coordinating with the orchestra members, she sometimes *smiles* and *nods* with *raised eyebrows*, as a sign of approval and praise because they are playing well.

*Expressing internal states.* Another important function of eyes when playing is to express internal states. Before giving some examples, let us see the difference between expression and communication (Poggi, 2022a).

We can speak of *communication* when a sender produces a signal carrying a certain belief – about the world, one's identity or one's mind – with an internal goal of transmitting it, often consciously but not necessarily so; we speak of *expression*, on the other hand, when the belief transmitted is not about the world but about the sender's own identity or about internal, physical or mental states, and the goal of making it known to others is an unconscious or tacit internal goal or an external, social or biological goal. Finally, we have cases of *noncommunicative expression*, in which the signal produced lets the meaning leak out but without any goal to communicate it: for instance, when a behaviour or trait is produced only to "put out", to give vent to the internal state. The pianist's eyes perform various expressive functions.

*Expression of cognitive processes.* Often the eyes display the pianist's cognitive states or processes: her *frowning eyebrows* express her concentration before the start or during performance; her *eyes upward* search for visual or acoustic images in memory or the recollection of a passage. The frequency or significance of *eyes upward* may vary according to the type of performance and the expertise of the pianist: in an improvisation, there will be more image-seeking than in playing a studied piece. And as for the *eyes upward* to recall a passage, the amateur playing a piece from memory will raise them more often than the professional more accustomed to memorisation.

*Expression of emotions.* In Marcella Crudeli's performance, some gaze items express her "process emotions". Her mirth is visible by her *shaking head to left and right rhythmically* but also by the eyes display that accompanies it: while she *smiles*, her smile is accompanied by *crow's feet* around her eyes that are typical of the sincere smile of happiness. On the other hand, she expresses the "outcome emotions" of satisfaction and pride about how the piece goes, by her *smile*, *chin up*, and *raised external eyebrows*, three typical displays of pride. Among "enacted emotions" is the "meaning-oriented" expression of sadness, with *inner parts of eyebrows raised* (A-shape eyebrows), displayed while playing a sad passage; whereas a "movement-oriented" emotion expression, functioning to facilitate the technical movement, are her *frowning eyebrows* which, by displaying anger, trigger the energetic activation needed to play louder.

According to the theory of facial feedback (Tourangeau & Ellsworth, 1979; Capella, 1993; Davis, Senghas & Ochsner, 2009), it is not only the emotion that produces the corresponding expression but also the opposite: just as forcing oneself to smile might lead to feeling more serene, frowning can make us feel angrier and more aggressive, and it can mobilise the energy that anger brings.

*Helping the technical gesture.* The example just seen also falls into this category. Sometimes the movement of the eyes, like other movements of the body in musical performance, is used to accompany and, almost, to help better perform the technical gesture of the hands. And this can occur with regard to various parameters of the music. A case in which the eyes seem to help the hands in the correct production of the melody, particularly in playing a high note, occurs in a passage of the concert in which, playing with her right hand a so-called acciaccatura, i.e. a very fast movement from E to E an octave above, Marcella Crudeli very quickly *moves first her thumb and then her right little finger*, and simultaneously *raises her right eyebrow*! As if there were a kind of "self-mirroring" from one to another part of the body, so that the movement of one almost helps to intensify the movement of the other.

In another passage, her eyes cooperate with her hands in the harmony parameter: the pianist plays some quatrains around the tonic, and then, as she repeats them a third below, she *lowers her eyebrows*; just as the melody is played two notes lower, she also lowers her eyebrows. In another passage, *raising the outer parts of the eyebrows* helps her to produce a tense timbre. *Raising the entire eyebrows*, finally, is a frequent movement, not only in this but also in other musicians, to help give the right intensity, more precisely to play softly or delicately – like someone who "walks on eggshells" and tries to play as softly as possible.

These uses of the eyes are probably not communicative – that's why I don't call them gaze items – but they are frequent and probably useful in musical performance.

## 12.2 The conductor's eyes

During a musical performance, the gaze is an important communication tool between the musicians, who look at one another to coordinate and can address reciprocal looks of understanding to synchronise (Bishop, Cancino-Chacón & Goebl, 2022). In a small ensemble, mutual gazing may link all the components, and coordination is rather "democratic", although one musician, e.g. the first violin in a string quartet, may still assume a leading function (Glowinski et al., 2013). But in an orchestra or choir, synchronisation is generally governed by a single member of the group: the conductor.

The figure of the Maestro sums up several roles (Poggi, 2011). First and foremost, he is a leader, the one who decides which pieces to perform and the interpretation to impart to each piece, and to do this, he must give technical indications on all the parameters of the music, melody, harmony, rhythm, tempo, timbre, intensity, expression. But in addition to being a technical leader, he must also be an emotional leader: knowing how to motivate musicians in their sometimes hard and difficult work, making them feel the beauty of making music or urging pride in a masterful performance, admiration or empathy for the author of the piece. And finally, the Maestro must be a master, he must teach how to make music: to this aim he uses ostensive and mimetic capacities, showing in first person the technical actions to be performed to obtain the desired sound or imitating the wrong actions to show what not to do; in response to the actions of the singers or musicians, he gives his feedback, approving the appropriate movements, disapproving the wrong ones. But if these more didactic functions are performed especially during rehearsals, whether in rehearsal or in concert, the conductor continues to be a leader and teacher, to motivate, to give feedback, to guide and teach: in rehearsal he can also use verbal communication, whereas in concert he must rely exclusively on bodily modalities. This is why his gestures, facial expression and gaze take on special importance.

Gestures in conducting have been studied both by conductors themselves and in the psychology of communication. But their gaze has not often been investigated (Poggi, 2002b). Indeed, in recent research (Poggi et al., 2020), interviews of five conductors revealed that they largely lack a high level of awareness of their use of gaze as a communicative tool during musical performance. And yet reports from orchestral players and music critics indicate that some conductors of the past and present made or do make systematic and conscious use of the gaze in rehearsals and concerts. Legendary is the case of Antonio Guarnieri, an early 20th-century conductor "with a gaze, sharp and penetrating, that bewitched the orchestral players (. . .) That gaze, those eyes that seemed to magnetise everyone, orchestral players, singers, choristers. It may have been suggestion, but it really seemed that Guarnieri, more than with the minimal gesture, barely prolonged (but by how much, then?) by that tiny butt of his baton, was conducting by looking" (Mandelli, 1997).

More recently, as we shall see, another Maestro had a profound awareness of the importance of gaze in conducting: Leonard Bernstein, who in 1989, during the encore of Haydn's Symphony No. 88 in G Major, put his hands behind his back and conducted only with his eyes and facial expression.

The Maestro's gaze is therefore also a language: at the very least a lexicon, i.e. a system of communication relating signals with meanings and a system that is quite universal, if the same conductor can use it today at La Scala in Milan, tomorrow at Tokyo's Suntory Hall or at the Metropolitan in New York and if orchestral players all over the world understand it. So let us try to discover the secret of this language.

### 12.2.1 The conductor's gaze words

To single out the signals of gaze used by a conductor and their meanings, an observational study was conducted on a corpus of musical performances in concert and rehearsal: 5 fragments by the choir Orazio Vecchi of Rome, conducted by Mr. Alessandro Anniballi, for a total of 99.43 minutes; 3 fragments in rehearsal and 2 in concert, drawn from Gabriel Fauré's Requiem; 2 in rehearsal and 1 in concert from Antonio Vivaldi's Magnificat, and 1 fragment in concert, from Gioachino Rossini's Petite Messe Solennelle (Poggi, 2018). These fragments of performance were analysed in terms of the annotation scheme in Table 12.1.

In col. 1, we write the piece title and the analysed minute; in col. 2, the words sung on the notes played at the same time of the analysed gaze; in col. 3, the concomitant communication in other modalities; col. 4 contains a description of the gaze; col. 5 contains a verbal paraphrasis of its literal

**TABLE 12.1** The Conductor's Gaze

| 1. Fragment Time | 2. Singing or music | 3. Verbal and other modalities | 4. Gaze | 5. Literal meaning | 6. Meaning in context | 7. Type of gaze | 8. Musical or interactive function | 9. Semotic device |
|---|---|---|---|---|---|---|---|---|
| 1 Req. PC 0.02 | | | Looks rightward | I ask for attention. | Ready to start | Request | Start | SPECIFIC CODIFIED |
| 2 Req. PS2 1.48 | Réquiem | | Raises eyebrows high | I mimic a raising. | Start from the high note. | Request | Pitch | DIRECT ICONIC |
| 3 Req. PC 2.44 | Piano: E C | Sings "mii" (E) pointing at tenors with index f. | Frowning eyebrows, looks at tenors | I strive. | Strive: Keep the intonaion | Request | Pitch | INDIRECT ICONIC Help Melody |
| 4 Mag.PS8 1.09 | | | Closed eyes | I am concentrating. | | Expression of cognitive state | Concentration | |
| 5 Mag.PS8 4.27 | (Strings) | Moves head to right and left and smiles | Closes eyes | I concentrate. | I concentrate on the pleasure I feel. ↑ I express pleasure. | Expression of outcome emotion | MOTIVATING (non-musical) | GENERIC CODIFIED |

meaning; col. 6, the meaning it takes up in context. This allows us to classify that gaze as to its type of meaning (col. 7) and, in col. 8, as to its interactional function (e.g. giving feedback, motivating) or technical function (melody, rhythm, intensity, etc.). Finally, col. 9 specifies the semiotic device, i.e. the connection between that particular gaze and the corresponding meaning.

*Some examples of analysis.*   At line 1, column 4, the conductor turns his gaze towards a section of the choir: this in everyday communication is a simple request for attention (col. 5), but here, more specifically, it is a request to prepare for the start (6), i.e. the beginning of the musical phrase: a glance with performative request (7) with the technical function of indicating the starts (col.8), i.e. who is to sing and when. From the point of view of the semiotic mechanism (col.9), as we shall see, this is a "specific codified signal" because in musical conduction it has a more specific meaning than in everyday life.

In line 2, the conductor raises his eyebrows high (col. 4): an imitation of an upward movement (5), hence a request (col. 7) to "start from the high note" (col. 6), i.e. an indication of musical pitch (col. 8) communicated through an iconic signal (col. 9) that represents, through a perceivable raising in the visual modality, another perceivable "raising" in the auditory modality: a higher frequency note, which we hear as "higher". The acoustic "height" is evoked by a spatial height.

In line 3, while the piano accompanist plays the notes E C (col. 2), the conductor, asking the tenors to intone the E with his *extended index finger*, intones it himself (col. 3), but while *looking at them*, he *frowns* (col. 4), thus miming an expression of effort (col. 5), he asks them (col. col. 7) to make an effort to maintain that difficult intonation (col. 6). This is again an indication of tonal pitch (col. 8) but communicated through an indirect iconicity (col. 9), which requires more inferential leaps: here the similarity is between a movement connected to a mental state of effort and the movements one makes in producing the high note (I express effort → you must do an effort → you must sing a high note that requires effort).

### 12.2.2   Semiotic devices

As was already seen for the orchestra conductor's gestures (Poggi, 2017), in his gazes, the same semiotic devices are also at work. Based on the way in which a signal is constructed starting from its meaning, six types of gaze can be distinguished:

1. GENERIC CODIFIED: A gaze that is usually employed in everyday communication is used in conduction with the same meaning. For example,

*turning the gaze towards someone* to ask for attention is a signal codified universally, not only in conduction.

2. SPECIFIC CODIFIED: A gaze generally employed in everyday communication but used in conduction with a meaning specific to communication in a musical ensemble: for example, *looking towards a section* not simply to ask for attention but to give the start.

3. DIRECT ICONIC: Aspects of music are mimicked with the body. Changes produced by bodily movements produce perceptions in the visual modality that, through a mechanism we may call modality transposition, refer to similar changes in the auditory modality: for example, *raising the eyebrows high* to evoke a pitch elevation of the sung tone.

4. INDIRECT ICONIC: The movements produced either by inference or through motor induction indirectly evoke the sound to produce, or other meanings: they are movements of three types:

   a. EXPRESSION OF MENTAL STATE: *Closing eyes*, which already in everyday language means "I am concentrating", in musical performance may let you infer, either "you concentrate too, to prepare for the start" or else "I concentrate because I want to enjoy the beauty of the music you are playing", perhaps with the aim of making the musicians appreciate it in order to motivate them more.

   b. EXPRESSION OF PHYSICAL STATE: The conductor who *squints his eyelids hard* while saying *"sforzatissimo"* imitates the expression of one who is making an effort, thus recalling the production of a "sforzato" sound.

   c. EXPRESSION OF EMOTION: *Frowning the eyebrows* as if out of anger, by inducing anger through contagion, evokes the connected energy and therefore asks for a high intensity: "forte".

Here, the movements connected to a physical or mental state are transmitted by the conductor to the musicians, to be performed by them too in order to better produce the technical gesture.

As we have seen with the pianist, sometimes mimicking the movements one makes in producing a certain sound helps to produce it. But this is also true, so to speak, even through third parties: even if it is the conductor who produces that movement and the choristers (because of mirror neurons) imitate him, this can help them to produce it. And the conductor perhaps adopts this technique precisely thinking, instinctively or consciously, that his movement can help the technical movement of the choristers.

From the point of view of the semiotic mechanism, in the corpus of fragments analysed the conductor's gaze items are in the majority generic codified (15), followed by specific codified (5), then by indirect (4) and direct iconic (3).

### 12.2.3  *Meanings and functions*

The analysis of the corpus allows us to outline a lexicon of the conductor's gaze (Poggi, 2018) that counts 17 gaze types, each with two or more tokens, and in certain cases, with both a literal and an indirect meanings (Table 12.2).

In Table 12.2, column 1 contains the description of the gaze signal at issue, col. 2 its most relevant parameter, and col. 3 its literal meaning; col. 4 the performative (whether request, praise, threat, information), col. 5 the semantic type, and col. 6 the semiotic device. However, since every gaze, beyond its literal meaning, can have an indirect meaning, the following four columns contain the indirect meaning (col. 7), its specific performative (col. 8), semantic type (col. 9), and semiotic device (col. 10). In some cases, the signal in col. 1 may assume, in the conductor's language, both the literal and the indirect meaning, according to context. For example, for the signal at line 1, "looks at (the chorister or musician) X", it may happen that the maestro looking at one or more choristers just wants to catch their attention (col. 3), perhaps during the rehearsal, to urge them not to disturb while another section sings, but more often this call for attention has been specialised with the indirect meaning "ready to start" (col. 7). Therefore, in its literal meaning, this gaze is a "generic codified" gaze (col. 6), that is, the same used in everyday life, with a meaning of request for attention, but its final idiomatisation as "ready to start" gives rise to a new meaning, again a codified one but specialised in the field of musical performance (col. 10). In other cases, the literal meaning loses validity, and the indirect one (idiomatised as "specific codified") becomes the only one really used in musical performance. For example, at line 7, the *wide open eyes* that *glare* at a chorister or the whole section when they make a mistake during performance would literally be a threatening gaze (cols. 3 and 4), but actually there is no threat; a threat is oriented on the future, but this is rather a gaze of reproach (column 8) that communicates: "you should not do so" (7): its true goal is to provide a negative feedback (9), stigmatising the error (see Chapter 10, Figure 10.12).

From the point of view of its meaning, a gaze, like some types of gestures – or among words, interjections – is a holophrastic communicative signal (Poggi, 1981, 2007, 2022b), that is, one that communicates both a performative and a content. For example, gaze n. 10, a *short eyebrow raising*, has a performative of request (col. 4), and the content is "sing a high pitch note" (col. 3); n. 12, an *eyebrow raising* accompanied by *head recessed in the shoulders*, is an expression of mental state (col. 4) and in particular conveys circumspection (cols. 3 and 5).

Further considerations allowed by Table 12.2 are summarised in Table 12.3 that, for each type of gaze, singles out the function it serves, in orchestra and choir conduction, distinguishing different types or degrees of communicativeness.

**TABLE 12.2** Conductor's Gaze Items

| 1. Signal | 2. Parameter | 3. Literal meaning | 4. Performative | 5. Type | 6. Semiotic device | 7. Indirect meaning | 8. Performative | 9. Type | 10. Semiotic device |
|---|---|---|---|---|---|---|---|---|---|
| 1. Looks at X | Eyes direction | Pay attention | REQUEST | Request for attention | GEN. COD. | Prepare for the start | REQUEST | Request to start | SPEC. COD. |
| 2. Stares at all | Eyes direction | I ask for your attention. | REQUEST | Broadcast Request for attention | GEN. COD. | | | | |
| 3. Looks at all | Eyes direction | I check whether you all pay attention. | INFORMATION ACQUISITION | Control gaze Noncommunicative | GEN. COD. | | | | |
| 4. Looks obliquely with raised eyebrows | Eyes direction/ head direction | Careful | WARNING | Warning gaze | GEN. COD. | | | | |
| 5. Raised eyebrow, wide open eyes | Eyebrows | It is important. | WARNING | Emphasis | GEN. COD. | | | | |
| 6. Wide open eyes, frowning eyebrows (extended index finger) | Eyebrows + Eyelids | Sing/play this. | REQUEST | Peremptory order | GEN. COD. | | | | |

| No. / Facial action | Modality | | | | | | | | |
|---|---|---|---|---|---|---|---|---|---|
| 7. Wide open eyes, fixed on X | Eyelids + direction + Duration | Woe to you! | THREAT | Threatening gaze | GEN. COD. | I reproach you for your mistake (Figure 10.12) | REPROACH | Negative feed-back | SPEC. COD. |
| 8. Raises eyebrows (nodding) | Eyebrows | I am amazed/I admire. | OUTCOME EMOTION EXPRESSION | Appreciation + approval | GEN. COD. | Bravo! | PRAISE | Positive Feedback | GEN. COD. |
| 9. Frowns eyebrows continuously (swinging head) | Eyebrows | Go on without stopping. | REQUEST | Request for continuity | GEN. COD. | | | | |
| 10. Shortly raises an eyebrow | Eyebrows | Sing/play the high note. | REQUEST | Pitch indication | DIR. ICON. | | | | |
| 11. Raises eyebrows all along the musical phrase | Eyebrows | I do things lightly. | EXPRESSION OF PHYSICAL STATE | Imitation of light movement | DIR. ICON. | Play/sing piano (Figure 12.1) | REQUEST | Intensity indication | IND. ICON. |
| 12. Raises eyebrows (head recessed in shoulders) | Eyebrows | I'm careful. | EXPRESSION OF MENTAL STATE | Circumspection gaze | GEN. COD. | Be precise and accurate. | REQUEST | Accuracy gaze | SPEC. COD. |

*(Continued)*

**TABLE 12.2** (Continued)

| 1. Signal | 2. Parameter | 3. Literal meaning | 4. Performative | 5. Type | 6. Semiotic device | 7. Indirect meaning | 8. Performative | 9. Type | 10. Semiotic device |
|---|---|---|---|---|---|---|---|---|---|
| 13. Internal eyebrows raised | Eyebrows | I feel sadness → feel/express sadness. | EXPRESSION ENACTED EMOTION Meaning | Sad gaze | GEN. COD. | Play yearning | REQUEST | Expression Indication | SPEC. COD. |
| 14. Frowning eyebrows | Eyebrows | I feel anger. | EXPRESSION ENACTED EMOTION Movement | Angry gaze | GEN. COD. | feel/ express anger → play forte | REQUEST | Intensity Indication | IND. ICON. |
| 15. Squints eyes | Eyelids | I strive. | EXPRESSION PHYSICAL STATE | Imitation effort movement | DIR. ICON. | Play/sing "sforzato" | REQUEST | Intensity Indication | IND. ICON. |
| 16. Closed eyes | Eyelids | I am concentrating. | EXPRESSION MENTAL STATE | Concentration gaze | GEN. COD. | I want to listen well/I'm enjoying this pleasure. (Figure 12.3) | EXPRESSION OF OUTCOME EMOTION | Motivational strategy | SPEC. COD. |
| 17. Tense squinted eyes (retracted torso) | Eyelids | I feel disgust. | EXPRESSION OUTCOME EMOTION | Disgusted gaze | GEN. COD. | It is not good like this. | REPROACH | Negative feedback | IND. ICON. |

**FIGURE 12.1**   Alessandro Anniballi *raised eyebrows*: "piano".

**TABLE 12.3** Functions and Meanings of the Conductor's Gaze

| Degree of communicativeness | Conduction function | |
|---|---|---|
| Communicative technical | Request | Start |
| | | Continuity |
| | | Intensity |
| | | Pitch |
| | | Expressivity |
| Expressive | Expression of physical state | |
| | Expression of mental state | |
| | Expression of outcome emotion | |
| | Expression of meaning-oriented enacted emotion | |
| | Expression of movement-oriented enacted emotion | |
| Communicative interactional | Warning | |
| | Threat | |
| | Reproach | |
| | Praise | |
| | Attention request | |
| Noncommunicative | Information acquisition | |

If the use of eyes by the performer is not always communicative, in the conductor it almost always has the goal of communicating. Most typically communicative are the cases in which his eyes order to start or to continue and when he provides indications of intensity or pitch or expressivity.

But in addition to the need to give technical instructions, the maestro, both in rehearsal and in concert, also engages in a social interaction with the ensemble, albeit always functional to the performance: his glances therefore also communicate "interactional" performatives, such as warnings, threats, requests for attention, praise and reproach (acts of feedback) or acts of general recommendation (e.g. the "accuracy" gaze n. 12).

Then come the signals that we have called expressive because they communicate, perhaps tacitly, instinctively, not as consciously calculated, physical states such as effort, mental states such as concentration, or emotional states.

In fact, the maestro's glances sometimes express emotions, just as we have seen in the pianist: "outcome felt emotions" (disgust, admiration, or pleasure of how the music is being played); "enacted emotions" such as sadness or anger (Table 12.2, lines 13 and 14). But even this is done by the conductor's eyes in order to communicate: within outcome felt emotions, the enjoyment about how the music is being expressed, to give feedback and to motivate: disgust, reproach for a low performance, and, within acted emotions, sadness – meaning-oriented – are expressed to let the musicians imprint it in the piece, anger – movement-oriented – to give the intensity indication "play forte".

On the other hand, the conductor seems to lack gaze items about "process emotions", that we have instead seen in the pianist, perhaps because, unlike the performer who directly produces music, the conductor does so "through third parties". His emotions are about a process put in place by others, so he only communicates the "outcome emotions"; while if he himself is excited or fearful about the performance, he may try not to let these emotions leak out so as not to infect the musicians.

Finally, what might be seen as a "zero degree" of communicativeness is the "control gaze" (Table 12.2, n. 3) by which the conductor *looks at all musicians* before starting. At a first level, this is not a "gaze to communicate", even in the sense of expressing anything, but a "gaze to look", i.e. not intended to give information to the ensemble, but only to get information for the conductor himself: to check if they are ready. However, even this seemingly uncommunicative way of looking gradually becomes a signal to the orchestra members asking to be ready: we start!

### 12.2.4 Bernstein's gaze

One might wonder whether identifying systematicity in the use of a single conductor's gaze is sufficient to support the existence of a shared lexicon.

It seems so: even in other conductors, such as Herbert von Karajan, Daniel Baremboim and Riccardo Muti, the same items of gaze identified in Anniballi are used with the same meanings.

One more qualitative study then (Poggi et al., 2020) examined the use of gaze by Leonard Bernstein in Haydn's symphony n° 88. The "Finale" of the symphony, "Allegro con spirito", was analysed by two independent judges while watching the video in mute mode to avoid being influenced by the corresponding sound (Table 12.4).

**TABLE 12.4** Leonard Bernstein's Gaze

| Time | Gaze | Meaning | Function |
|---|---|---|---|
| 0.23 | Raised eyebrows | Play piano | Intensity |
| 0.29 | Half-closed eyes | I feel ecstasy, enjoyment. → | Outcome emotions → |
| | | You are playing well. | Feedback |
| 0.33 | Irises leftward + Raised eyebrows | I address you to my left. → | Attention request → |
| | | Prepare for the start. | Start (Figure 12.2) |
| 0.38 | Fast eye closure | Yes → | Approval → |
| | | This is good. | Feedback |
| 0.43 | Frowning eyebrows | Play with determination. | Expression |
| 0.47 | Half-open eyes + Raised eyebrows | I am serene. → | Meaning-oriented emotion |
| | | Play in a serene way. | |

**FIGURE 12.2**   Attention – Start.

**TABLE 12.5** Functions and Meanings of Bernstein's Gaze

| Function | Meaning | n. |
|---|---|---|
| Communicative technical | Start | 16 |
| | Intensity | 11 |
| | Pitch | 1 |
| | Tempo | 1 |
| | Duration | 2 |
| | Expression | 12 |
| Expressive | Concentration | 4 |
| | Outcome emotion | 5 |
| | Meaning-oriented emotion | 4 |
| Communicative interactional | Attention request | 8 |
| | Feedback | 10 |
| Total | | 74 |

In the analysed fragment of Haydn's symphony, Leonard Bernstein produces 74 gaze signals, that can be grouped into 11 types of gaze, having the same meanings and the same functions as those of Table 12.2 (see Table 12.5).

## 12.3 Can we all understand the maestro?

So far, we can say that the gaze in conducting constitutes a fairly systematic and shared lexicon, at least on the production side: different conductors use the same gazes to communicate the same meanings, functional to the same elements of the performance. But let us now turn to the side of signal comprehension: are these meanings understood – and easily understood – by the musicians in an ensemble? Moreover, can they be understood by a layman who does not sing in a choir or play in an ensemble? In order to answer this question, a perceptual study was carried out (Poggi & Ansani, 2018b).

Eight types of gaze, drawn from the ones in Table 12.2, were selected, meaning, respectively: "I am concentrating", "play forte", "play piano", "this is a high pitch note", "play sforzato", "play in a poignant way", "start now", "I reproach you: error". An experiment was designed taking these eight gaze items and the level of expertise of participants (expert/not expert) as independent variables and the comprehension of the meanings of the eight gaze items as the dependent variable. The research question was whether participants attribute to each gaze the same meanings as those hypothesised in Table 12.2, resulting from the previous qualitative study. A questionnaire was built using as a stimulus for each of the eight gaze items a videoclip of one of four conductors, Anniballi, von Karajan, Muti or Barenboim, while adding two "neutral" gazes as control stimuli. Each stimulus was followed by two questions, an open one and a multiple-choice one: the open question asked to view the video (without audio) and to explain in words what the conductor wanted to communicate by that face and what let the participant think the meaning was just that one. The multiple-choice question asked to assess, on a 5-points Likert scale, how plausible it was, for that gaze, each of 13 interpretations: "play piano", "play passionately", "play loud", "with anger", "more accurately", "start now", "play in a poignant way", "play progressively louder and louder", "this is a high note", "play sforzato", "I am concentrated", "play softer and softer", "I reproach you". Finally a set of questions followed aimed at establishing the participant's level of musical expertise, on the basis of one or more of the following criteria: (1) taking part in an orchestra, a choir, or a band, (2) playing an instrument, (3) regularly attending concerts. The questionnaire was submitted to 197 participants, 133 females and 64 males, mean age 22.3.

The results tell us that the gaze items most frequently correctly interpreted are the technical ones: "start", "forte" and "piano". In the cases where the meaning chosen by a participant is different from the hypothesised one, there is often a connection with it: for example, instead of interpreting as "forte", the subject answers *with anger* or *euphoric*, instead of "piano", *with precision*.

The same for open questions; for example, the gaze for "strong" is interpreted as *scolding someone, anger, violence, grit, eagerness*: these are all meanings alluding to high arousal movements such as those performed to play or sing loudly. They are further proof for the existence of a device of indirect iconicity, whereby emotional or physical states are used for indications of intensity.

Coming to the second independent variable, the participants' level of musical expertise, no differences result between musicians and non-musicians in the recognition of the gaze items presented. Actually, even a previous work on the comprehension of conductors' gestures had shown their generalised comprehensibility for non-musicians too (Poggi & Ansani, 2016; Poggi, D'Errico & Ansani, 2021).

Therefore the conductor's signals, whether gazes or gestures, are not a specific jargon because they exploit the same devices of signal creation as do gestures and verbal languages, such as modality transposition through metaphor and metonymy, and they communicate meanings making use of codified, emotional and iconic expressions.

## Note

1 My special gratitude goes to the pianist Marcella Crudeli and to the conductors Fabrizio Santi and Alessandro Anniballi, who gave me the gift of so many precious data for my studies, as well as so many hours with the joy of music.

# CONCLUSION: THE RICHNESS OF GAZE

The language of our eyes follows systematic and complex rules. It has a phonology and perhaps even a morphology; it has no syntax, since its messages count as complete sentences. But it does have a semantics, governed by principles similar to those of verbal languages, such as polysemy and synonymy, and of considerable richness, since it can convey many different kinds of meaning: not only emotions but also events and properties of the world, our relations of affection or power with others, the intentions of our verbal and nonverbal communicative acts, the relations between parts of our speech, the acts of asking and giving turn and providing backchannel in conversation. Our gaze is also governed by sociolinguistic, social and situational rules of opportunity that tell us not only how to communicate a specific meaning with our eyes but also if, where, how and when to do so. And while the rules that determine what a particular gaze means are largely universal, the norms of use are culturally determined. Moreover, the meanings we convey with our gaze are intertwined with the multimodality of our communication, deliberately or unconsciously supplementing, complementing, sometimes contradicting what we say with words or gestures.

Thanks to this rich structure, gaze allows us not only to influence others through communication, persuasion or charisma but also to make teaching more efficient and learning easier and more motivating. In music-making, as well as conveying emotions, it can give technical indications and promote synchrony in singing or playing together.

What is our gaze, then? A complex and sophisticated communication system, the nature of which can be further explored by future research.

DOI: 10.4324/9781032678344-13

# REFERENCES

Ajello A.M., Pontecorvo C., Zucchermaglio C. (1991), *Discutendo si impara: interazione sociale e conoscenza a scuola*, La Nuova Italia, Roma.

Alibali M.W., Nathan M.J. (2012), *Embodiment in mathematics teaching and learning: Evidence from learners' and teachers' gestures*, in "Journal of the Learning Sciences" 21, 2, pp. 247–286.

Allwood J. (2003), *Meaning potential and context. Some consequences for the analysis of variation in meaning*, in H. Cuyckens, R. Dirven, J.R. Taylor (Eds.), *Cognitive approaches to lexical semantics*, Mouton de Gruyter, Berlin and New York, pp. 29–65.

Allwood J., Nivre J., Ahlsén E. (1992), *On the semantics and pragmatics of linguistic feedback*, in "Journal of Semantics" 9, pp. 1–26.

Amidon E.J., Hunter E. (1966), *Improving teaching: The analysis of classroom verbal interaction*, Holt, Rinehart and Wilson, New York.

Anolli L. (2011), *Fondamenti di Psicologia della Comunicazione*, Il Mulino, Bologna.

Ansani A. (2020), *Geert Brône and Bert Oben (Eds.): Eye-tracking in interaction*, in "Corpus Pragmatics" 4, pp. 473–477.

Antinucci F. (1975), *I presupposti teorici della linguistica di Franz Bopp*, in U. Vignuzzi, G. Ruggiero, R. Simone (a cura di), *Teoria e Storia degli studi linguistici*, Bulzoni, Roma.

Argyle M. (1990), *Bodily communication*, Routledge, London.

Argyle M., Cook M. (1976), *Gaze and mutual gaze*, Cambridge University Press, Cambridge.

Attardo S., Eisterhold J., Hay J., Poggi I. (2003), *Multimodal markers of irony and sarcasm*, in "Humor. International Journal of Humor Research" 16, 2, pp. 243–260.

Attardo S., Pickering L. (2023), *Eye tracking in linguistics*, Bloomsbury Publishing, New York.

Austin J.L. (1962), *How to do things with words*, Oxford University Press, Oxford.

Babad E. (2005), *Nonverbal behavior in education*, in J. Harrigan, R. Rosenthal, K. Scherer (Eds.), *The new handbook of methods in nonverbal behavior research*, Oxford University Press, Oxford, pp. 283–311.

Bandler R., Grinder J. (1979), *Frogs into princes: Neuro linguistic programming*, Real People Press, Boulder, CO.

Bara B.G. (1999), *Pragmatica cognitiva: I processi mentali della comunicazione*, Bollati Boringhieri, Torino.

Baron-Cohen S., Wheelwright S., Jolliffe T. (1997), *Is there a "language of the eyes"? Evidence from normal adults, and adults with autism or Asperger syndrome*, in "Visual Cognition" 1997, 4, pp. 311–331.

Bateson M., Nettle D., Roberts G. (2006), *Cues of being watched enhance cooperation in a real-world setting*, in "Biology Letters" 2, 3, pp. 412–414.

Baumgartner E., Devescovi A., D'Amico S. (2000), *Il lessico psicologico dei bambini*, Carocci, Roma.

Berlin B., Kay P. (1969), *Basic colour terms: Their universality and evolution*, University of California Press, Berkeley, CA.

Bevacqua E., Heylen D., Pelachaud C., Tellier M. (2007), *Facial feedback signals for ecas*, in *Proceedings of AISB'07: Artificial and ambient intelligence*, Newcastle University, Newcastle upon Tyne, UK.

Bishop L., Cancino-Chacón C., Goebl W. (2022), *Beyond synchronization: Body gestures and gaze direction in duo performance*, in "arXiv preprint arXiv:2201.13297", https://doi.org/10.48550/arXiv.2201.13297

Bonsignore R. (2002), *Il lessico dello sguardo: una verifica empirica*, Tesi di Laurea non pubblicata, Università Roma Tre, Roma.

Boyes-Braem P. (1981), *Significant features of the handshape in American sign language*, Unpublished PhD. Thesis, University of California, Berkeley.

Brône G., Oben B. (Eds.) (2018), *Eye-tracking in interaction*, John Benjamins, Amsterdam.

Brookes H. (2004), *A repertoire of South African quotable gestures*, in "Journal of Linguistic Anthropology" 14, 2, pp. 186–224.

Brossard A. (1992), *La psychologie du regard: de la perception visuelle aux regards*, Delachaux et Niestlé, Paris.

Calbris G. (1990), *The semiotics of French Gestures*, Indiana University Press, Bloomington, IN.

Calbris G. (2003), *L'expression gestuelle de la pensée d'un homme politique*, Ed. du CNRS, Paris.

Calbris G. (2011), *Elements of meaning in gesture*, John Benjamins, Amsterdam.

Cañigueral R., Hamilton A.F.D.C. (2019), *The role of eye gaze during natural social interactions in typical and autistic people*, in "Frontiers in Psychology" 10, p. 560.

Capella J.H. (1993), *The facial feedback hypothesis in human interaction: Review and speculation*, in "Journal of Language and Social Psychology" 12, pp. 13–29.

Castelfranchi C. (1975), *Le voci del sedere*, in D. Parisi (a cura di), *Studi per un modello del linguaggio*, Quaderni della ricerca scientifica CNR, Roma, 89, pp. 55–88.

Castelfranchi C. (1981), *Scopi esterni*, in "Rassegna Italiana di Sociologia" XXII, 1, pp. 329–381.

Castelfranchi C. (1988), *Che figura. Emozioni e immagine sociale*, Il Mulino, Bologna.

Castelfranchi C., Parisi D. (1980), *Linguaggio, conoscenze e scopi*, Il Mulino, Bologna.

Castelfranchi C., Poggi I. (1990), *Blushing as a discourse: Was Darwin wrong?*, in R. Crozier (Ed.), *Shyness and embarrassment. Perspectives from social psychology*, Cambridge University Press, New York, pp. 230–251.

Castelfranchi C., Poggi I. (1998), *Bugie, finzioni, sotterfugi. Per una scienza dell'inganno*, Carocci, Roma.

Cavé C., Guaïtella I., Bertrand R., Santi S., Harlay F., Espesser R. (1996), *About the relationship between eyebrow movements and F0 variations*, in *Proceedings of the 4th international conference on spoken language processing (ICSLP)*, Philadelphia, pp. 2175–2179, https://doi.org/10.21437/ICSLP.1996-551

Cavicchio F., Magno Caldognetto E., Poggi I. (2005), *Functions and cues of Irony, Humour and Ridicule in a political trial*, Oral presentation at the 9th international pragmatics conference, Riva del Garda, 15–20 July 2005, International Pragmatics Association.

Cerrato L. (2005), *Linguistic functions of head nods*, in J. Allwood, B. Dorriots, S. Nicholson (Eds.), *Multimodal communication. Proceedings from the second nordic conference on multimodal communication*, Gothenburg Papers in Theoretical Linguistics, Department of Linguistics, Goteborg University, Goteborg, pp. 137–152.

Chiera A., Ansani A., Sessa I., Cataldo V., Schettino L., Poggi I. (2022), *Gestures and pauses to help thought: Hands, voice, and silence in the tourist guide's speech*, in "Cognitive Processes".

Chomsky N. (1965), *Aspects of the theory of Syntax*, The MIT Press, Cambridge, MA.

Clift R. (2024) What's in a look? The accountability of gaze in trajectories to conflict, in *Frontiers in Psychology* 15.

Conte R. (1997), *L'obbedienza intelligente. Come e perché si rispettano le norme*, Laterza, Bari.

Conte R., Castelfranchi C. (1995), *Cognitive and social action*, University College, London.

Cook M. (1977), *Gaze and mutual gaze in social encounters: How long – and when – we look others "in the eye" is one of the main signals in nonverbal communication*, in "American Scientist" 65, 3, pp. 328–333.

Costa M., Ricci Bitti P.E. (2003), *Il chiasso delle sopracciglia*, in "Psicologia Contemporanea", 176, pp. 38–47.

Csikszentmihalyi M. (1990), *Flow: The psychology of optimal experience*, Harper & Row, New York.

Dal Monte R. (2001), *L'occhionario. Una ricerca sul lessico dello sguardo*, Tesi di Laurea non pubblicata, Università Roma Tre, Roma.

Dalton K.M., Nacewicz B.M., Johnstone T., Schaefer H.S., Gernsbacher M.A., Goldsmith H.H., Alexander A.L., Davidson R.J. (2005), *Gaze fixation and the neural circuitry of face processing in autism*, in "Nature Neuroscience", 8, 4, pp. 519–526.

Darwin C. (1872), *The expression of emotions in man and animals*, Murray, London.

Davis J.I., Senghas A., Ochsner K. (2009), *How does facial feedback modulate emotional experience?*, in "Journal of Research in Personality" 43, 5, pp. 822–829.

De Carolis B., D'Errico F., Macchiarulo N., Palestra G. (2019), *"Engaged faces": Measuring and monitoring student engagement from face and gaze behavior*, in *Proceedings of IEEE/WIC/ACM international conference on web intelligence-companion volume*, pp. 80–85, https://doi.org/10.1145/3358695.3361748

De Paolis F. (2005), *Il lessico dello sguardo*, Tesi di Laurea non pubblicata, Università di Roma La Sapienza.

D'Errico F., Poggi I. (2013), *Pride in mind and face*, in A. Freitas-Magalhães (Ed.), *Emotional expression: The brain and the face*, University Fernando Pessoa Press, Porto, pp. 281–309.

D'Errico F., Poggi I. (2016), *Social emotions. A challenge for sentiment analysis and user models*, in M. Tkalčič, B. De Carolis, M. de Gemmis, A. Odić, A. Košir (Eds.), *Emotions and personality in personalized services. Models, evaluation and applications*, Springer, Berlin, pp. 13–34.

D'Errico F., Signorello R., Demolin D., Poggi I. (2013), *The perception of charisma from voice. A cross-cultural study*, in *Proceedings of the 2013 humaine association conference on affective computing and intelligent interaction (ACII)*, pp. 552–557, https://doi.org/10.1109/ACII.2013.97

Descartes R. (1649), *Les Passions de l'ame*, Henry Le Gras, Amsterdam.

Dionisio D.P., Granholm E., Hillix W.A., Perrine W.F. (2001), *Differentiation of deception using pupillary responses as an index of cognitive processing*, in "Psychophisiology" 38, 2, pp. 205–211.

Dodd M. (1939), *Through embassy eyes*, Harcourt Brace, New York.

Doherty-Sneddon G., Phelps F.G. (2005), *Gaze aversion: A response to cognitive or social difficulty?*, in "Memory & Cognition" 33, 4, pp. 727–733.

Dovidio J.F., Ellyson S.L., Keating C.F., Heltman K., Brown C.E. (1988), *The relationship of social power to visual displays of dominance between men and women*, in "Journal of Personality and Social Psychology" 54, 2, pp. 233–242.

Duchenne G.B.A. (1862), *The mechanism of human facial expression* (Edited and Translated by R.A. Cuthbertson), Cambridge University Press, Cambridge.

Duranti A. (1992), *Language and bodies in social space: Samoan ceremonial greetings*, in "American Anthropologist" 94, 3, pp. 657–691.

Egurtzegi A., Blasi D.E., Bornkessel-Schlesewsky I., Laka I., Meyer M., Bickel B., Sauppe S. (2022), *Cross-linguistic differences in case marking shape neural power dynamics and gaze behavior during sentence planning*, in "Brain and Language" 230, July, p. 105127.

Eibl-Eibesfeldt I. (1972), *Similarities and differences between cultures in expressive movements*, in R. Hinde (Ed.), *Non-verbal communication*, Cambridge University Press, Cambridge.

Ekman P. (1979), *About brows: Emotional and conversational signals*, in M. von Cranach, K. Foppa, W. Lepenies, D. Ploog (Eds.), *Human ethology: Claims and limits of a new discipline*, Cambridge University Press, Cambridge, pp. 169–202.

Ekman P., Friesen W.V. (1971), *Constants across cultures in the face and emotion*, in "Journal of Personality and Social Psychology" 17, pp. 124–129.

Ekman P., Friesen W.V. (1978), *Facial action coding system*, Consulting Psychologists Press, Palo Alto.

Ekman P., Friesen W.V. (1982), *Felt, false, and miserable smiles*, in "Journal of Nonverbal Behavior" 6, 4, pp. 238–252.

Ekman P., Friesen W.V., Simons R.C. (1985), *Is the startle reaction an emotion?*, in "Journal of Personality and Social Psychology" 49, 5, pp. 1416–1426.

Emery N.J. (2000), *The eyes have it: The neuroethology, function and evolution of social gaze*, in "Neuroscience and Biobehavioral Reviews" 24, pp. 581–604.

Engelhardt P.E., Ferreira F., Patsenko E.G. (2010), *Pupillometry reveals processing load during spoken language comprehension*, in "Quarterly Journal of Experimental Psychology" 63, 4, pp. 639–645.

Englehart J.M. (2009), *Teacher–student interaction*, in *International handbook of research on teachers and teaching*, Springer US, Boston, MA, pp. 711–722.

Ewbank M.P., Jennings C., Calder A.J. (2009), *Why are you angry with me? Facial expressions of threat influence perception of gaze direction*, in "Journal of Vision" 9, 12, pp. 16–16.

Ewing L., Rhodes G., Pellicano E. (2010), *Have you got the look? Gaze direction affects judgements of facial attractiveness*, in "Visual Cognition" 18, 3, pp. 321–330.

Exline R.V. (1963), *Explorations in the process of person perception: Visual interaction in relation to competition, sex, and need for affiliation*, in "Journal of Personality" 31, 1, pp. 1–20.

Falck-Ytter T., Carlström C., Johansson M. (2014), *Eye contact modulates cognitive processing differently in children with autism*, in "Child Development" 86, 1, pp. 37–47.

Fele G., Paoletti I. (2003), *L'interazione in classe*, il Mulino, Bologna.

Ferrara F., Nemirovsky R., Terc C. (2005), *Connecting talk, gesture, and eye motion for the microanalysis of mathematics learning*, in "International Group for the Psychology of Mathematics Education" 1, p. 138.

Feyereisen P., Lignian A. (1981), *Gaze direction in aphasics during speaking: A pilot study*, in "Current Psychology of Cognition" 1, pp. 287–298.

Fiske S.T. (2012), *Managing ambivalent prejudices: Smart-but-cold and warm-but-dumb stereotypes*, in "Annals, AAPSS" 639, January.

Flanders N.A. (1965), *Teacher influence, pupil attitudes, and achievement: Ned A. Flanders* (No. 12), Cooperative research monograph, US Department of Health, Education, and Welfare, Office of Education.

Fornés Pallicer M.A., Puig Rodríguez-Escalona M. (2011), *Mirar de reojo y fijar la mirada en los textos latinos/Looking sideways and staring in Latin texts*, in "Cuadernos de Filología Clásica. Estudios Latinos" 31, 2, pp. 213–234.

Fornés Pallicer M.A., Puig Rodríguez-Escalona M. (2019), *Comunicar con la mirada en la Roma antigua: el movimiento de párpados*, in "Faventia" 38, pp. 7–21. ISSN: 0210–7570, https://revistes.uab.cat/faventia/article/view/v38-fornes-puig

Fornés Pallicer M.A., Puig Rodríguez-Escalona M. (2024), *Non-verbal communication in Ancient Rome: Eyebrow gestures*, in "Languages" 9, 3, p. 92, https://doi.org/10.3390/languages9030092

Fox E., Damhanovic L. (2006), *The eyes are sufficient to produce a threat superiority effect*, in "Emotion" 6, 3, pp. 534–539.

Fukuda K. (2001), *Eye blinks: New indices for the detection of deception*, in "International Journal of Psychophysiology" 40, pp. 239–245. http://doi.org/10.1016/S0167-8760(00)00192-6

Galli de' Paratesi N. (1969), *Le brutte parole. Semantica dell'eufemismo*, Mondadori, Milano.

Giacomantonio M., Jordan J., Federico F., van den Assem M.J., van Dolder D. (2018), *The evil eye: Eye gaze and competitiveness in social decision making*, in "European Journal of Social Psychology" 48, 3, pp. 388–396.

Glaholt M.G., Reingold E.M. (2011), *Eye movement monitoring as a process tracing methodology in decision making research*, in "Journal of Neuroscience, Psychology, and Economics" 4, 2, p. 125.

Glowinski D., Mancini M., Cowie R., Camurri A., Chiorri C., Doherty C. (2013), *The movements made by performers in a skilled quartet: A distinctive pattern, and the function that it serves*, in "Frontiers in Psychology" 4, p. 841.

Goldin-Meadow S., Kim S., Singer M. (1999), *What the teacher's hands tell the student's mind about math*, in "Journal of Educational Psychology" 91, 4, p. 720.

Goodwin C. (1981), *Conversational organization: Interaction between speakers and hearers*, Academic Press, New York.

Grammer, K., Schiefenhövel, W., Schleidt, B., Eibl-Eibesfeldt, I. (12 January 1987), *Patterns on the face: The eyebrow flash in crosscultural comparison*, in "Ethology" 77, 4, pp. 279–299. https://doi.org/10.1111/j.1439-0310.1988.tb00211.x

Guaïtella I., Cavé C., Santi S. (1993), *Relations entre gestes et voix: le cas des sourcils ed de la fréquence fondamentale*, in *Actes du colloque Images et Langage*, Vol. I, CNRS, Paris, pp. 261–268.

Gullotta G., Tuosto E.M. (2017), *Il volto nell'investigazione e nel processo*, Giuffrè, Milano.

Hess E.H. (1965), *Attitude and pupil size*, in "Scientific American" 212, 4, pp. 46–55.

Hess E.H. (1975), *The role of pupil size in communication*, in "Scientific American" 233, 5, pp. 110–119.

Hess E.H., Polt J.M. (1960), *Pupil size in relation to mental activity during simple problem-solving*, in "Science" 143, 3611, pp. 1190–1192.

Hietanen J.O., Syrjämäki A.H., Zilliacus P.K., Hietanen J.K. (2018), *Eye contact reduces lying*, in "Consciousness and Cognition" 66, pp. 65–73.

Hyönä J., Radach R., Deubel H. (Eds.) (2003), *The mind's eye. Cognitive and applied aspects of eye movements research*, Elsevier, Amsterdam.

Iizuka Y. (1994), *Gaze during speaking as related to shyness*, in "Perceptual and Motor Skills" 78, 3 (suppl.), pp. 1259–1264.

Ijuin K., Horiuchi Y., Umata I., Yamamoto S. (2015), *Eye gaze analyses in L1 and L2 conversations: Difference in interaction structures*, in *International conference on text, speech, and dialogue*, Springer, Cham, pp. 114–121.

Ijuin K., Jokinen K. (2020), *Exploring gaze behaviour and perceived personality traits*, in "Human Computer Interaction" 14, 2020, pp. 504–512.

Ijuin K., Umata I., Kato T., Yamamoto S. (2018), *Difference in eye gaze for floor apportionment in native- and second-language conversations*, in "Journal of Nonverbal Behavior" 42, pp. 113–128.

Jakobson R., Halle M. (1971), *Fundamentals of language*, Mouton, The Hague.

Jokinen K. (2011), *Turn taking, utterance density, and gaze patterns as cues to conversational activity*, in *Proceedings of ICMI 2011 workshop multimodal corpora for machine learning: Taking stock and road mapping the future*, Alicante, Spain, pp. 31–36. Association of Computing Machinery, New York.

Jokinen K., Furukawa H., Nishida M., Yamamoto S. (2013), *Gaze and turn-taking behavior in casual conversational interactions*, in "ACM Transactions on Interactive Intelligent Systems (TiiS)" 3, 2, pp. 1–30.

Kajimura S., Nomura M. (2016), *When we cannot speak: Eye contact disrupts resources available to cognitive control processes during verb generation*, in "Cognition" 157, pp. 352–357.

Kalma A. (1992), *Gazing in triads: A powerful signal in floor apportionment*, in "British Journal of Social Psychology" 31, 1, pp. 21–39.

Kampe K.K., Frith C.D., Dolan R.J., Frith U. (2001), *Reward value of attractiveness and gaze*, in "Nature" 413, 6856, p. 589.

Kang O., Wheatley T. (2017), *Pupil dilation patterns spontaneously synchronize across individuals during shared attention*, in "Journal of Experimental Psychology: General" 146, 4, pp. 569–576.

Kendon A. (1967), *Some functions of gaze-direction in social interaction*, in "Acta Psychologica" 26, pp. 22–63.

Kendon A. (1988), *Sign languages of aboriginal Australia. Cultural, semiotic, and communicative perspectives*, Cambridge University Press, Cambridge.

Kendon A. (1992), *Abstraction in gesture*, in "Semiotica" 90, 3–4, pp. 225–250.

Kendon A. (2004), *Gesture. Visible action as utterance*, Cambridge University Press, Cambridge.

Kendon A., Cook M. (1969), *The consistency of gaze patterns in social interaction*, in "British Journal of Psychology" 60, 4, pp. 481–494.

Kita S., Essegbey J. (2001), *Pointing left in Ghana: How a taboo on the use of the left hand influences gestural practice*, in "Gesture" 1, 1, pp. 72–95.

Krahmer E., Ruttkay Z., Swerts M., Wesselink W. (2002), *Pitch, eyebrows and the perception of focus*, in *Proceedings of speech prosody 2002*, Aix en Provence, France, pp. 443–446. International Society for Conversational Analysis, Los Angeles, CA.

Kreidlin G.E. (2002), *Neverbal'naia semiotika: Iazyk tela i estestvennyi iazyk* [Non-verbal semiotics: Body language and natural language], Novoe literaturnoe obozrenie, Moscow (Academic Library Series).

Kret M.E., Sjak-Shie E.E. (2019), *Preprocessing pupil size data: Guidelines and code*, in "Behavior Research Methods" 51, pp. 1336–1342. http://doi.org/10.3758/s13428-018-1075-y

Lanthier S.N., Jarick M., Zhu M.J., Byun C.S.J., Kingstone A. (2019), *Socially communicative eye contact and gender affect memory*, in "Frontiers in Psychology" 10, p. 1128.

Larsson M., Pedersen N.L., Stattin H. (2007), *Associations between iris characteristics and personality in adulthood*, in "Biological Psychology" 75, 2, pp. 165–175.

Lavater J.K. (1772), *Physiognomische fragmente, zur befoerderung der menschenkenntniss und menschenliebe*, Winterthur, Leipzig (trad. it. *Regole fisionomiche o sia osservazioni su di alcuni lineamenti caratteristici e su le relazioni della fisionomia della umana razza con quellade' bruti*, Vallardi, Milano 1819).

Leal S., Vrij A. (2008), *Blinking during and after lying*, in "Journal of Nonverbal Behavior" 32, pp. 187–194. http://doi.org/10.1007/s10919-008-0051-0

Leder H., Mitrovic A., Goller J. (2016), *How beauty determines gaze! Facial attractiveness and gaze duration in images of real world scenes*, in "i-Perception" 7, 4, p. 2041669516664355.

Lefcourt H.M., Wine J. (1969), *Internal versus external control of reinforcement and the deployment of attention in experimental situations*, in "Canadian Journal of Behavioral Science" 1, pp. 167–181.

Lewis M. (1995), *Self-conscious emotions*, in "American Scientist" 83, 1, pp. 68–78.

Lewis M. (2008), *Self-conscious emotions: Embarrassment, pride, shame, and guilt*, in M. Lewis, J.M. Haviland-Jones, L.F. Barrett (Eds.), *Handbook of emotions*, The Guilford Press, New York, pp. 742–756.

Liberati M.F. (2002), *Lo sguardo dell'insegnante*. Unpublished Degree thesis, Roma Tre University, Rome.

Lopis D., Conty L. (2019), *Investigating eye contact effect on people's name retrieval in normal aging and in Alzheimer's disease*, in "Frontiers in Psychology" 10, p. 1218.

Lorini E., Castelfranchi C. (2007), *The cognitive structure of surprise: Looking for basic principles*, in "Topoi" 26, 1, pp. 133–149.

Lumbelli L. (1981), *Educazione come discorso: quando dire è fare educazione*, Il Mulino, Bologna.

Macedonia M. (2019), *Embodied learning: Why at school the mind needs the body*, "Frontiers in Psychology" 10.

Magli P. (1995), *Il volto e l'anima, Fisiognomica e passioni*, Bompiani, Milano.

Mandelli A. (1997), *Antonio Guarnieri*, Edizioni MC Musica Classica, Milano.

Marchak F.M. (2013), *Detecting false intent using eye blink measures*, in "Frontiers in Psychology" 4, https://doi.org/10.3389/fpsyg.2013.00736

Mathôt S. (2018), *Pupillometry: Psychology, physiology, and function*, in "Journal of Cognition" 1, 1, pp. 1–23.

McCarthy A., Lee K., Itakura S., Muir D.W. (2006), *Culturaldisplay rules drive eye gaze during thinking*, in "Journal of Cross-Cultural Psychology" 37, 6, pp. 717–722.

McIntyre N.A., Mulder K.T., Mainhard M.T. (2020), *Looking to relate: Teacher gaze and culture in student-rated teacher interpersonal behaviour*, in "Social Psychology of Education" 23, 2, pp. 411–431.

McKay K.T., Grainger S.A., Coundouris S.P., Skorich D.P., Phillips L.H., Henry J.D. (2021), *Visual attentional orienting by eye gaze: A meta-analytic review of the gaze-cueing effect*, in "Psychological Bulletin" 147, 12, pp. 1269–1289.

McNeill D. (1992), *Hand and mind*, University of Chicago Press, Chicago.

Merola G., Poggi I. (2003), *Multimodality and gestures in the teacher's communication*, in A. Camurri, G. Volpe (Eds.), *Gesture-based communication in human-computer interaction*, Springer, Berlin, pp. 101–111.

Miceli M. (1992), *How to make someone feel guilty: Strategies of guilt inducement and their goals*, in "Journal for the Theory of Social Behavior" 22, 1, pp. 81–104.

Miceli M. (2008), *Il pianto. Cause e scopi*, in I. Poggi (a cura di), *La mente del cuore. Scienze cognitive delle emozioni*, Armando, Roma, pp. 138–162.

Miceli M., Castelfranchi C. (2003), *Crying: Discussing its basic reasons and uses*, in "New Ideas in Psychology" 21, pp. 247–273.

Miceli M., Castelfranchi C. (2014), *Expectancy and emotions*, Oxford University Press, London.

Miller M., Galanter E., Pribram K.H. (1960), *Plans and the structure of behavior*, Holt, Rinehart and Winston, New York.

Minarikova E., Smidekova Z., Janik M., Holmqvist K. (2021), *Teachers' professional vision: teachers'gaze during the act of teaching and after the event*, in "Frontiers in Education", 3 September, Section Teacher Education, https://doi.org/10.3389/feduc.2021.716579

Mizzau M. (1997), *Il falso e il finto*, in M.A. Bonfantini, C. Castelfranchi, A. Martone, I. Poggi, J. Vincent (a cura di), *Menzogna e simulazione*, Edizioni Scientifiche Italiane, Napoli, pp. 121–129.

Moriuchi J.M., Klin A., Jones W. (2017), *Mechanisms of diminished attention to eyes in autism*, in "American Journal of Psychiatry" 174, 1, pp. 26–35.

Morris D. (1977), *Manwatching: A field guide to human behavior*, Jonathan Cape, London.

Morris D., Collett P., Marsh P., O'Shaughnessy M. (1979), *Gestures. Their origins and distribution*, Jonathan Cape, London.

Müller C. (2004), *Forms and uses of the palm up open hand: A case of a gesture family?*, in C. Müller, R. Posner (Eds.), *The semantics and pragmatics of everyday gestures*, Weidler, Berlin, pp. 233–256.

Musicus A., Tal A., Wansink B. (2015), *Eyes in the aisles: Why is Cap'n Crunch looking down at my child?*, in "Environment and Behavior" 47, 7, pp. 715–733.

Nation K., Penny S. (2008), *Sensitivity to eye gaze in autism: Is it normal? Is it automatic? Is it social?*, in "Development and Psychopathology" 20, 1, pp. 79–97.

Niedźwiecka A. (2020), *Look me in the eyes: Mechanisms underlying the eye contact effect*, in "Child Development Perspectives" 14, 2, pp. 78–82.

Ochs M., Niewiadomski R., Brunet P., Pelachaud C. (2012), *Smiling virtual agent in social context*, in "Cognitive Processing" 13, 2, pp. 519–532.

Ohlsen G., van Zoest W., van Vugt M. (2013), *Gender and facial dominance in gaze cuing: Emotional context matters in the eyes that we follow*, in "PLoS ONE" 8, 4, https://doi.org/10.1371/journal.pone.0059471

Orletti F. (2015), *Partecipazione e gestione dei turni in una interazione in classe con bambini in difficoltà. Il ruolo dei segnali verbali e multimodali*, in *Parole, gesti, interpretazioni*, pp. 129–145, Aracne, Roma.

Osgood C.E., Suci G.J., Tannenbaum P.H. (1957), *The measurement of meaning*, University of Illinois Press, Urbana.

Pacori M. (2010), *I segreti del linguaggio del corpo*. Sperling & Kupfer, Milano.

Palanica A., Itier R.J. (2012), *Attention capture by direct gaze is robust to context and task demands*, in "Journal of Nonverbal Behavior" 36, 2, pp. 123–134.

Parisi D. (a cura di) (1975), *Studi per un modello del linguaggio*, Quaderni della Ricerca Scientifica, CNR, Roma.

Parisi D. (a cura di) (1979), *Per una educazione linguistica razionale*, Il Mulino, Bologna.

Parisi D. (2010), *Simulazioni: la realtà rifatta nel computer*, Il Mulino, Bologna.

Pelachaud C., Bilvi M. (2003), *Modelling gaze behavior for conversational agents*, in *International workshop on intelligent virtual agents*, Springer, Berlin, pp. 93–100.

Pelachaud C., Pogg I. (2002a), *Subtleties of facial expressions in embodied agents*, in "Journal of Visual Computer Animation" 13, pp. 301–312.

Pelachaud C., Poggi I. (2002b), *Multimodal embodied agents*, in "The Knowledge Engineering Review" 17, 2, pp. 181–196. http://doi.org/10.1017/S0269888902000218

Peters C., Pelachaud C., Bevacqua E., Mancini M., Poggi I. (2005), *A model of attention and interest using gaze behavior*, in *International workshop on intelligent virtual agents*, Springer, Berlin, pp. 229–240.

Pezzato N. (1998), *Parlare con gli occhi. Aspetti espressivi e comunicativi dello sguardo*, Unpublished M.A. thesis, Roma Tre University, Rome.

Pezzato N., Poggi I. (1999), *Le funzioni comunicative dello sguardo*, in A. Tronconi (a cura di), *Atti del 6° Convegno Nazionale Informatica, Didattica e Disabilità*, Andria, Bari, 4–6 novembre, pp. 27–31.

Plutchik R. (1980), *Emotion: A psychoevolutionary synthesis*, Harper & Row, New York.

Poggi I. (1981), *Le interiezioni. Studio del linguaggio e analisi della mente*, Boringhieri, Torino.

Poggi I. (1983), *La mano a borsa: analisi semantica di un gesto emblematico olofrastico*, in G. Attili e P.E. Ricci Bitti (a cura di), *Comunicare senza parole. La comunicazione non-verbale nel bambino e nell'interazione sociale tra adulti*, Bulzoni, Roma, pp. 219–238.

Poggi I. (2001), *Le sopracciglia dell'insegnante: un contributo al lessico della faccia*, in *Atti delle XI Giornate di Studio del Gruppo di Fonetica Sperimentale*, in *Multimodalità e Multimedialità nella Comunicazione*, Padova, 29 novembre–1 dicembre 2000, Unipress, Padova, pp. 57–65.

Poggi I. (2002a), *Symbolic gestures. The case of the Italian gestionary*, in "Gesture" 2, 1, pp. 71–98.

Poggi I. (2002b), *The lexicon of the conductor's face*, in P. McKevitt, S. O'Nualláin, C. Mulvihill (Eds.), *Language, vision, and music. Selected papers from the 8th international workshop on the cognitive science of natural language processing (Galway, 1999)*, John Benjamins, Amsterdam, pp. 271–284.

Poggi I. (2005), *The goals of persuasion*, in "Pragmatics and Cognition" 13, 2, pp. 297–336.

Poggi I. (2006a), *Le parole del corpo. Introduzione alla comunicazione multimodale*, Carocci, Roma.

Poggi I. (2006b), *Body and mind in the Pianist's performance*, in M. Baroni, M.R. Addessi, R. Caterina, M. Costa (Eds.), *Proceedings of the 9th international conference on music perception and cognition, ICMPC (Bologna, 22–26August,2006)*, Bononia University Press, Bologna, pp. 1044–1051.

Poggi I. (2007), *Mind, hands, face and body. A goal and belief view of multimodal communication*, Weidler, Berlin.

Poggi I. (a cura di) (2008), *La mente del cuore. Scienze cognitive delle emozioni*, Armando, Roma.

Poggi I. (2011), *Music and leadership: The Choir Conductor's multimodal communication*, in M. Ichino & G. Stam (Eds.), *Integrating gestures. The interdisciplinary nature of gestures*, John Benjamins, Amsterdam, pp. 341–353.

Poggi I. (2017), *Signals of intensification and attenuation in orchestra and choir conduction*, in "Normas" 7, 1, pp. 33–47. http://doi.org/10.7203/Normas.7.10423

Poggi I. (2018), *Lo sguardo del maestro*, in C. Corradi (a cura di), *Cultura popolare, religione diffusa, analisi qualitativa: un sociologo italiano a cavallo tra due secoli. Studi in onore di Roberto Cipriani*, Morlacchi, Perugia, pp. 233–252.

Poggi I. (2022a), *Psicologia della comunicazione. La mente, il corpo, gli altri*, Mondadori, Milano.

Poggi I. (2022b), *Interjections and other emotional communicative acts*, Volume 1, edited by Gesine Lenore Schiewer, Jeanette Altarriba, Bee Chin Ng, De Gruyter Mouton, Berlin, Boston, pp. 442–471, https://doi.org/10.1515/9783110347524-021

Poggi I., Ansani A. (2016), *Forte, piano, crescendo, diminuendo. Gestures of intensity in orchestra and choir conduction*, in *Proceedings of the MMSYM (MultiModal Symposium) 2016 (Copenhagen, September 29–30, 2016)*, Liu Electronic Press, Linköping, pp. 111–119.

Poggi I., Ansani A. (2018a), *'Alzò gli occhi al cielo'. Semantics of an item in the lexicon of gaze*, in *Cognitive science of communication and action, MidTerm conference AISC 2018 "Levels of cognition"*, Genova, 25–27 June, AISC, Genova.

Poggi I., Ansani A. (2018b), *The lexicon of the conductor's gaze*, in *Proceedings of the 5th international conference on movement and computing*, Genoa, Italy, 28–30 June, pp. 1–8. Association for Computing Machinery, New York.

Poggi I., Ansani A. (2022), *Multimodality and music performance. The lexicons of gesture and gaze in orchestra and choir conductors*, in "Acta Polytechnica Hungarica" 19, 5, pp. 215–234.

Poggi I., Ansani A., Cecconi C. (2018), *The meanings of the sigh. Vocal expression along the route of our desires*, in "Lebenswelt" 13, pp. 27–42. https://riviste.unimi.it/index.php/Lebenswelt/article/view/11106/10502

Poggi I., Ansani A., Cecconi C., Origlia A. (2018), *Virtual body signals to understand human signals. The meaning of "alzare gli occhi al cielo"*, in *Comunicazione al Convegno dell'AIP Sociale (Associazione Italiana di Psicologia, Sezione Psicologia Sociale)*, Bari, 19–21 Settembre, AIP, Bari.

Poggi I., Cavicchio F., Magno Caldognetto E. (2005), *Persuasive goals of Irony in a political trial, Presentation at the workshop WP8 of Humaine EU project*, Trento, 17–18 November.

Poggi I., D'Errico F. (2012), *Pride and its expression in political debates*, in F. Paglieri, L. Tummolini, R. Falcone, M. Miceli (Eds.), *The goals of cognition. Festschrift for Cristiano Castelfranchi*, College Publications, London, pp. 221–253.

Poggi I., D'Errico F. (2020), *Comunicazione multimodale e influenza sociale. Il corpo e il potere*, Carocci, Roma.

Poggi I., D'Errico F. (2022), *Multimodality, power, and social influence*, Routledge, London.

Poggi I., D'Errico F., Ansani A. (2021), *The conductor's intensity gestures*, in "Psychology of Music" 49, 6, pp. 1478–1497, https://doi.org/10.1177/0305735620963179

Poggi I., D'Errico F., Spagnolo A. (2010), *The embodied morphemes of gaze*, in S. Kopp, I. Wachsmuth (Eds.), *GW 2009, gesture in embodied communication and human-computer interaction*, Springer, Berlin, pp. 34–46.

Poggi I., D'Errico F., Vincze L. (2013), *Comments in words, face and body*, in "Journal of Multimodal User Interface" 7, 1, pp. 67–78. http://doi.org/10.1007/s12193-012-0102-z. ISSN 1783–7677

Poggi I., Merola G., Liberati M.F. (2003), *The Teacher's gaze*, Oral presentation at the *International conference ECFE 2003*, Rimini, 18–20 September 2003, European Conference on Facial Expression.

Poggi I., Pelachaud C. (1998), *Performative faces*, in "Speech Communication" 26, 1–2, pp. 5–21. http://doi.org/10.1016/S0167-6393(98)00047-8. ISSN:0167–6393

Poggi I., Pelachaud C. (2000), *Performative facial expressions in animated faces*, in J. Cassell, J. Sullivan, S. Prevost, E. Churchill (Eds.), *Embodied conversational agents*, The MIT Press, Cambridge, MA, pp. 155–188.

Poggi I., Pelachaud C. (2002), *Signals and meanings of gaze in animated faces*, in P. McKevitt, S. O'Nualláin, C. Mulvihill (Eds.), *Language, vision, and music. Selected papers from the 8th international workshop on the cognitive science of natural language processing (Galway, 1999)*, John Benjamins, Amsterdam, pp. 133–144.

Poggi I., Pelachaud C., de Rosis F. (2000), *Eye communication in a conversational 3D synthetic agent*, in "AI Communications" 13, 3, pp. 169–181.

Poggi I., Pezzato N., Pelachaud C. (1999), *Gaze and its meaning in animated faces*, in P. McKevitt (Ed.), *Proceedings of the workshop on "language, vision and music", CSNLP-8 (Cognitive Science and Natural Language Processing)*, Galway, Ireland, 9–11 August, pp. 33–40.

Poggi I., Ranieri L., Leone Y., Ansani A. (2020), *The power of gaze in music. Leonard Bernstein's conducting eyes*, in "Multimodal Technologies Interaction 2020" 4, 2, p. 20. Special issue *"Musical Interactions"*, https://doi.org/10.3390/mti4020020, https://www.mdpi.com/2414-4088/4/2/20

Poggi I., Roberto E. (2007), *Meaningful eyes*, in E. Ahlsén, P.J. Henrichsen, R. Hirsch, J. Nivre, A. Abelin, S. Stroemqvist, S. Nicholson, B. Dorriots (Eds.),

*Communication – action – meaning. A festschrift to Jens Allwood*, Department of Linguistics, Goteborg University, Goteborg, pp. 325–341.

Poggi I., Spagnolo A., D'Errico F. (2010), *The morphemes of the eyelids*, in *Atti del Congresso La Comunicazione Parlata*, Napoli, 23–25 febbraio 2009, SLI - GSCP, Università degli Studi L'Orientale, Napoli.

Poggi I., Vincze L. (2009a), *The persuasive import of gesture and gaze*, in M. Kipp, J.C. Martin, P. Paggio (Eds.), *Proceedings of the workshop on multimodal corpora: From models of natural interaction to systems and applications*, *LREC*, pp. 46–51. ELRA Language Resources Association, Paris.

Poggi I., Vincze L. (2009b), *Gesture, gaze and persuasive strategies in political discourse*, in *Proceedings of the workshop on multimodal corpora*, *LREC* (Marrakech, May 2008), Springer, Berlin, pp. 73–92.

Poggi I., Zuccaro V. (2008), *Admiration*, in *Proceedings of the workshop AFFINE: Affective interaction in natural environment, post-conference workshop of ICMI 2008*, Chania, Crete, 24 September, ACM, New York.

Poole K.L., Schmidt L.A. (2021), *Vigilant or avoidant? Children's temperamental shyness, patterns of gaze, and physiology during social threat*, in "Developmental Science" 24, 6, p. e13118.

Posner R. (2003), *Everyday gestures as a result of ritualization*, in M. Rector, I. Poggi, N. Trigo (Eds.), *Gestures. Meaning and use*, Edicoes Universidade Fernando Pessoa, Porto.

Posner R., Serenari M. (2001), *Il grado zero della gestualità: dalla funzione pratica a quella simbolica – alcuni esempi dal Dizionario berlinese dei gesti quotidiani*, in E. Magno Caldognetto, P. Cosi (Eds.), *Atti delle 11e Giornate del Gruppo di Fonetica Sperimentale: Multimodalità e multimedialità della comunicazione* (Padova, November 29–December 1, 2000), Unipress, Padova, pp. 81–88.

Rajecki D.W., Ickes W., Tanford S. (1981), *Locus of control and reaction to strangers*, in "Psychology and Social Psychology Bulletin" 7, 2, pp. 282–289.

Ravinal R. (2022), *Eye contact is everything in public speaking*. https://rosemary-ravinal.com/eye-contact-importance-when-public-speaking/, consultato 6–12–22.

Rayner K. (1977), *Visual attention in reading: Eye movements reflect cognitive processes*, in "Memory & Cognition" 5, 4, pp. 443–448.

Rector M., Poggi I., Trigo N. (Eds.) (2003), *Gestures. Meaning and use*, Universidade Fernando Pessoa, Oporto.

Remondini V. (2000), *I comportamenti non verbali dell'insegnante. Comunicazione facciale e strategie didattiche*, Tesi di laurea non pubblicata, Dipartimento di Scienze dell'Educazione, Università Roma Tre.

Roget P.M. (1962), *Roget's thesaurus of English words and phrases*, Longmans Green, London.

Rosenthal R., Jacobson L. (1968), *Pygmalion in the classroom*, in "The Urban Review" 3, 1, pp. 16–20.

Rossano F. (2013), *Gaze in conversation*, in J. Sidnell, T. Stivers (Eds.), *The handbook of conversation analysis*, Wiley-Blackwell, Oxford, pp. 308–329.

Schiffrin D. (1987), *Discourse markers*, Cambridge University Press, Cambridge.

Serenari M. (2003), *Examples from the Berlin dictionary of everyday gestures*, in M. Rector, I. Poggi, N. Trigo (Eds.), *Gestures. Meaning and use*, Edicoes Universidade Fernando Pessoa, Porto.

Serenari M. (2004), *The struture of dictionary entries: Results of empirical investigations*, in C. Müller, R. Posner (Eds.), *The semantics and pragmatics of everyday gestures*, Weidler, Berlin.

Shang J., Liu Y., Fu X. (2008), *Dominance modulates the effects of eye gaze on the perception of threatening facial expressions*, in *2008 8thIEEE international conference on automatic face & gesture recognition*, IEEE Computer Society, Los Alamitos, CA, pp. 1–6.

Shimojo S., Simion C., Shimojo E., Scheier C. (2003), *Gaze bias both reflects and influences preference*, in "Nature Neuroscience" 6, pp. 1317–1322.

Shirer W. (1941), *Berlin diary: The journal of a foreign correspondent, 1934–1941*, Alfred A. Knopf, New York.

Signorello R., D'Errico F., Poggi I., Demolin D. (2012), *How charisma is perceived from speech. A multidimensional approach*, in *Proceedings of IEEE social computation* (Amsterdam, 3–5 September 2012), IEEE Computer Society, New York, pp. 435–440.

Signorello R., D'Errico F., Poggi I., Demolin D., Mairano P. (2013), *Charisma perception in political speech: A case study*, in H. Mello, M. Pettorino, T. Raso (Eds.), *Proceedings of the VIIth GSCP international conference: Speech and corpora*, Firenze University Press, Firenze, pp. 343–348.

Sirois S., Brisson J. (2014), *Pupillometry*, in "Wiley Interdisciplinaire Review" 5, 679–692, https://doi.org/10.1002/wcs.1323

Sparhawk C. (1978), *Contrastive – identificational features of persian gestures*, in "Semiotica" 24, pp. 49–86.

Stokoe W.C. (1978), *Sign language structure: An outline of the communicative systems of the American deaf*, Linstock Press, Silver Spring.

Strick M., Holland R.W., van Knippenberg A. (2008), *Seductive eyes: Attractiveness and direct gaze increase desire for associated objects*, in "Cognition" 106, 3, pp. 1487–1496.

Suetonius (335), *De vita Caesarum*. Eng. Tr. *The twelve ceasars*, Penguin, New York.

Teigen K.H. (2008), *Is a sigh "just a sigh"? Sighs as emotional signals and responses to a difficult task*, in "Scandinavian Journal of Psychology" 49, 1, pp. 49–57.

Terburg D., Hooiveld N., Aarts H., Kenemans J.L., van Honk J. (2011), *Eye tracking unconscious face-to-face confrontations: Dominance motives prolong gaze to masked angry faces*, in "Psychological Science" 22, 3, pp. 314–319.

Tipples J., Atkinson A.P., Young A.W. (2002), *The eyebrow frown: A salient social signal*, in "Emotion" 2, pp. 288–296.

Tirassa M. (1991), *Fallimenti della comunicazione*, in "Ricerche di Psicologia" 3, pp. 59–88.

Tomasello M., Hare B., Lehmann H., Call J. (2007), *Reliance on head versus eyes in the gaze following of great apes and human infants: The cooperative eye hypothesis*, in "Journal of Human Evolution" 52, 3, pp. 314–320.

Torres O., Cassell J., Prevost S. (1997), *Modeling gaze behavior as a function of discourse structure*, in *First international workshop on human-computer conversations*, Bellagio, Italy, https://citeseerx.ist.psu.edu/document?repid=rep1&type=pdf &doi=e03656c66f50e531485899371aca1b79d48d9837.

Tourangeau R., Ellsworth P.C. (1979), *The role of facial response in the experience of emotion*, in "Journal of Personality and Social Psychology" 37, pp. 1519–1531.

Tracy J.L., Robins R.W. (2004), *Show your pride: Evidence for a discrete emotion expression*, in "Psychological Science" 15, pp. 194–197.

Trevarthen C. (1979), *Communication and cooperation in early infancy*, in "Before Speech", pp. 321–347.

Tsuji Y., Shimada S. (2018), *Socially anxious tendencies affect impressions of others' positive and negative emotional gazes*, in "Frontiers in Psychology" 1, 9, p. 2111. http://doi.org/10.3389/fpsyg.2018.02111

Vincze L., Poggi I. (2011), *Communicative functions of eye closing behaviours*, in A. Esposito, A. Vinciarelli, C. Vicsi, C. Pelachaud, A. Nijholt (Eds.), *Proceedings of the conference "analysis of verbal and nonverbal communication and enactment: The processing issues"*, Springer, Berlin, pp. 401–416.

Vincze L., Poggi I. (2016), *I am really certain of this! Towards a multimodal repertoire of signals communicating a high degree of certainty*, in *Proceedings of the multimodal symposium 2016*, Copenhagen, 29–30 September, pp. 102–110, Linköping University Electronic Press, Linköping, SE.

Vincze L., Poggi I. (2022), *Multimodal signals of high commitment in expert-to-expert contexts*, in "Discourse and Communication", 16, 16, https://doi.org/10. 1177/09579265221109091

Viola M. (2022), *Seeing through the shades of situated affectivity. Sunglasses as a socio-affective artifact*, in "Philosophical Psychology". https://doi.org/10.1080/09 515089.2022.2118574

Volterra V. (cur.) (1987), *LIS. La Lingua Italiana dei Segni*, Il Mulino, Bologna.

Volterra V., Roccaforte M., Di Renzo A., Fontana S. (2019), *Descrivere la lingua dei segni italiana. Una prospettiva cognitiva e sociosemiotica*, Il Mulino, Bologna.

Wardhaugh R., Fuller J.M. (2021), *An introduction to sociolinguistics*, Blackwell, Oxford.

Weast T. (2008), *Quantified eyebrow motion: New evidence from American sign language questions*, in "Proceedings form the Annual Meeting of the Chicago Linguistic Society" 44, 2, pp. 227–242.

Weber M. (1920), *Wirtschaft und Gesellschaft, Verlag Mohr Siebeck*, English version, *The theory of social and economic organization*, Oxford University Press, New York.

Wellens A.R. (1987), *Heart-rate changes in response to shifts in interpersonal gaze from liked and disliked others*, in "Perceptual & Motor Skills" 64, pp. 595–598.

Whalen P.J., Kagan J., Cook R.G., Davis F.C., Kim H., Polis S., Johnstone T. (2004), *Human amygdala responsivity to masked fearful eye whites*, in "Science" 306, 5704, pp. 2061–2061.

Wilbur R. (1994), *Eyeblinks & ASL phrase structure*, in "Sign Language Studies" 84, 1, pp. 221–240.

Wirth J.H., Sacco D.F., Hugenberg K., Williams K.D. (2010), *Eye gaze as relational evaluation: Averted eye gaze leads to feelings of ostracism and relational devaluation*, in "Personality and Social Psychology Bulletin" 36, 7, pp. 869–882. https:// doi.org/10.1177/0146167210370032

Yamazaki K., Yamazaki A., Ikeda K., Liu C., Fukushima M., Kobayashi Y., Kuno Y. (2016), *"I'll be there next" A multiplex care robot system that conveys service order using gaze gestures*, in "ACM Transactions on Interactive Intelligent Systems (TiiS) 5, 4, pp. 1–20.

Zani B., Selleri P., David D. (1994), *La comunicazione. Modelli teorici e contesti sociali*, Carocci, Roma.

Zuczkowski A., Bongelli R., Riccioni I. (2017), *Epistemic stance in dialogue: Knowing, unknowing, believing*, John Benjamins, Amsterdam.

# INDEX

Printed and bound by CPI Group (UK) Ltd, Croydon, CR0 4YY

06/11/2024

01784841-0002